INDIANA
HISTORICAL SOCIETY
PUBLICATIONS

Planting

CORN BELT CULTURE

THE IMPRESS OF THE UPLAND SOUTHERNER AND YANKEE IN THE OLD NORTHWEST

Richard Lyle Power

GREENWOOD PRESS, PUBLISHERS
WESTPORT, CONNECTICUT

Library of Congress Cataloging in Publication Data

Power, Richard Lyle, 1896–
    Planting Corn Belt culture.

    Reprint. Originally published: Indianapolis :
Indiana Historical Society. 1953. (Indiana Historical
Society publications ; v. 17)
    Includes bibliographical references and index.
    1. Northwest, Old--Civilization. I. Title.
F484.3.P6 1983   977   83-8491
ISBN 0-313-24060-4

Reprinted in 1983 by Greenwood Press
A division of Congressional Information Service, Inc.
88 Post Road West, Westport, Connecticut 06881

Printed in the United States of America

10 9 8 7 6 5 4 3 2 1

For Florence, Marcia, and Richard

FOREWORD

What cannot totally be known, ought not to be totally neglected; for the knowledge of a part is better than ignorance of the whole.

Abulfeda*

This volume undertakes to discover the content of two variants of early American culture, that of the upland Southerner, who came from the plateaus and valleys westward of the Atlantic Coastal Plain, and that of the Yankee, the man from New England and New York.† It describes the conditions of their transit to the Old Northwest and attempts headway at understanding their contact and blending there. It is assumed that the interaction between what the school histories used to call the "New England" and the "Virginia" types of early American constitutes one of the significant features in the development of our republic, and the pages that follow should lend weight and character to the assumption.

The present study seeks therefore to break down into specific elements a process of cultural genesis which has been hitherto blanketed with generalities. It introduces new data in an effort to sketch with some detail the cultural diversities in the area it deals with.

An undertaking of this sort calls for consideration of at least three elements—the Yankee East, the Upland South, and the Northwest itself. The special significance of the Old Northwest (Ohio, Indiana, Illinois, Michigan, Wisconsin) is that it was a large area settled early enough and with sufficient

* This is inscribed by G. W. H. Kemper on the flyleaf of his *A Medical History of the State of Indiana* (Chicago, 1911), copy in IHS.

† The author has found one reference to "New Jersey Yankees." *Diary of C. K. Laird*, IHS.

concentration of the two peoples to afford a satisfactory field for observation. Also, the Northwest became in turn a seedbed for populating states such as Iowa, Minnesota, Kansas, and places more remote.

This limitation of emphasis, of course, denies fair attention to the migration from the Middle States to the Northwest and to the considerable numbers of Germans, Irish, English, and Scandinavians who came thence. The westward migration of natives of Ohio to near-by states presents another special case since the Ohio-born had doubtless undergone a tempering within that older, favorably known and comparatively wealthy state. Also, several thousands of Quakers who removed to the Northwest, mostly from the Carolinas though originally from Nantucket, were not typical Uplanders and would deserve study in their own right. But it will become clear that the Yankee deserves singling out for special treatment because of his influential role in shaping the Northwest.

Although attention is necessarily devoted to the Old Northwest in general, geographical circumstances often bring the study to focus upon the states of Indiana and Illinois, sometimes upon their southern portions. These two states lay at the upper end of a "corridor" through which uncounted thousands worked northward from the Uplands; which recalls Professor Paxson's remark that the southern heritage became more complete as the frontier moved down the Ohio Valley. Both received much the same sort of early settler—Indiana became a state in 1816, Illinois in 1818—and were later infiltrated with an increasing migration from the Northeast.

As to southern Indiana–Illinois (the earliest portions of those states to be populated), their area lies to the southward of the belt of most fertile glacier-borne soils, another way of saying that it missed inclusion in the agriculturally favored area known as the Corn Belt. More than any other area of the North, this became an outpost of southern folkways which the

Yankees could never quite understand or modify. Indiana, more "southernized" than any other northern state, became for the Yankees a sort of special problem and thus occupies a prominent place, especially in passages where the comparative effects of physical factors are discussed.

The study bears upon the sixty-year period from 1800 to 1860, giving special attention to the last thirty years of that period, after the "Yankee drift" had set in. Beyond regional interest, these pages may help in understanding that larger process wherein regional variety became blended into a common national culture. These pages also venture to synthesize some of the views and conclusions of historians such as Channing, Turner, Mathews, Wertenbaker, Fox, and perhaps a score of others.

The sources upon which this writing depends originated close to the level of everyday living. Of printed materials, agricultural and religious periodicals have been conspicuously useful. Much used among manuscripts were the papers of the American Home Missionary Society, held by Hammond Library, Chicago Theological Seminary. These materials originated for the most part after the Society was reorganized in 1827, and represent a sort of Puritan equivalent of the *Jesuit Relations*. Objectivity has been sought through allowing individuals whenever possible to speak for themselves and their groups.

As the twentieth century has uncoiled, a new and practical interest in the American past has appeared, a desire to discover what America is and what America means. Peril from without, the pressure of unsolved problems within, and surety that significant changes are in the making, have driven many to a thoughtful reconsideration of our past in the hope of finding guidance. These chapters will be justified if they help to stimulate pride in America's cultural elements, for these afford a certain spiritual ballast in times of stress like the present.

INDIANA HISTORICAL SOCIETY

My thanks are due to scores of friends, teaching colleagues, and librarians for all sorts of aid and helpful suggestions. It is a matter of regret that these abettors are so numerous that it is impossible to cite them by name. Especial thanks are due to my former colleagues in the Department of History and Government at St. Lawrence University, and to the staff of Herring Library; also to the officers and staff of the Indiana Historical Society. Gratitude further extends to the American Philosophical Society held at Philadelphia for Promoting Useful Knowledge, for grants of funds which encouraged completion of the undertaking.

The base maps for the Ohio, Indiana, and Illinois land-wealth maps were furnished through the courtesy of the George F. Cram Company, Indianapolis. The corn production map for 1860 was taken from *Historical Atlas of the United States,* by Clifford and Elizabeth H. Lord (New York, 1944); and the one for 1949 from U. S. Bureau of the Census, *U. S. Census of Agriculture: 1950,* V, pt. 3 (Washington, D. C., 1952). The map showing the areas of the eastern United States under co-operative drainage is a section of *Map of the United States Showing Location of Drained Agricultural Lands: 1950,* published by U. S. Bureau of the Census. Photographs of the Louisiana gourdseed and northern flint varieties of corn were furnished by Edgar Anderson of the Missouri Botanical Garden, St. Louis. Wilbur Peat, of the John Herron Art Museum, Indianapolis, supplied a photograph of the New England-style house. The photograph of the Southern Federalist-style house was from a collection made by the Historic American Buildings Survey, in the Indiana Historical Society Library.

R. L. P.

INDIANAPOLIS
June, 1953

CONTENTS

ILLUSTRATIONS

ABBREVIATIONS USED IN CITING
PRINCIPAL MANUSCRIPT SOURCES

AHMS Papers of the American Home Missionary Society, Hammond Library, Chicago Theological Seminary (Photostatic copies of these papers originating in Indiana before the end of 1835 were consulted in the Indiana Division, Indiana State Library, Indianapolis.)

CHS Chicago Historical Society Library

DU Duke University Library, Durham, N. C.

ILLSL Illinois State Historical Library, Springfield

IHS Indiana Historical Society Library, Indianapolis

ISL Indiana State Library, Indianapolis

McHC McCormick Historical Collection, State Historical Society of Wisconsin, Madison

MHC Michigan Historical Collections, University of Michigan, Ann Arbor

OAHS Ohio State Archaeological and Historical Society, Columbus

UV Alderman Library, University of Virginia, Charlottesville

WHS State Historical Society of Wisconsin, Madison

INTRODUCTION

The Southerners Got There First

Taking a long-time view, one might summarize the earlier settlement of the Old Northwest in this way: The Southerners had at least forty years' start. They had reached the Blue Grass of Kentucky and even made settlements on the Wabash while the New Yorkers were still fighting the Indians along the upper Mohawk. But Yankeedom presently seemed bent on making up lost time in reaching out for the northern Mississippi Valley. Emigrants were soon multiplying on the various routes by land or water to the Northwest.[1] But the Uplanders had won the first heat in the race. They had by 1830 planted their modes of living in the then settled portions of the Northwest—their farmways and speech, their educational and religious views, their dietary and cookery, ways of conducting business and politics, their homeways, social life, and amusements.[2]

To historians this dominance by the Uplanders is commonplace. One remarks, for example, that the Old Northwest was, until 1850 at least, "peculiarly the child of the South." Another specifies that the Ohio Valley as a whole "was an extension of the Upland South. . . ." Still another, that "In most of the civilizations which developed in the West—for there were numerous clearly defined civilizations—the influence of the South was profound." And most emphatic of all: "Various studies have made clear and it needs only to be repeated that in the early decades of the nineteenth century, West and South were hardly distinguishable terms."[3] It is also of material interest that the Uplanders considered themselves western men whether they resided in North Carolina,

(1)

Kentucky, or Indiana: They "had come not from *the* South, but from an older West."[4]

Sundry onlookers remarked similarity between the South and the West. Gifted with tenacious memory, at least two writers accounted for the educational backwardness in southern Indiana and Illinois by calling up Governor Berkeley's unabashed thanks to God for the absence from Virginia, two centuries before, of free schools and printing presses.[5] The rustic society of "Egypt," the southernmost quarter of Illinois, they related to the southern Uplands. In Ohio the similarity appeared in political behavior. "You are acquainted with the manner of holding Elections in the Southern States," wrote Vermont-bred Calvin Fletcher from Urbana, "so I need not mention the intreague and stratiges used here . . .," as he went on to designate nocturnal caucuses, slander, animosities, the carrying of weapons, mobs, and gougings as part of electoral activity.[6]

Easterners described Hoosier speech, for example, as a peculiar dialect "common to a great extent among the lower class of people in the South."[7] A savage editorial in the Springfield, Massachusetts, *Republican* at the time of the Civil War burdened Indiana with a singular infamy which the editors linked with the southern origins of its people.[8] At the same moment, unfriendly comment said the northern people who lived near the Ohio River cheered for Jefferson Davis, wore the butternut uniform, spoke the southern dialect, hated Negroes and abolitionists, and had no religious training. Even after Appomattox the leopard's spots remained: the eastern viewpoint insisted that "Western men and society, strictly speaking, are largely of Southern origin . . . full of prejudice against 'Yankees.' "[9]

Despite the Southerners' advantageous start, Yankee immigration became by 1840 what a distinguished historian called, referring to Illinois, a "Yankee invasion."[10] But a "Yankee invasion" signified more than the addition of another popular element. It was probably the most dynamic thing that played upon the social genesis of the Old Northwest or any other portion of America. In a large view, two native types had met in the Great Interior Valley to enact latter scenes of a drama begun in England two centuries before. For the Yankees were determined to refashion the men of the West (and of the nation, for that matter) in the Yankee image, and whenever one group of men sets out to make over another, the story is pretty certain to be worth following up.

NOTES

[1] Edward L. Burchard, "Early Trails and Tides of Travel in the Lead Mine and Blackhawk Country," in *Journal of the Illinois State Historical Society,* XVII (January, 1925), 599.

[2] Logan Esarey, *A History of Indiana* (2 volumes. Fort Wayne, 1924), I, Chapter IX; Theodore C. Pease, *The Frontier State, 1818-1848* (*Centennial History of Illinois,* Volume II, Chicago, 1918), p. 7.

[3] William E. Dodd, "The Fight for the Northwest, 1860," in *American Historical Review,* XVI (July, 1911), 774; Frederick Jackson Turner, *The Frontier in American History* (New York, 1920), p. 164; Thomas J. Wertenbaker, *The Old South: The Founding of American Civilization* (New York, 1942), pp. 17-18; H. C. Hubbart, "Pro-Southern Influences in the Free West, 1840-1865," in *Mississippi Valley Historical Review,* XX (June, 1933), 46.

[4] Roger H. Van Bolt, "The Indiana Scene in the 1840's," in *Indiana Magazine of History,* XLVII (December, 1951), 338-39. See also Frederick Jackson Turner's essay "The Old West," in *The Frontier in American History,* pp. 67-125.

[5] Charles A. Church, *History of Rockford and Winnebago County, Illinois . . .* (Rockford, 1900), p. 341; Aaron Wood, D. D., *Sketches of Things and Peoples in Indiana* (Indianapolis, 1883), p. 19. For a statement that Berkeley was in error about free schools see *Dictionary of American Biography* (20 volumes + index. New York, 1937), II, 218.

[6] Calvin Fletcher, Urbana, Ohio, to Jesse Fletcher, Ludlow, Vermont, November 21, 1818, IHS.

[7] *Great Republic Monthly* (New York), I (June, 1859), 635.

[8] Springfield (Mass.) *Republican,* January 31, 1863, as quoted in the Lafayette (Ind.) *Daily Journal,* February 11, 1863.

[9] *Home Missionary* (New York), XXXVII (September, 1864), 113; also XXXI (October, 1858), 146; XXXIX (February, 1867), 248.

[10] Allen Johnson, "Stephen A. Douglas," in *Dictionary of American Biography,* V, 399.

Chapter I

THE CULTURAL IMPERIALISM OF THE YANKEES

1. Religion the Spearhead

"a thirty years war"

A nineteenth-century journalist remarked that the Yankee considered himself established in America "as a sort of religious, political, industrial, agricultural and commercial missionary."[1] The late Professor Hansen, in search of the essence of "immigrant Puritanism," decided that it lay in a certain passage in Governor Winthrop's *Journal*. To repeat the significant words, wrote Hansen, "strict discipline . . . more needful in plantations than in a settled state."[2] Each writer had acceptably paraphrased the theme of this chapter.

The first belief of the Puritan–Yankees was that the rising West would eventually affect, for good or for evil, the entire nation; the second, that the West would "yield to the plastic hand of a *master*." The West would be "just what the *people* of the West make it; and *they* will be what the influences sent out from the East make them." New England and eastern interests generally must therefore be alert lest the "refluent wave" of ignorance, skepticism, and sin rise higher and higher until "it rolls over the beautiful monuments of Puritan intelligence and piety."[3]

The simplest way to classify the Yankee's motives is to say tritely that they were religious, economic, and political, though these were never quite separable from one another. Beyond this the means of discipline were determined by the problem in hand, often respecting the principle that "old societies of men need nervines; new communities, anodynes rather."[4] Or in

the belief that "there is not a human institution that can bear
to be neglected." Taxed with being busybodies and meddlers,
apologists own that the instinct for meddling, as divine as that
of self-preservation, runs in the Yankee blood; that the typical
New Englander was entirely unable, when there were wrongs
to be corrected, to mind his own business.[5]

The odds are considerable that one will discover this mili-
tancy in one of its religious rather than its secular phases. For
religion provided a principal vehicle, much of the emotional
push, and many of the proposed controls and correctives. Thus
among "clerical schemes and pompous undertakings of the
present day under the pretense of religion" which *The Reformer,* a small, tightly printed Philadelphia periodical of the
early 1820's aimed to expose, was a "plot" attributed to certain
New England churchmen to fashion the rising American nation
entirely after the Yankee image.[6]

The ire of *The Reformer's* editors had been aroused by a
passage in one of Lyman Beecher's tracts which declared:

> The integrity of the Union demands special exertions to pro-
> duce in the nation a more homogeneous character, and bind us
> together by firmer bonds. . . . A remedy must be applied to this
> vital defect. . . . But what shall that remedy be? There can be
> but one. The consolidation of the State Governments would make
> a despotism. But the prevalence of pious, intelligent, enterprising
> ministers through the nation; at the ratio of one for 1000, would
> establish schools, and academies, and colleges, and habits, and
> institutions of homogeneous influence. These would produce a
> sameness of views, and feelings, and interests, which would lay
> the foundation of our empire upon a rock.

To Beecher's term "homogeneous influence" the editors
rejoined:

> These ministers to produce this *homogeneous influence* must,
> of course, be all of one religious persuasion . . . his own. . . .
> From such a *homogeneous influence* as *they* might effect, it be-
> comes us to pray from the bottom of our hearts "good Lord deliver
> us." The fate to which it might doom us, we fear, would not be
> much better than that of Old Spain sometime since. Four pious

persons, we remember, were once hung at Boston by reason of such *homogeneous influence.*

Leaving aside any personal or doctrinal animosities involved, it is significant that Beecher had designated something he thought a weakness in the nation's make-up, and urged a nationwide remedy. It is also significant that the editors of *The Reformer* recognized the implications of the proposal and lavished their wrath upon it.[7]

But solicitude for the West was not confined to any one group of eastern churchmen a century ago. New England Baptists were accused by western men, who "smelled the New England rat," of "setting up an ecclesiastical hierarchy over the Baptist denomination which in the end would undermine the liberties of the entire nation." A meeting of Baptists at Cincinnati was warned that New England had the West by the hand, and intended to keep hold of it.[8] Likewise the Unitarians and Transcendentalists of New England felt a special responsibility for the West. Ralph Waldo Emerson referred in 1832, for example, to a "late special meeting of the Am. Unitarian Association" at which "The West" was the leading topic, and discussion of the appointment of missionaries and of an agent were "well received." Indeed there was talk of asking Emerson to go to the Middle West as a Unitarian missionary or editor, or to become a regular pastor there.[9]

Whatever reticence Yankees may have felt about discussing the "plan," especially after it had been publicly challenged, the flow of extravagant language released by the Civil War demonstrates that the idea of a cultural assimilation of the West by the Yankees—"a thirty years war," one writer called it—had never been suffered to lapse.[10]

2. MERCANTILE MORALITY

"one dollar by way of prevention"

Though it would be unjust to charge the Yankees with parsimony or of expecting the balance to be always in their favor, the dollar was by any reckoning an instrument of strategy. Yankee awareness of the reforming efficacy of his dollars is itself a story of arresting interest. It ranges from petty benevolences to needy groups—used Sunday school literature, church bells, pianos, and miscellaneous items—through carefully wrought inducements to western communities to match the Yankee dollar in order to build women's colleges, to bold proposals to Christianize the nation (indeed the planet, if Britain would only aid) by means of an effort of twenty years' duration. The latter gigantic project, educational and evangelical, was to be supported by the proceeds of a 10 per cent capital levy on individual wealth, the entire venture to be self-liquidating at the end of the period.[11]

Material reasons for planting Yankee mores throughout the nation were expressed without subtlety: "One dollar by way of *prevention,* is of more value than a hundred by way of *reparation.*"[12] This was particularly true in relation to the newer states. Businessmen therefore *"owe it to their own interests to aid in this enterprise"* because "the very wealth . . . which adorns our cities, and gives . . . influence to its possessors, they owe, in some measure, to the operation of christian principles diffused through the community by christian teachers."[13] The same vein of argument besought merchants to "give nobly." It was "Far better . . . to give his money, not to say his prayers, to make the *people good,* where he entrusts millions of property, than to spend it upon bailiffs, to apprehend his runaway creditors, or to collect his debts among a dissolute people, without either responsibility or principle."[14]

Meanwhile eastern men of money did not take a passive view of "strict discipline." Looking upon commerce as a "great divine instrumentality for civilizing and Christianizing the world,"[15] a Boston merchant insisted:

The same resources that can support trade can throw a religious influence into every part of it, until New England institutions are established from the lakes to the shores of the Pacific, and you may travel from the Atlantic to the Pacific, and every six miles find a New England village, with its church spires pointing to the skies, and the school by its side.[16]

A method more direct is illustrated by the activity of Charles Butler, a retainer of eastern creditors who labored successfully to induce the Michigan legislature to keep with financial regularity. Butler presently became agent for a similar cause before the Indiana legislature. After working through an exhausting period of about ten months beginning in May, 1845, Butler wrote:

> The influence of my operations is not limited to Indiana itself, but will tell on the destiny of the other States and the country at large. The measure is not yet sufficiently estimated, nor, indeed, can it be. A few years will develop its fruits and effects more strikingly, and it will be regarded with admiration.[17]

If one were expecting Massachusetts, Boston, and State Street to make a case of especial earnestness he would not be disappointed. The Reverend H. B. Hooker bespoke the anxiety of Massachusetts for her financial commitments as well as for her sons and daughters who had gone West. Fifty million dollars had gone by 1864, mostly from Massachusetts, into railroads; fifty million into lands, manufactures, and loans; and another twenty-five million into mining. Men shrewd enough to make money, he concluded, "know that bonds and stocks and mortgages are all the more valuable for being within the sound of the *church*-going bell." But Mr. Hooker was ringing the changes on an old theme. Nothing essential remained to be said after a field worker wrote from Wisconsin Territory in 1839: *"The Gospel is the most economical police on earth."*[18]

3. Politics Yankee Fashion

"Come on, then, and help us"

Whether the need of the moment was more thorough family discipline in the West,[19] or the application of the Puritan system as a "rational and effective antidote for the multitudinous 'isms',"[20] political control was implicit in almost every point of Yankee aggressiveness. Such control was present in a theocratic sort of proposal that "some two or three good ministers in the neighborhood" designate the "natural" business center of western townships regardless of existing activity at the point decided upon.[21]

Non-Yankees early suspected the New Englander's willingness to see his political influence extended. Southerners at the Continental Congress insisted that "Boston aims at nothing less than the sovereignty of the whole continent."[22] Timothy Dwight did little to dispel such belief when he wrote in 1793 to Oliver Wolcott:

Not only young gentlemen from our sister States, but from every quarter of the globe would do well to pass a few years of their lives amongst us, and acquire our habits of thinking and living. Half a dozen legislators or even scholars bred in New England and dispersed throughout the different countries of Europe every year would in half an age change the face of Political affairs in the old world.[23]

As the nineteenth century unfolded, headlines such as "political power moving westward" expressed Yankee dismay at the prospect of being ruled by "people strong in their impulses, conscious of their rapidly growing strength . . . ambitious of using it . . . but comparatively undirected and unrestrained by the influence of institutions of religion and education."[24]

Here then was the crux of the matter: the danger of political dominance by the rising West. Facing it, Yankee vigilance was unrelaxing.

One obvious means of control was to outvote the opposition; hence the tenor of a letter of George Churchill, a Vermonter settled in territorial Illinois, concerning the proposed state constitution. Because slavery was not tolerated by the document, Churchill expected a large proportion of immigrants thenceforth to be Yankees and other friends of liberty and of election by ballot. Though the coming election was to be conducted "on the old plan, that is, *Viva voce,*" he hoped soon to see elections conducted in Yankee fashion. But in any case the liberty men would soon be able to manage the slaveholders "if we can get some more Yankees. Come on, then, and help us."[25]

The motive of the New England men (as well as of their opponents) who hastened to Kansas in 'fifty-four is familiar, but it is interesting to hear it acknowledged by one who saw fellow Yankees passing through Chicago, Kansas-bound. Only New England could produce such men: "In fine, they looked as though they were destined to be 'sovereigns' not only in *word,* but *deed*:—& such Sovereigns too, as Petty Demagogues would in vain appeal to for positions of power & influence."[26]

Yankees in far away California felt equally certain they held the key to civic welldoing: "As yet the native 'greasers' rule," was the word from Santa Barbara, "but a year or two more will put office and power out of their hands. We long for the day. They hate enterprise and ignore public improvements. Our main street even is impassable. It might be a fine drive. . . . Well, the Lord cut short their day, and give his people dominion."[27]

It has already been noted that the Civil War dissolved restraints on Yankee speech. During these years Henry Ward Beecher, for example, proclaimed in rhetoric of volcanic grandeur the benefits and virtues to be associated with Yankee control. "It is the gospel that has saved the West and Northwest to this nation," thundered Beecher the summer of Gettysburg; it was eastern missionaries who carried Puritan ideas of human rights to the West. That the war was impoverishing the South while the North was engrossing wealth was simply God's way of preparing the North for the grand work before it.

We are to have charge of this continent. The South has been proved, and has been found wanting. She is not worthy to bear rule. She has lost the scepter in our national government, she is to lose the scepter in the States themselves; and this continent is to be from this time forth governed by Northern men, with Northern ideas, and with a Northern gospel.

"Is this sectional?" No, Christ was not born all over the world. "There must be a nest somewhere from out of which the bird, the eagle, can fly."

We hold the vitalizing principles of national life; and the nation is to be given to us because we have the bosom by which to nourish it. As a child feeds at the breast of its mother, so the nation is to feed upon us. . . . Our diocese will be little less than the whole continent.[28]

Nor did it forecast anything happy for the South when other men of zeal said, as cannon and muskets spoke their parts, that the fields of the South needed "Puritanizing, 'Yankee-izing,' if you will, as well as her institutions."[29] This is typical of statements implying rigorous treatment for the post-bellum South. From Terre Haute the Reverend Lyman Abbott wrote, as Sherman was about to march to the sea, "We have not only to conquer the South,—we have also to convert it."[30] An agent who toured the subdued area in 1866 justified strong measures because the Confederacy was then "as never before, Our Country." "As the Puritan has now triumphed over the Cavalier, he should take possession of his conquest." Another condoned the southward drift of "Northern capital, Northern enterprise, and Northern culture" because "an effete race and a semi-barbarism are to be supplanted by a hardier stock and a higher civilization."[31]

Such statements accord all too well with the view of W. J. Cash that the War and Reconstruction "represent in their primary aspect an attempt on the part of the Yankee to achieve by force what he had failed to achieve by political means . . . the will to make over the South in the prevailing American image and to sweep it into the main current of the nation."[32]

4. MECHANISMS AND METHODS

"Christian emigration and centralization"

"colleges among the wildflowers"

In addition to Sunday schools, missions, temperance pleas, Bibles, and tracts, one of the agencies by which Yankees hoped to curb the West was migration by colonies. A typical reference describes how, around 1836, a company of "intelligent Christian men in Connecticut" purchased a large tract near Peoria in Illinois. "By their laws, no undesirable characters could purchase land, and were so kept away, while those who were worthy were in every way encouraged, which insured good society from the start."[33] The special object of another such colony, organized at Bergen, New York, was "to plant institutions of religion and education, and at the same time consider the betterment of their growing families."[34] From Auburn Seminary a "Western Fraternity" was reported in 1827, whose members planned to settle in the West "contiguously, so as to form one Presbytery if possible."[35]

But the strongest calls for collective removal came from Yankees already in the West. From Galena, in 1830, the Reverend Aratus Kent wished his voice to "reverberate among the hill-tops of my loved New England, saying 'Brethren come over to the Mississippi and help us.'" It was duty; ministers should emigrate with their congregations pledged to settle in a body. From Jacksonville the Reverend J. M. Ellis wrote, the same year, that if eastern laymen had "one particle of missionary zeal or Christian enterprise,—it will kindle, it will burn and thousands will come."[36] Not ephemeral, this appeal was unchanged a generation later. "If I do not mistake," wrote a Yankee from Denmark, Iowa, "we greatly need some individual that holds the pen of a ready writer, to hold up distinctly before the churches the importance and duty of *Christian emigration and centralization.*"[37]

Yet it is not intended to say that only the Yankees saw the advantages of migrating in such numbers as to afford a congenial concentration. The Germans often went in force to rural as well as city destinations. Presbyterians from Kentucky and Quakers from the Carolinas concentrated on certain counties in Ohio, Indiana, and Illinois. To one Quaker remaining in North Carolina it seemed as though "all the good and wise were gathering in that free country."[38] A North

State man was pleased to say from Washington County, Indiana, that "the most of us hereabouts are old Carolinians or their descendants, & Old Pasquotank [County] is well represented." A settler near Mt. Morris, Illinois, was happy at the prospect of having "all of my old Marylanders around me. . . ."[39]

But the leaders of these groups never dreamed of equaling the stiff control undertaken by a Connecticut colony at Wethersfield, Illinois, as recited in a letter to its agents on location. The agents would see to sundry practical matters: surveys and subdivision; would ascertain how far from the village were the standing waters of Winnepeseoga Swamp; was there a stream that would carry a mill, and what should be the price of farms? Then, after the usual charge that all prospective settlers should give full evidence of proper character, the instruction concludes:

Begin your own labors in place with morning & evening prayers & reading the Scriptures. On your first Sabbath & every following one till you have a preacher, hold a prayer meeting & read a sermon. In this be neither negligent nor discouraged. And while you make it a steady object to promote the public good of the Connecticut Association & of the settlement as a whole, regard especially the literary, moral & religious improvement of the town of the region of country.[40]

Mass migrations were indeed congenial to the Puritan tradition. Whole parishes, parson and all, had sometimes migrated from Old England.[41] Lois Kimball Mathews mentions twenty-two colonies in Illinois alone, all of which originated in New England or New York, most of them planted between 1830 and 1840. She refers as well to such colonies in a half-dozen states outside the Old Northwest.[42] It is not surprising that at the close of the Civil War there was talk in the North of mass migrations to control the conquered Confederacy.[43] But such movements of people to the frontiers had their drawbacks; they were extravagant of Yankee manpower; they provoked irritation among non-Yankees in regions in which the colonists settled.[44]

Yankees also relied heavily upon collegiate training. In a powerful rationalization of the import of higher learning, the Reverend Richard Salter Storrs held that colleges are centers of that moral power which pervades, supplements, and controls all others. There is no limit to the diffusion of their influence which, in an order as socially fluid as the American, is universal. They nurture democracy, commerce, patriotism, and philanthropy, and ply for the security and interests of all classes. They endanger not the common schools; indeed the lower had sprung from the higher, after which they flourish side by side as reciprocals. The "tower and armory" of the entire Yankee movement, all other devices were by comparison superficial and fugitive.[45]

Others believed with Dr. Storrs that the colleges had "in no small measure made the people what they were," that they informed "the educated and ruling mind"—editors, authors, ministers, teachers.[46] "Whoever educates the great West, gains possession of the helm of the nation and controls the destinies of the world," declared the report of one organization.[47] How better achieve this control, queried another, than by "founding colleges among the wild flowers, and in the very footprints of the savages?"[48] An agent sent to the East to procure funds for Illinois College promised: "Give me this sum and the Mississippi Valley is ours." A professor in the same college avowed: "What New Haven is in Connecticut, I would make Jacksonville in Illinois."[49] Moreover, colleges would help to define and defend the paths of trade and ensure the kind of "mercantile morality" the Yankees wished to prevail at large.[50]

Small wonder that with stakes so high Lyman Beecher "thought seriously of going over to Cincinnati, the London of the West,"[51] and did so. Or that Illinois College was mentioned among activities which excited among non-Yankees alarm "nearly equal to that of Belshazzar. . . ."[52] But meanwhile non-Puritan churchmen also, aware of the leverage of higher education and believing that "the President of a superior college had it in his power to do more harm or good than the President of the United States," were building their own colleges in the Northwest.[53]

Because the Yankee outreach was broadly popular, teachers, tradesmen, artisans, farmers were, each in their way, servants of destiny.[54]   It is not surprising that an individual attached to a great organization should feel the high import of his work, as did the one who wrote from Illinois: "When I look upon the vast and beautiful prairie surrounding our town, and think that in a few years it will be covered with cultivated fields, and inhabited by thousands, I feel a most intense desire that the right kind of moral institutions should grow up with the increasing population."[55]   But it is a little surprising to find that individual teachers from New England, not attached to an institution, entertained a similar feeling.   Writing from the village of Ontario, La Grange County, Indiana, a teacher who signed himself "H.V.W." told how several teachers from various towns in Massachusetts had by chance settled near that Indiana village.   Teaching he considered vital: ". . . you cannot serve your country better than by assisting to lay well (after New England style) the foundations of the institutions of learning that are springing up throughout this western land."[56]

For the general improvement of western people the individual Yankee was urged to "mingle freely and unsuspiciously with his neighbors, and while he sinks his manners to their level, strive to bring up their habits, by successful example, to the New England standard."[57]   Yankees in southern Illinois would do more to elevate the farming technique of their southern-bred neighbors "than all the agricultural papers in the world; for them they never read."[58]   Even isolated Yankee families could present examples of the stricter family discipline favored by Yankees, "a sacred duty which parents owe to their children and to society. . . ."[59]

Individuals were instruments of the movement in at least one other interesting way.   Certain eastern workers in the West, unwilling to await the eventual fruits of preaching, teaching, and commerce, asked that Easterners of designated callings and financial rating be sent to them. Thus Samuel Merriwether wrote from Jeffersonville, Indiana, on July 31, 1833, to Absalom Peters in New York City, suggesting that a cabinetmaker, "a young Brother in the Lord," might migrate thence and take over the Sunday school.[60] Another such "rebuilder" besought the migration to Illinois of some of the "christian mechanics" of New York—paper makers, tanners— yet he advised that their recruitment be gone about quietly.[61]

More importunate and detailed was the appeal of the Reverend Moses H. Wilder, writing from China, in southern Indiana:

We want 3 intelligent Pious Farmers who love souls to emi- grate and settle among us. One could buy a farm now owned by a Baptist Universalist drin[king?][62] Preacher who is a deadly enemy to everything like improvement price say $500. Another could in another neighborhood purchase a farm now owned by a *campbelite* and when he moves away their strength is gone in the neighborhood—$600.

A third could purchase a valuable farm now owned by the Elder which we have just dismissed to go to Mr. R's ch[urch] in Madison and with him Mr. R[ussell] would leave the neighbor- hood for he would have no one to hold up his hand—price $800. In each of these places such a man would be able to sustain a Sabbath School . . . and . . . would soon relieve your Society from further aid to us. Can you not send us these men?[63]

5. THE YANKEES SHOUT VICTORY

"little less than the whole continent"

Only rarely during the generation after the *Reformer's* editors had scolded Beecher in the early 1820's did any son of the Puritans express misgiving about the "great tide of light & truth . . . settling westward so powerfully & rapidly."[64] They intended to touch and fashion American life in its totality, and for a time, especially during the two decades following the Mexican War, they felt themselves highly successful. Victory and the benefits of victory were proclaimed in many ways, and the exuberance of these boastings supplies additional detail as to what the Yankees intended to accomplish.

A "vast deal of true Yankee ingenuity" had enabled the West to overcome certain of its economic difficulties. Deep plowing, among other meritorious practices, had shown what "northern energy" could accomplish on the worn out lands of Virginia.[65] But a letter written by a lay Yankee from California in 1848 shows most readily the "total" character of the presumed conquest, also the intenseness of an irreverent layman's sense of mission. Recovering from a pang of misgiving at his country's breath-taking growth, the writer proceeded:

Yet, why should I regret? Louisiana, Florida, Texas, were once, and but a few years since, the territories of France and Spain. Ultra foreigners in language, birth, race, habits, manners, and religion! but now naturalized, fraternized—incorporated with that all-pervading solvent and amalgam, the universal Yankee nation. . . . Thus push we the bark of enterprise, adventure, conquest and commerce along, till we are fairly installed on the mountain heights that overlook the broad Pacific. Here am I, a confirmed emigrant, one of the foremost of that pioneer, pilgrim band, that starting from the North Atlantic shore, pursue the setting sun in his course. . . . This looks to me as the destiny of the Saxon, or Anglo-American race. If they fail to carry it out, it will be from their losing a part of that roving, restless (and if it were not for the alliteration, I would say) resistlessly-reforming principle, that has hitherto impelled them to come in contact with everything, and renovate everything they touched. So operative will be these national characteristics, that California will soon be California no longer. The hordes of emigrants and adventurers, (now or soon to be on their way here,) will speedily convert this wild, cattle-breeding, lasso-throwing, idle, bigoted, bull-baiting race, into an industrious, shrewd, trafficking, Protestant set of thorough-going Yankees.[66]

Commentary as to how the victory was being achieved ranged from trifling anecdote to analyses admirable for their depth of understanding. A New Englander thrilled at winning the confidence of a southern squatter in Iowa by introducing him to mince pie and candles. "He would be 'consarned' if he would not have some of them Yankee fixings," the squatter exclaimed on return to his rail-pen home. Upon which the Easterner exulted: "Thus has the power of example been felt widely; and the process of assimilation to New England tastes and the conquest to New England principles have been extended, until their complete triumph has been made certain throughout the Northwest."[67]

When Washington feared western parties he did not foresee home missions, began another's explanation conventionally enough, but his remarks quickly transcended the commonplace: "Your pioneer evangelism carries nationality along every parallel of latitude," he assured. There were indeed "century-long processes of society and history" which would eventually bind divisive elements into nationality. "But we cannot wait for these. Under the ministry of your missionaries, the thing is often done suddenly, as it were in the twinkling of an eye." Therefore, "Let missions, like freedom, follow the flag everywhere. The cannon of Fremont and Halleck will set before them many an open door. So, but gently and silently will the Homestead Bill, the Pacific Railroad . . . set before them many more."[68]

The Reverend H. D. Kitchel of Detroit assured hearers that "Puritanized Saxon Blood, as pure as that which flows in the veins of Boston," had worked the miracle. "By far the most operative and influential, wherever it goes," its work was evident throughout a vast "New England zone."

It is the plastic and organizing force. It is not number, but weight, that tells in the formative process of a colonial state. A single family of genuine Puritan substance . . . is a germ, around which a whole flood of miscellaneous population will take form, and serve as nutriment. More than by its numbers, the innate validity of this element molds the rising communities of the West, and unconsciously fashions all after the ideas with which it comes charged.

Even non-Christian New England families could be influential; they knew what a school, a church, a town meeting was, "and the subtle presence has a mastery. . . . It works dimly for a time, amid the colonial chaos; but presently, as the social web turns right side up, the figure appears—it's the New England pattern."[69]

Another pleasing belief was that New England, in addition to giving western communities shade trees, colleges, good morals, and temperance, had at last made good the great sea-to-sea patent of 1620; had harmonized discordant elements, "given character" to states such as Iowa and Kansas, and even bound to the Union "by a telegraphic and moral sympathy" the "chaotic mass" of California's population.[70] Perhaps the Chilean cleric, Melchior Martinez, was correct when years before he referred to the United States as "the Boston republic."[71]

Whether New England might pay overdearly for her role of *"seminarium heroum"* was long a disturbing question. Early in the nineteenth century spokesmen were imploring that the bleeding by migration be stanched. "For more reasons than I have time to assign," pleaded one, "New England is the place in which to live and to die."[72] But even sectional decline could have its glory. Said one periodical in summarizing this disturbing topic:

New England has declined only because she has been translated. We go back and look in the old nest and find nothing there but shells; on the trees, all through the forests, are the winged ones that rose from the house of straw to fill the whole land with beauty and music. New England has declined—into America. Plymouth Rock is only the doorstep of a house that reaches to the Golden Gate.[73]

Deliberate, calculating, even "scientific," the engineers of this cultural movement were perfectly aware of the implications of their words and acts. Often their language attained a poetic level as they spoke of their task as they conceived it—the fashioning of diverse materials, "like those of the image which was of gold, silver, brass, iron, and clay," into the symmetry of one body. One wonders whether any other essay in the propagation of a culture was ever undertaken—within a free social order—on a similar scale, with a fuller consciousness of the ends to be achieved and the agencies employed, or in a spirit of more militant sincerity.[74]

NOTES

[1] *The Country Gentleman* (Albany, N. Y.), III (June 15, 1854), 383, quoting New York *Courier and Enquirer.*

[2] Marcus L. Hansen, *The Immigrant in American History* (Cambridge, 1940), p. 103.

[3] *Home Missionary,* XII (March, 1840), 246; XI (January, 1839), 209; XIII (April, 1841), 266.

[4] *Ibid.,* XXXVI (August, 1863), 88.

[5] *New England Magazine* (Boston), III (1832), 198; Howard A. Bridgman, *New England in the Life of the World* (Boston, 1920), pp. 10-11.

[6] Quoted in Albert H. Smyth, *The Philadelphia Magazines and Their Contributors, 1741-1850* (Philadelphia, 1892), p. 203.

[7] *The Reformer* (Philadelphia), I (October, 1820), 236-37. For more discussion of the "design," see Volume I (November, 1820), 241-58, and Volumes II and III. In Volume IV, Theophilus R. Gates was listed as "Proprietor and principal editor."

[8] John F. Cady, "The Religious Environment of Lincoln's Youth," in *Indiana Magazine of History,* XXXVII (March, 1941), 24; *Proceedings of the Western Baptist Education Society . . .* (Cincinnati, 1850), pp. 26-27.

[9] Ralph L. Rusk (ed.), *The Letters of Ralph Waldo Emerson* (6 volumes. New York, 1939), II, 122, note 78; I, 185, 350; III, 118; V, 200.

[10] *Home Missionary,* XXXVI (August, 1863), 91. See also Part 3 of this chapter.

[11] *The Reformer,* III (March, 1822), 49-57 (quoting the *Boston Recorder,* January 26, 1822), describes the twenty years' effort. See also Mae E. Harveson, *Catharine Esther Beecher, Pioneer Educator* (Philadelphia, 1932), pp. 120-21, and Donald G. Tewksbury, *The Founding of American Colleges and Universities before the Civil War . . .* (New York, 1932), pp. 9-15.

[12] *Home Missionary,* XVI (July, 1843), 49 ff.

[13] *Ibid.,* X (January, 1838), 137-38; XI (January, 1839), 209-10; XI (February, 1839), 225.

[14] *Ibid.,* III (June, 1830), 27; XXIV (September, 1851), 109.

[15] Henry Ward Beecher, *Freedom and War, Discourses on Topics Suggested by the Times* (Boston, 1863), p. 421.

[16] Philip D. Jordan (ed.), *Letters of Eliab Parker Mackintire to William Salter, 1845-1863* (New York, 1936), p. 7.

[17] George Lewis Prentiss, *The Union Theological Seminary . . . with a Sketch of . . . Charles Butler, L. L. D.* (Asbury Park, N. J., 1899), pp. 452 ff., 474, 498. See also sketch of Butler in *Dictionary of American Biography,* III, 359; Esarey, *History of Indiana,* I, 431-34.

[18] *Home Missionary,* XII (May, 1839), 10, and XXXVII (August, 1864), 86-87; see also III (June, 1830), 27, and XXIV (September, 1851), 109.

[19] Henry Barnard, "Observations on the West and South, 1840's," in *Journal of Southern History,* VIII (May, 1942), 246.

[20] *Home Missionary*, XXXVI (August, 1863), 88; XVI (August, 1843), 87-88, Socialism; XVII (March, 1845), 251-52, Fourierism.

[21] *Ibid.*, XIII (February, 1841), 228-29.

[22] John C. Miller, *Sam Adams, Pioneer in Propaganda* (Boston, 1936), p. 315.

[23] Quoted by Bernard Fay in *The Revolutionary Spirit in France and America* (New York, 1927), p. 363.

[24] *Home Missionary*, XIV (April, 1842), 277; XXIV (July, 1851), 58.

[25] "Letter of George Churchill of Madison County, Illinois, to Mr. Swift Eldred, Warren, Connecticut, September 9, 1818," in *Journal of the Illinois State Historical Society*, XI (April, 1918), 65.

[26] Benjamin E. Gallup, Chicago, to Richard E. Ela, Rochester, Wisconsin, September 30, 1854, in *Wisconsin Magazine of History*, XX (September, 1936), 88.

[27] Reverend J. A. Johnson, in *Home Missionary*, XLI (May, 1868), 6.

[28] *Ibid.*, XXXVI (September, 1863), 109-12. For similar views by others see XXXVII (September, 1864), 113; XXXVI (August, 1863), 85-91.

[29] *Ibid.*, XXXV (August, 1862), 90.

[30] *New Englander* (New Haven), XXIII (October, 1864), 701.

[31] *Home Missionary*, XXXVIII (March, 1866), 253, 261; XXXIX (August, 1866), 91-92.

[32] *The Mind of the South* (New York, 1941), p. 103. For corroboration of many phases of this chapter see an able article by George Winston Smith, "Some Northern Wartime Attitudes toward the Post-Civil War South," in *Journal of Southern History*, X (August, 1944), 253-74. Use by Northerners of schoolteachers as an instrument of policy has been studied recently. From 1862 to 1872 probably five to six million dollars were spent for teaching. Of the 9,503 teachers in Freedom schools in 1869 perhaps 5,000 were northern natives. A heavy New England influence is evident. The Boston *Advertiser* said there must be a Yankee school in every county so that in the future the people should "march arm in arm with Massachusetts." Leaders calculated expendables: at the cost of a "light brigade of school mistresses," ran one view, a colony worth more than any English possession might be achieved and a market developed for northern-made furniture, cutlery, cloth, yarn, rope, sewing machines, staves, kettles, and dry goods; the profits would at once enrich the North and pay for schooling the Negroes. Henry Lee Swint, *The Northern Teacher in the South 1862-1872* (Nashville, Tenn., 1941), pp. 3, 32-34, 46, 56, 58.

[33] Stories of Pioneer Mothers of Illinois. MSS collected in 1893, in ILLSL.

[34] Ella Hume Taylor, "A History of the First Congregational Church of Geneseo [Illinois]," in *Journal of the Illinois State Historical Society*, XX (April, 1927), 113.

[35] Letter of A. S. Wells, Auburn, New York, January 24, 1827, AHMS. The American Home Missionary Society was organized in 1826 by societies of Congregational, Presbyterian, Associate Reformed, and Dutch Reformed

churches. After 1861 it was entirely Congregational. Absalom Peters, who
was a leader in its establishment, served as corresponding secretary from
1825 to 1837, and from 1828 to 1836 he edited the *Home Missionary*. Letters
from missionaries in the field were usually addressed to Peters.

Vermontville, Michigan, was praised as a model product of mass migration. See *Home Missionary*, III (May, 1830), 14; XIV (May, 1841),
editorials. Also XXI (November, 1848), 164; XXXVIII (December,
1865), 197; *Luminary* (Lexington, Ky.), May 25, 1831, p. 391.

[36] Letters of Kent, February 9, July 31, 1830, and Ellis, March 8, 1830,
AHMS; see also James Crawford, Delphi, Indiana, July 10, 1832, AHMS.

[37] *Home Missionary*, XXXVIII (January, 1866), 212.

[38] George R. Wilson, *History of Dubois County [Indiana]* . . . (Jasper,
Ind., 1910), p. 102; Emma A. and James Arthur Donnell, *The Donnells and
Their Macdonald Ancestors* . . . (Greenfield, Ind., 1928), Chapter III;
Branson L. Harris, *Some Recollections of My Boyhood* (Indianapolis, c.
1906), p. 58; "S. B." to Elizabeth Stanton, Guilford County, North Caro-
lina, April 1 [early 1830's], IHS; *Life and Travels of Addison Coffin
Written by Himself* (Cleveland, 1897), p. 61.

[39] Henry Gregory, Canton, Indiana, to "Dear Willy," February 24, 1869,
William Morris collection, DU; James H. Smith, Mt. Morris, Illinois, to
David Ports, Boonesborough, Maryland, November 23, 1846, ILLSL.

[40] C. J. Tenney to John F. Willard and Henry G. Little, 1836, Illinois
Historical Survey, Urbana.

[41] Edward Channing, *A History of the United States* (6 volumes +
supplementary map volume. New York, 1905-26), I, 426-27.

[42] Lois Kimball Mathews, *The Expansion of New England* (Boston,
1909), pp. 215-16.

[43] Smith, "Some Northern Wartime Attitudes Toward the Post-Civil
War South," in *Journal of Southern History*, X (August, 1944), 259.

[44] "But 'colonies' make a very small portion of the emigration to this
State." Editorial in Springfield *Sangamo Journal*, May 5, 1838.

[45] Richard Salter Storrs, Jr., D. D., *A Discourse . . . for the Promotion
of Collegiate Education at the West* (New York, 1856), pp. 4-21.

The address of Governor Everett of Massachusetts at the Essex cattle
show (1836) extols education as New England's "proudest boast": "Hus-
bandmen, sow your seed of instruction in your sons' and daughters' minds.
It will grow up and bear fruit, though the driving storm scatter the blos-
soms of spring, or untimely frost overtake the hopes of autumn. Plant the
germ of truth in the infant understandings of your children; save, stint,
spare, scrape,—do anything but steal—in order to nourish that growth; and
it is little,—nothing to say, that it will flourish when your grave-stones,
crumbled into dust, shall mingle with the dust they covered;—and it will
flourish, when the over-arched heaven shall pass away like a scroll, and the
eternal sun, which lightens it shall set in blood!" Quoted from *Salem
Gazette* in *The Cultivator* (Albany, N. Y.), O. S. III (December, 1836), 161.

[46] Quoted by Tewksbury in *The Founding of American Colleges and
Universities*, p. 5.

[47] Quoted by Harveson, *Catharine Esther Beecher*, p. 121. See also Albert Barnes, *Home Missions, A Sermon* (New York, 1849), p. 40, and *passim*.

[48] *New Englander*, IV (April, 1846), 277.

[49] Quoted in Pease, *The Frontier State*, pp. 417, 419.

[50] Tewksbury, *The Founding of American Colleges and Universities*, pp. 12-13.

[51] Charles Beecher (ed.), *The Autobiography and Correspondence . . . of Lyman Beecher* (2 volumes. New York, 1866), II, 224.

[52] Samuel Mallory and William Proctor, Lewiston, Illinois, to Absalom Peters, corresponding secretary, December 28, 1829. See also Robert K. Richardson, "The Mindedness of the Early Faculty of Beloit College," in *Wisconsin Magazine of History*, XIX (September, 1935), 32-70.

[53] George P. Schmidt, *The Old Time College President* (New York, 1930), pp. 29-30. See Chapter V below, Part 5.

[54] Bridgman, *New England in the Life of the World*, p. 6. Among the first ten graduating classes of Illinois College were 32 clergymen, 7 physicians, 6 lawyers, 2 educators, 2 farmers, and 1 inventor. Among the first 25 graduates of Knox College were 11 clergymen. See Ernest G. Hildner, "Colleges and College Life in Illinois 100 Years Ago," in *Papers in Illinois History, 1942* (Springfield, 1944), p. 25.

[55] *Home Missionary*, XXXIII (October, 1860), 150.

[56] *Boston Cultivator*, XIV (November 27, 1852), 380.

[57] Abner D. Jones, *Illinois and the West* (Philadelphia and Boston, 1838), p. 156.

[58] Herbert A. Kellar (ed.), *Solon Robinson, Pioneer Agriculturist* (2 volumes. *Indiana Historical Collections*, XXI, XXII, Indianapolis, 1936), I, 424.

[59] *Prairie Farmer* (Chicago), VI (April, 1848), 123. Vermont boasted no police, that no murder had been committed in the state within ten years, and eulogized its ". . . homes, genuine homes, that are the center of the world to its inmates, for which the father works, votes and talks—where the mother controls, educates, labors and loves—where she rears men, scholars and patriots." Quoted in *Ohio Farmer* (Cleveland), February 2, 1854, from Rutland (Vt.) *Herald*.

[60] AHMS.

[61] Reverend John F. Brooks, Belleville, Illinois, to Peters, October 8, 1832, AHMS.

[62] The manuscript is torn at this point.

[63] Letter dated February 3, 1834, AHMS.

[64] Reverend J. R. Wheelock, Greensburg, Indiana, to Peters, May 9, 1833, AHMS.

[65] *The Cultivator*, O. S. IX (October, 1842), 154; *The Country Gentleman*, V (June 25, 1855), 391.

[66] *American Agriculturist* (New York), VIII (February, 1849), 58-59.

[67] *Home Missionary*, XXXIX (February, 1867), 248.

[68] *Ibid.*, XXXV (August, 1862), 87-90. A waggish version of this idea

also appears: "Warlike Wit, a farmer in southern Illinois, seeing the cannon at Cairo, remarked that 'Them brass missionaries had converted a heap of folks.'" *Yankee Notions* (New York), X, (August, 1861), 229.

[69] *Congregational Quarterly* (Boston), III (October, 1861), 341-42.

[70] *Home Missionary*, XXXVI (August, 1863), 85-91.

[71] Bernard Moses, *The Intellectual Background of the Revolution in South America* (New York, 1926), p. 39.

[72] *New England Farmer* (Boston), II (January 24, 1824), 203.

[73] *Home Missionary*, XLII (November, 1869), 174, quoting *Liberal Christian.*

[74] Even in the 1940's the old warmth rekindles when Yankees recall their past—and consider the national future: "America is striving toward unity. In that process the Yankee has a big part to play. In the Middle West he is strong. He has 'vanished' only from New England. With the Anglo-Saxon of the South he is the largest part of the American 'melting pot.' This does not mean that a Yankee mould should be imposed upon America. Unity cannot be won by coercion. America is a new thing in the world. The Puritans played probably the biggest part in its development. Decade by decade they may lose themselves in a new American type, but if America is to go on being America it must preserve or call to rebirth the spiritual strengths of Puritan character." Editorial in *Christian Science Monitor* (Boston), December 30, 1940.

Chapter II

THE MEN AS COLONIZERS

1. Chattels and Live Lumber

Suckers: "an unwanted excrescence"

A notice which originated in a Danville, Kentucky, newspaper of the 1820's can be taken as broadly descriptive of a large portion of the southern settlers who pressed northward:

> Emigrants—the number of movers passing daily through this place westward, is astonishing. They are generally poor, having their plunder packed on horses, or in carts drawn by calves, cows, and horses, or in some instances by oxen and horses. Several days during the last week the road was literally filled with movers.
>
> Nine-tenths of these movers are from North Carolina, South Carolina, Georgia, Virginia, and other southern and eastern slaveholding states; the remainder are all our citizens, all pressing to the free states on our western frontier.[1]

Contemporaries were impressed by the poverty of early southern comers to the Northwest, especially those who came to Indiana and Illinois. A New Hampshire man believed that migrants to Indiana in 1816 were from some cause not so wealthy as the settlers of the other territories. A Scottish traveler contrasted Pennsylvania where the "most extensive" farmers prevailed, and Ohio where the "first" and "second" classes were most numerous, with Indiana where "backwoodsmen and second-rate settlers" predominated.[2]

A German traveler in the 1820's was assured by his landlord that at least two hundred wagons full of emigrants had crossed the Ohio River at Vevay, Indiana, that season in flight from the insolent behavior of their more wealthy neighbors. Writing in the 1870's, Judge Charles H. Test of Indiana recalled seeing "a family of eight or ten following on foot a cow, on the back of which was thrown a sack containing all their worldly goods," quitting states where the poor white man was regarded as little superior to slaves or cattle. References to the early population of Illinois are similar. One explanation of the nickname "Sucker" was that the poorer class, like the sucker on the tobacco plant, was an unwanted excrescence. The proportion of very poor people is great, wrote a home-missions worker from Illinois in 1831.[3]

The shelters and households of these southern-bred people also indicate poverty.[4] As late as 1859 a Yankee missionary was surprised that not a single family in his southern Illinois congregation possessed a glass lantern to light the way home from church in mud and darkness, and charitably explained that they were "not accustomed to many of the conveniences of life." Western women were amused at the use by Yankees of clothes lines—the former dried their wash on fences or bushes—also at clothes pins, "them little boys ridin' a rope." A similar absence of "fixings" is illustrated by a Virginia farmer living (1832) near New Philadelphia, Ohio, in a two-story house on four hundred acres. Here the victuals were good, yet a whole knife, fork, or spoon was not to be had. Every aspect of the household was as deficient except the beds.[5]

The inference that poverty pursued these men across the Ohio River is supported by a review of farmland values in Ohio, Indiana, and Illinois, based upon the Federal census of 1850. The criterion of $100 value of farmland per capita was adopted for this comparison.[6] Two conclusions stand out: Ohio's superiority in landed wealth; only nine Ohio counties fell below, while many ranged several fold above the criterion of $100; which adds interest to a traveler's commendation of the middle-class quality of Ohio's society: born aristocrats had been excluded by early hardships, and the "free beggars" by the high price of land.[7] The other conspicuous point is the inferiority in land wealth in areas settled predominantly by southern stock. Some fifty contiguous counties of south-

Map of Ohio showing counties having less than a $100
valuation of farmland per capita, 1850.
(U. S. Census, 1850)

western Indiana and southern Illinois—an area which long
baffled reforming New Englanders[8]—fell with the exception
of one county below the criterion.

Of Williamson County, located in the heartland of Egypt, a
resident historian wrote that no other county of Illinois was
settled with so little capital—not until after 1830 could he find
record of an individual worth as much as a thousand dollars.
Yet the fifty counties in southern Indiana–Illinois suggest
that Williamson County, notwithstanding two thirds of its
population were, until 1835, hunters, was far from singular
in the meagerness of its wealth, and that its claim might have
been successfully challenged.[9]

As one historian advised his readers to stand at Cumberland
Gap to observe the southern emigration, so one may study the

Map of Indiana showing counties having less than a
$100 valuation of farmland per capita, 1850.
(U. S. Census, 1850)

Yankee migration, admixed with "natives of all climates and
countries," at the quays and docks of Buffalo. "Canal boats,
filled with emigrants, and covered with goods and furniture,
are almost hourly arriving," a correspondent wrote to the
Genesee Farmer in the spring of 1832.

Several steamboats and vessels daily depart for the far west,
literally crammed with masses of living beings. . . . Some days,
near a thousand thus depart. Hundreds and hundreds of horse

Map of Illinois showing counties having
less than a $100 valuation of farmland per
capita, 1850.
(U. S. Census, 1850)

wagons arrive every spring and fall with emigrants from our own
state; and when at Buffalo, the whole caravan, consisting of
family, horses, dog, wagon and furniture, are put on board the
steamboats, and landed either in Ohio or Michigan. Some even
go round through the upper lakes and land at Chicago, and pursue
their courses to Indiana, Illinois or Missouri.

Not fourteen years since, in August, 1818, the first steamboat built on Lake Erie, the "Walk-in-the-Water," had left

Buffalo for Detroit to begin a financially hazardous enterprise.
"She made a trip every eight days, and hardly supported
herself. Now, two steamboats leave Buffalo daily for the
ports west . . . besides several schooners of 50 to 150 tons
burthen; and for the last two years their average profits, de-
ducting all expenses, have been from 50 to 75 percent. . . ."[10]

The following spring the Buffalo waterfront was equally
busy. Over six hundred passengers had cleared for the West
in a single boat. Included in the freight—as pretty an assortment as heart might desire to see—were pigs, poultry, dogs,
cats, cattle and sheep, boxes, bales, barrels, hogsheads, crates,
wagons, carts, implements, spinning wheels, and cradles.[11] In
addition to the westward lake traffic originating at Buffalo
there were by 1833 at least three scheduled upriver steamers a
week, as well as an occasional schooner, from Ogdensburg,
New York, and Prescott, Ontario, at the foot of Great
Lakes–St. Lawrence navigation.[12]

These glimpses at Buffalo set the Yankees apart in variety
and bulk of personal goods transported: luxury possessions
brought to Illinois in the 1830's, fine clothing, which aroused
envious curiosity in the Westerners, clocks, a handsome saddle
from New York City.[13] Meanwhile a letter from Illinois to
Connecticut illustrates early traffic in bulky goods as well as
desire to carry westward as much as possible of New England.

When you come, I wish you to bring me *onion seed,* of the real old
fashioned (Wethersfield?) also, some of the crooknecked squash
and summer squash. You will also do well to bring a good assortment of *garden seeds,* and *fruit tree seeds,* such as *pears, plums,
cherries,* etc., and not forget *clover* and *timothy* seed. Do not be
satisfied with bringing enough for your own use, but bring some
to speculate upon, and some for your humble servant.[14]

Indeed from the beginnings of settlement the Yankees
brought to the Northwest goods of bulk and heft—"chattels
and live lumber," one Marylander called it. A letter directed
to Senator Thomas Worthington in 1804 represents that the
frontiersmen of Trumbull County, Ohio, depended upon

Yankee incomers for supplies of Genesee whiskey, boots, shoes, hats, and axes. The Buckeye men protested the levying of import duties at the present site of Erie, Pennsylvania, on such goods which, in their transport, had been temporarily outside the United States.[15]

In bringing "seed corn and irish tators" across the mountains to Kentucky one William Calk, according to his journal, March, 1775, achieved enviable priority.[16] But most examples of pioneer commerce turn a little pale beside the 2,500 pounds of freight brought by Col. John May from Boston to the Marietta settlement in the summer of 1788. The Colonel considered it "not a little extraordinary" that his party and cargo, which included as a minor item eighty quarries of window glass, should achieve the thirty days' journey to Pittsburgh having lost nothing of more worth than a penknife. From Pittsburgh Colonel May proceeded in a boat crowded with twenty-seven men, two cows and two calves, seven hogs, and nine dogs, besides eight tons of luggage. Yet we may perhaps expect the unusual from a party which included New England men "of the first respectability" who doubtless later shared the Colonel's contempt for five "poor devils" who, discouraged with the Ohio settlement, turned homeward in mid-June, 1788, as they had come, "moneyless and brainless."[17]

A second inference from a visit to the docks of Buffalo is that with the Yankees, far more than with the Uplanders, migration meant an immediate cash outlay. The elaborate transport system of the canals and lakes necessarily relied upon patrons with cash in hand. A New Hampshire man in Wisconsin said in apparent sincerity that only Yankees from fertile spots of New England could afford to migrate. If a man on a poor farm ceased laboring long enough for the idea to shoot across his brain, his whole family would starve. Only the naked fact of being a bachelor "saved my bacon," he added.[18]

Yankee writings are much concerned with finances. A New England woman writing from Indiana in 1838 advised her cousin that a migrant "wants at least a thousand dollars

to start with."[19]   An Illinois minister makes it clear that three
of his poorer but benevolent parishioners—together they had
contributed forty dollars to church support—had recently
removed from the East on a money basis; one from York
State eighteen months before with twenty-one dollars in
cash; another had borrowed to pay the freight on his goods; a
third from New England a few years since with seventy-five
cents in cash.[20]   One may be sure that possession of any surplus
at the end of so costly an experience implies access to considerable funds at the start.

At the same time a better-to-do sort of settler was reported
in northern portions of the Northwest.   James Crawford, a
Yankee missionary, referred in 1827 to the incredibly large
migration to southern Indiana: "Our State is literally filling
up with poor—but generally industrious people. . . ."   Five
years later he reported the people of a northern Indiana community, settling chiefly from Ohio and the East, "more wealthy
and enterprising and perhaps more intelligent than first settlers
generally are."   Wisconsin could boast that in a single land
district farmer-settlers paid $800,000 in cash to the government
during one month; while from Michigan came the word that
lands were available only for cash, which brought from
Absalom Peters, editor of the *Home Missionary* on a western
tour in 1830, hearty approval: "The moral character of the
population of Michigan must surpass that of any new country
whose settlers are encouraged to take up their lands on the
credit system, which opens the door to idle and profligate
men, and in the end operates as an embarrassment to the
wealth and good morals of the community."[21]

A Virginian sightseeing in New England over a century
ago reported "not a hundredth part of the appearance of
abject, squalid poverty, that our state presents."[22]   Such a
remark prepares us to suspect that the poverty of the Uplanders
would disparage them in the minds of Yankees, with whom it
was conventional opinion that by "a fixed and inevitable law,
ignorance is allied with poverty, and intelligence with wealth,"

and who prided themselves that in no other part of the civilized
world were so few indigent poor to be found as in New England: "This forms one of the best traits of our character. . . ."[23]

2. SOCIETY, MIXED AND PURE

"some leven [sic] of a better character"

Helpfully differentiative, a historian of early American
culture remarks that New England was to a large degree "East
Anglia transplanted to America," while the older part of
Virginia eastward of the Blue Ridge was "a cross section of all
England shaken apart and reunited in a different pattern."[24]

From whatever cause—cohesiveness of her social institutions or sharply defined natural boundaries—New England remained, until the 1830's at least, more continuously homogeneous than most American regions had been, comparatively
unaffected by the variety of stocks that had occupied other
parts of the country.[25]

Yet those Englishmen who were shaken apart and reunited
had, for Southerners, no unique experience. Later comers
found themselves within a mixing bowl containing humanity
still more oddly assorted. In the valley of western Virginia,
for example "Tuckahoe" (lowland) and "Cohee" (upland)
elements, including Germans, Scotch-Irish, former servants,
men of means, slaveholders, the slaveless, and men of divers
faiths, mingled and merged ways of living.[26] Indeed this
great troughlike valley which extended behind the Blue Ridge
from Pennsylvania to Georgia eventually channeled thousands
of these men of mixed backgrounds through Cumberland
Gap, which in turn headed them toward Tennessee, Arkansas,
Missouri, Kentucky, and the Old Northwest.[27]

It is historically important that by the time the Upland
Southerner reached the Northwest as a settler he had traveled
circuitously and far. Compared with the Yankee, his migration
had been prolonged and devious, often lasting through several
generations and stages. Frequent change in surroundings had

modified his blood, feeling, and faith. It is not surprising
that the Yankees, fresh from an order they considered
superior to any other, proud of their "common character"—
even the Chinese were scarcely more homogeneous—[28] reacted
sharply to stock so hopelessly miscellaneous. Yankees also
looked unfavorably upon western men because of their mobility
and restlessness; and because of a damaging lag in community
improvement, a consequence, Yankees thought, of the preceding faults.

Of all descriptives applied to the western people "heterogeneous" was probably the word or idea most frequently
drawn. Indiana's populace was "most heterogeneous," a
"heterogeneous mass," and "a crude raw mass." Its social
order was "in an unfortunate State composed of persons from
every part of the Union."[29] On the eve of midcentury the
Hoosier populace was still described by a worldly-wise
Easterner as "the strangest mixture" he had ever seen.

Illinois was called "peculiarly notable for its diversity."[30]
In addition to the expected melange reports depicted various
strata and classes.[31] While the holding of slaves was not
tolerated, a Southerner wrote from Shawneetown in 1819 of
a "certain class of people who supply their place." Another
explained that these pariahs presently left "Egypt" for destinations such as Missouri, Arkansas, and Texas. But the riddance
must have been incomplete. After the Civil War there was
still reported a "deplorable system of caste"—a "Brahmin or
Northern" group, middle-class natives who imitated its superior
ways, and outcasts from the South of such "hideous depravity"
as the writer had never before seen. Between these classes, the
writer added, there was no communion.[32] Thus it appears
that the "complex social structure" of white elements in the
ante-bellum South was appreciably visited upon the Northwest.[33]

Also, an early textbook in geography explains that Indiana
was settled "for the most part by young men, either unmarried
or without families," which implies a greater than common
footlooseness.[34] Indiana's people were termed a "floating

unsettled class, waiting an opportunity to sell and move out farther," of "a moving character," and "very floating." Others mentioned the "prevailing thirst for immigration," complained of the "changeableness of our population" or remarked that "few people seemed to be settled."[35]

At Kaskaskia in southern Illinois the velocity of moving population was so brisk that workers, far from able to establish a church, were content "to recover here and there one from the *moving* families as they remained in place for a few months of the year & then pass to other parts of the country, as one would stand upon the bank of a river and save what he could of a wreck which was floating swiftly down the current."[36]

Thus, the question was whether people from the four quarters of the world would ever "settle down into anything like the moral and religious society of New England. . . ."[37] A Massachusetts farmer found in the Northwest in 1839 "little of that harmony and kindly feeling which exists among the people of New England; and a long period must elapse before the whole population will become assimilated and melted down into one homogeneous mass. Good society may be found in the West, even in the newest settlements, but it must be selected."[38]

What transiency and delayed improvement meant to a young southern-bred physician was left for the record by Dr. Charles Hay, father of diplomat John Hay. "The word 'moving,' " he noted in 1830 at Salem (on a main route across southern Indiana), "is almost as odious to me as the term revolution is said to be in France." Every kind of business suffered whether of merchant, mechanic, or physician, said Dr. Hay, who also feared that western Indiana and Illinois were settling "with a great deal of the sweepings of Indiana itself." Yet he presumed there would be "some leven of a better character."[39]

In their turn the pious element reasoned that only a "pure morality" could draw the better class of people who would "increase still more the value of property." But morality was handicapped in communities where there were as many as

"twenty different denominations . . . so mixed that a
congregation can scarcely be found dence enough to assemble
statedly . . . strong enough to support a pastor." Desirable
settlers were reluctant to tarry where a preferred affiliation
was too weak to remain organized, a complaint seconded by
those who dreaded living without a pastor over the church.[40]

One must calculate the risk in designating certain areas as
more beset than others with frontier ills. From Chicago to
Cairo men filed complaints that the local populace was from
"everywhere in general & nowhere in particular," or that "this
Western Country is as Complete a Jargon as ever was Shinars
plain. . . ."[41] It is probable, too, that critic-viewers of the
West followed the worn grooves of travel, saw the "heterogeneous, disorderly" sort, but failed to see the "regular
people . . . chiefly settled back upon the head waters."[42]

Moreover, southern Indiana–Illinois lies below the soil
area most fertilized by glaciation. "This part of Indiana,"
wrote an onlooker in 1829 from Clark County (bordering the
Ohio River), is "considered old and poor . . . and a spirit of
emigration is quite prevalent."[43] A Kentuckian who followed
the Vincennes (Buffalo) Trace from Louisville to Vincennes
the next year said the "great majority of the land I passed
through was very poor, and a miserable population."[44] Nearly
a half century previously John Filson, explorer, surveyor, and
historian of early Kentucky termed the same stretch of country
diverse in its soil "but in no part so fertile as Kentucky. . . ."[45]

With terrain more rugged, heavier rainfall (40-60 inches
annually), and more pronounced damage from erosion, southern Indiana–Illinois was less agriculturally stable than the
Corn Belt to the northward (with 28 to 40 inches of rainfall).
This recalls certain pockets of "ten-year soil" (in the southern
belt) so designated because after a decade of cropping, erosion
had made them unprofitable to cultivate.[46]

It also appears that in addition to its handicap in soil
southern Indiana–Illinois lay at the outlet of a "corridor" which
spilled human beings northward across the Ohio River between

Cincinnati and Cairo. Through this passageway tens of thousands—some of them Poor Whites, more of them white and poor merely—fled from what was called "good states—to emigrate from."[47] Sundry points of historical geography suggest why the rate of human mobility should have remained brisk over several generations of time (for a pronounced northward drift is evident in the present century).[48]

For the Uplanders who migrated to escape the presence of slavery, Indiana and Illinois remained for several decades the nearest free soil. Iowa, the next free commonwealth in their latitude, did not reach territorial status until 1838 or enter the Union until 1846. Ohio, scarcely a poor man's stopping place, lay too far to the eastward to receive the full force of this migration: "Water flows Northwest" from Cumberland Gap, someone has remarked. Also the chief land routes tended, like the waterways, to bring migrants across the Ohio River at points below Cincinnati.[49]

Farm seekers by the thousands must have worked their way northward from the numerous river crossings in order to give Indiana in 1860 the highest concentration of southern-born population (11 per cent) of any state in the Northwest. Illinois was close behind with 10 per cent, but of Ohio's people only 5 per cent had been born in slave states.[50] Indeed population-density maps show that the early movement of the settlement frontier in the Northwest was as much northward as westward.[51]

Other thousands crossed Indiana westward from the Falls of the Ohio at Louisville via the Vincennes Trace, one of the oldest Indiana roadways and the first to carry a stage route. Virtually a projection westward of the Wilderness Road which ran from Cumberland Gap to Louisville, the Vincennes Trace has been rated as the "chief route" by land from the South to Illinois.[52] Five thousand people are estimated to have followed it toward Missouri in 1819; which calls to mind the Tennesseean who spurned Illinois for Missouri: "Well sir, your *sile* is mighty *fartil,* but a man can't own niggers here, God-durn you." Thus there appears to have been, at the simplest, in southern Indiana–Illinois a crisscrossing of westward and northward streams of population. In addition, lesser paths, trails, and river crossings were so numerous as to make possible pioneering advance through the forest on an almost solid front.[53]

So after allowance for error and exaggeration there is substance for saying that the conditions the Yankees deplored were present in southern Indiana–Illinois. Hope of avoiding casual society is precisely the reason why Yankees and Yorkers removed to the West in groups large enough to dominate the new community. Scarcely any other trait would have pained Yankee–Puritans more keenly than ways of living which appeared tentative or unsettled: Did not the Connecticut legislature once affirm that "good people do not need any asylum?"[54]

3. Paper, Ink, and Print

"I will write you some circumstances. . . ."

"The Substances of what we think
Tho' born in THOUGHT, must live in INK."
—Motto, since 1744, of the Dietz Press,
Williamsburg and Richmond

And now we have them—the types and ink and paper in their bed; with a strong hand we lay hold of this projecting lever. What are we about to do? We are about to join together material and immaterial—to unite the senseless Thing to the deathless Thought—we are going to press Immortality into these frail sheets and send it hither and thither, up and down in the earth on a mission that shall never, never end.

DAVID TURNER

Fondness for the aroma of the print shop has not been restricted to any single group or region. Exercisers of the art of print have been gripped with the extraordinary meaning of their vocation. This is witnessed—in spite of print-fearful Governor Berkeley—by the birth cry of Virginia's first publishing house, or by the lively joy of David Turner, a country printer of York State.[55]

Of all the ways and accomplishments which set off the

Uplanders from the Yankees as colonists, more general possession by the latter of the instruments and habits of letters is perhaps of most importance. For scrivening men and women could keep records, strengthen group solidarity, maintain contact with the mother hive, recruit helpers to the West, compete to better advantage in business, and tell not only their own story but, due to the inarticulateness of the Uplanders, provide much of the written records concerning the Southerners themselves.

The fact that a man came from the South would tend to associate him with a lesser prevalence of writing and print and penmanship than Yankees were accustomed to. First, as to public schools and libraries. The national census of 1850 indicates that in New England and New York an average of 23 per cent of the population was enrolled in public schools; whereas the average for six southern states which supplied the bulk of upland folk to the Northwest (Maryland, Virginia, the Carolinas, Tennessee, and Kentucky) was 7 per cent.

By the same source the average number of people per school in the seven northeastern states was 211; for the southern states, including Negroes, 531.[56] Even conceding that one third of the population of the southern states were Negroes for whom, presumably, no public schools kept, the average would be approximately 360 persons per school.

These figures point up the remarks of a young Vermonter who had seen something of the West with the eyes of a teacher that "New England and I will say Vermont is one of the best countries in the world to get an education in." He also explained that his Kentucky-born wife was a lagging correspondent because she did not gain a fondness for writing in her childhood. An Ohio pioneer, noting the lack of autobiographical or historical material on citizens of Chillicothe, said that this was in fact not remarkable "for the Chillicotheans were of Virginia origin, a people little given to writing of their political achievements, being better satisfied in exerting influence and making history. *Esse quam videre* should be their epitaph."[57]

Again using the Census of 1850, the average number of potential borrowers per volume in libraries other than private ones in the seven northeastern states was three; in the southern states it was nineteen. As between Massachusetts and Tennessee, the extremes, one finds less than one person against each volume in the former, and forty-five persons in the latter.

TABLE I—(Based on 1850 Census)

COMPARISON OF SCHOOLS, LIBRARIES, AND PUBLICATIONS

	Approx. % of population enrolled in public schools	Average number of persons per school	Average number of persons per volume in public libraries	Avg. number of periodicals & newspapers published
Northeastern States				
Maine	33	141	5	7.3
New Hampshire	24	133	4	9.7
Vermont	29	115	5	8
Massachusetts	18	270	1–	64
Rhode Island	16	354	1–	11.5
Connecticut	19	224	2	18
New York	21	265	2	37
Average	23	211	3	22.2
Southern States				
Maryland	6	642	5	34
Virginia (including W. Virginia)	4.7	483	16	6.5
N. Carolina	12	327	30	2.3
S. Carolina	2.5	923	6	10.7
Tennessee	10	376	45	6.9
Kentucky	7.2	439	12	6.7
Average	7	531	19	11.1
Old Northwest				
Indiana				4.3
Illinois				6
Ohio				15
Michigan				8.2
Wisconsin				8.7
Average				8.4

A man from the Old Dominion traveling in New England in the mid 1830's observed that "a man or woman who cannot read, is here a prodigy"; also that nine tenths of the people in Massachusetts took or read newspapers, while in Virginia not more than half the white population had similar habits of reading.[58] The same midcentury census shores up the Virginian's views. The number of newspapers and periodicals printed annually per capita in the seven northeastern states averaged somewhat over twenty-two copies, for the six southern states about eleven, for the five states of the Old Northwest over eight copies. But it is worth noting that in the Northwest, Indiana and Illinois fell below the other three states, where larger fractions of settlers had been drawn from the East, notwithstanding the late settlement of Michigan and Wisconsin.

Compared with the handwritten materials left by the Yankees a silence hangs over the feelings of the Uplanders as they grubbed, chopped, and hewed in the Northwest. Instances are much more numerous when the ordinary Yankee farmers and their wives wrote letters from the Northwest. The preceding data touching public schools, newspapers, and periodicals must provide part of the explanation. It is interesting, too, that historians concerned with the ante-bellum South have recently reported an almost complete lack of personal letters of the nonslaveholder, the small slaveholder, and even the small planter.[59]

Letter writing and the diffusion of print explain why the Yankees knew more about the West in advance of migration than the Uplanders evidently knew. Recourse to print and script also made the Yankees more deliberate and selective in deciding where to migrate than were the men who came westward through Cumberland Gap. Witness descriptions of how "western fever" attacked them, and their painful weighing of the pros and cons of migration.[60] Before deciding to remove to Wisconsin a New Hampshire man wrote: "It is very difficult I find to make up ones mind in regard to the best spot or section of the country in which to settle at the West. A person may read Flints geography till he is blind, and then he must have an uncommonly grasping mind in order to combine all the circumstances of every place and compare them so as to make a selection."[61] This while at least two Yankees, one in Ohio, the other in Illinois, charged the local residents with ignorance of civil geography, especially the names of townships, but also of local towns and counties.[62]

Dominating proprietorship and patronage of the press by the Yankees was moreover a means of favorably representing to the world their homeland as well as certain western areas, especially those where Yankees settled numerously; and of disparaging other localities (if only by ignoring them), notably places where Southerners were predominant.[63] A South Carolinian struck the nail squarely with the remark that "The Yankees have a way of writing and engraving their country into notice, and thereby of making it the resort of all who have money to spend." Another, a Virginia teacher, complained against competition from a Yankee pedagogue who "by dint of impudence and advertisements" had completely overshadowed him and taken away his pupils and fees.[64] Also, the Yankee's readiness to record his thoughts makes him vivid and readily understood—"methinks I have a pretty exact measure of Jonathan's foot," one Southerner put it—whereas many of our impressions of the upland Southerner rest on less direct evidence, often on the records left by Yankees.

What the joy and satisfaction of writing to relatives and friends—the sweets of a correspondence by letter, one Vermonter called it—we can only imagine. But we can glean from the old letters some of the matters they wrote about.

"I will write you some circumstances," volunteered a Connecticut man as he relayed the exciting facts of corn farming in Illinois: "corn grows here without hoing. . . . it is nothing for a man that has got a goin to raise 2,000 bushel. I now of a good many that has planted 200 Acres, you will think this a great story."[65]

To Virginia went an importuning inquiry: "And further I want you to let me know wats become of my Mother whare she is or wats become of her whether she is still a living and how she is a doing."[66] To an oncoming Quaker relative a travel hint or two: "When you come on the canall boats select your births, before the best are taken. Thee will find the middle ones most desirable keep out of the night air on the canall and carefully avoid the bridges for there is something like 750 the captain informs us—do not forget cloaks. . . ."[67]

A letter to York State spells out the wrench of family separation: ". . . you have not been out of my mind one day since I left you O my thought back to you my Dear friends I cant express with my pen at this time as I have so mutch to rite the first to relate is my journey to the Ohio."[68]

An exhortation on parental duty and family government (directed, curiously, from Indiana to Massachusetts):

Have you a growing family. Set before them no other example but such as you would be willing for them to follow teach them to profit by every means in your power or to instruct them, spare no pains in schooling your children, let your government [be] by mind and steady use no harsh correction but guide and govern without anger. If you love your family and wish for their welfare set a good example before them at all times, use no language before your children but such as you would like to hear them use, be sure to correct or repremand them as the case may require for every wilful disobedience train them up to virtue that they may be likely to be a blessing in their day to you, and to all who may [be] intimate with them.[69]

At least one man regretted that letter writing was lapsing into vain ornamental display: "I am well aware that great advantages arise out of frequent correspondence if it is carried on in the proper manner; but nowadays, a person writes to another & if not filled with fashionable sentences, expressions & extracts from the French or Latin Authors, it is considered out of date."[70]

Lastly, to Maryland a request for homely favors: "tell Susan to ask Mrs. Booth for a quilt pattern called tangle britches wich she has peised with pale blue calico replace a flat iron to old Mr. Stone wich we took in a mistake and we will give you one when you come bring Mulkyes sylabic spelling book and Kirkmuns gramer."[71]

4. ATTITUDES AND AFFIRMATIONS

*"One feels more than he expresses,
the other expresses more than he feels."*

A little girl is said to have finished her sampler "with the proud line, 'New England is my nation.' "[72] This might be an incident without significance if there were no other signs that New Englanders were to an unusual degree tied together by feelings akin to nationality. Non-Yankee colonists at the first Continental Congress feared "there was 'too great a nationality among Bay-men' for the good of America as a whole." A Yankee who was able to contemplate Yankees objectively stated as a generally conceded view that they, perhaps with the exception of the Scotch, have "more national feeling" than any other people. Hezekiah Niles, a spirited supporter of the War of 1812 and no admirer of New England, referred ironically in his *Register*—recognizing what was to him unpleasant truth—to "The NATION *of New England.*"[73]

While the word "nationality" may sometimes have been used by chance, context often indicates its appropriateness: "A Yankee is a Yankee over the globe," wrote a western editor, "and you might know him if you meet him on the mountains of the moon in five minutes by his nationality. We love and honor him for it, whenever it is not carried by a blinding prejudice." Fortunately the Yankees could mix a dash of humor into serious subjects, but it is hard to tell where humor left off when nationality was the theme: "The live Yankee is but the eccentricity of a truly wonderful people; the moral and physical impress of New England is stamped upon the universe; we owe her our nationality, and the world owes her admiration and respect." As one author put it, New England was a "holy land," for only within the narrow limits of Palestine does one find a true historical parallel to the type of power represented by the New England dynamic.[74]

Of New Englanders collectively the mark of nationality most apparent to outsiders was the belief, borrowing seventeenth-century phrasing attributed to Elder Thomas Faunce, that the Pilgrims "brought in themselves the germs of every quality essential to national greatness." Harriet Beecher Stowe affirmed that New England was "the seed-bed of this great American republic and all that is likely to come of it. . . ." She looked upon New England Puritans as "especially called and chosen by God for some great work on earth." Others Puritan-minded saw the coming of the Pilgrims as "the most sacred story since the story of Bethlehem," and explained that Massachusetts and New England stemmed directly from East Anglia, "for more than three centuries the conspicuous seat of the English genius and power."[75]

For the individual, "being a New England man" included love of the native soil, reluctance to emigrate, dread of expatriation, and a shared sense of special destiny or mission. From such feeling came a singular sense of obligation to New England, to the Republic, to God, and to posterity. "Now for one," was the pledge of the Reverend John Todd before a rural audience in 1835, "I not only glory in being a New England man, but I want to transmit this character down to posterity."[76]

Being a "New England man" made difficult choices inevitable. The decision which tapped the richest vein of sentiment was whether or not to migrate from the homeland. While the organized call came largely from the religious, individual Yankees beckoned constantly: Sometimes it was earnest entreaty. "Every mail from the West teems with the Macedonian cry, come over and help us." Sometimes it was peppery banter. From Wisconsin: "Some of you lazy devils ought to be out here." From Illinois: "Poor Souls how I pitty you," wrote a youth to his family in Maine, "contented to drag out a miserable life in a land where grass hoppers can hardly live, where toads can be seen crying for a little sorrel, and even the poor *weevils* had to *emigrate* in order to get a little *wheat,* & I don't blame them . . . it . . . should teach man an important lesson."[77]

But whencesoever the impulse the pain of actual decision

remained. To go West was perilous and disagreeable. "At the East, society is the rock; at the West, sand."[78] Not to go was to sidestep duty. Proponents of removal by communities met the warning that too abundant emigration could cause New England's hopeless eclipse within the greater republic. The earnestness of such importuning still glows:

O could I reach the ear of our young men in New England, I would say to them: Here is land enough—take it. Here is enterprise enough, and here is the sheet anchor of this nation; stay by the sepulchres of your fathers; stay by the soil which none but free-men may tread; stay by the fountain which is for the salvation of the land; and when you have covered our soil, and millions swarm here, then go out and seek other homes. But, above all, I would say, whether you stay here, or go away, remember that New England is your mother, and never act unworthy of your parentage.[79]

There were indeed the stubbornly unbudging, like the one who "would rather live on a dinner of herbs in Connecticut, than dine on a stalled ox in Illinois," who declined to consider seriously the question of leaving home. Others, who went out, seemed threatened by a sort of spiritual death by leaving:

"A long life scarcely serves to wean a person of common sensibility from the faces of his friends and the tombs of his ancestors. To thousands who have gone out from among us, New England will still be their 'home,' and their western valley their place of exile." Thus spoke Jeremiah Spofford before the Essex County, Massachusetts, Agricultural Society in 1833. A New Hampshire émigré in Illinois reciprocated: Will County, Illinois, where he intended to remain, would one day be "the *garden of the world,*" but New England "with her mountains and lakes—her hill and dale—and rapid coursing rills—and all her varied charms, yet stand foremost in my admiration and affections."[80]

But the showing of group loyalty is not confined to one side. Among southern states Kentucky and Virginia contest honors. "No State in the Union," a New Hampshire man advised his father, "is so national in its character as Kentucky.

They are certainly an unique people." The well-informed
James Hall acknowledged in his *Western Monthly Magazine*
Kentucky's "marked nationality." Perhaps this nationality had
been the more readily achieved if it was true that "the first
population of Kentucky was from the purest spring that ever
fertilized a country, and there was little to defile its waters."[81]

But to a competent latter-day witness, Virginia, perhaps
more than any other state, enjoyed the enduring affection of
her sons after they had made new homes beyond her borders.
One of these felt deprived in Indiana of his tobacco and
whiskey from the Old Dominion. He desired his sons to
return to Lexington for at least part of their college life "either
at the College or the Institute," that they might "understand
the manners and customs and form attachments for Virginia
and the South." Another was pleased to find in the Northwest
certain men from the Old Dominion "to whom the name of
that venerable state comes Not without its divine effect &
hallow'd associations."[82] Forty years later, 1880, reaper-maker
Cyrus H. McCormick, the first president of the Virginia
Society of Chicago, distinguished between love of one's nation,
"a noble virtue of the mind," and love of one's native state, "a
pure affection of the heart." "I may say of Virginia, as
David said of the city of his love: 'If I forget thee, O Jerusalem,
let my right hand forget her cunning.' "[83]

With the upper-class Kentuckian or Virginian love of the
native soil was one thing. With the land-questing Virginian
yeoman it was quite another. Wrote Matthias Bowman from
central Indiana to his brother in Rockingham County:

> I bin in formed that thare is a roomer in circulation if i was
> back on my old home and fixt like i was i would Stay my Deare
> Sirs i am fixt here and if i was Dare nothinge boud Sickness or
> Deths would keepe me Dare and i think if Some more of you
> would come oud here you would Do whell. . . . and if you Dount
> intent to come out here for God Sake try and ged youre chillrin
> out as fast as they turn out for them Sefs So they make Some
> thing for them Selfs thare ar as fined Nabers here as thare is

Dare. . . . buid the deavil goodby and come out here or Some
ware in the west now I will guo to my Diner[84]

Despite their aggressiveness the Yankees held concerning
the West a set of hopes, premonitions and anxieties which were
complex and paradoxical. They feared depopulation and
political submergence of the homeland.[85] In the "Macdeonian
cry" fear of being swamped balanced determination to place
Yankee trademarks on the new region. They feared the
dark-green corn of the Muskingum, Scioto, Miami, and
Wabash valleys—not the dwarfish thing of New England, but
a larger variety of that *king of vegetables* whose topmost
leaf was higher than the walls of the farmer's dwelling; farms
whose acres and herds numbered hundreds and thousands; soils
"containing more feet of rich vegetable mold than the New
England states could on the average boast of inches"; farmers
who considered manure useless for soil maintenance.[86]

Moreover western soil incited men to easy wealth and un-
productive speculation. "If you accost even a farmer in these
parts, before he returns your civilities he draws from his pocket
a lithographic city, and asks you to take a few building lots, at
half their value . . . as a personal favor conferred on you."
But, the writer concluded, ". . . the inhabitants will starve!
their work is altogether of the head, and not of the *hands*—they
are trying to live by speculation more than by labor."[87]

That travelers from the East expected to find Pittsburgh
"immersed in sin and sea-coal" is an amusing version of a
common New England anxiety. The unimpeded terrains of
the West offered but little physical restraint to men, were in
short an incitement to anarchy. Accepting the maxim that in a
new country "the *second generation is inferior to the first,*" the
Yankees cautioned against the "astonishing" deterioration
which followed migration and insisted that all but the most
spiritually fortified needed "the concentrated heat of an eastern
sun to ripen them for heaven."[88]

The Southerner was, by Yankee standards, content to let
matters take their course, content to let others alone and he

wished to be left alone. He had few plans involving others than himself. A remark of Charles S. Sydnor's bears on the attitude of Southerners generally, for the yeoman resembled the gentleman in feeling no compulsion to change things. "Lacking the New Englander's zeal for improvement and reform, he could enjoy rest with a free conscience."[89]

Neither does it appear that the Uplander often associated the Northwest with any form of degeneracy. Less societally conscious than the Yankee (his description of local society was rarely more elaborate than "civil" or "very civil"), he was not actively concerned over the establishment of social controls or whether his ways would predominate over others. Tall corn and thick topsoil meant merely opportunity to the upland Southerner.

Both men enjoyed the prestige of being authentically native. Both had the fibre from which enduring folk characters are made. "One feels more than he expresses; the other expresses more than he feels. The pride of one is his acuteness, of the other, his bluntness."[90] To recall that the Uplander was a man of tempered feelings and attachments need not mean that he was a man of indecision or weak loyalties. Indeed the unwary could be badly deceived by his apathetic ways and tendency to represent himself as a much worse fellow than he actually was. Worth its page for illustrating this latter point, as well as the make-up and temper of the Uplander, is the story "How Cairo Got Her Bad Reputation," recounted by an editor of the Cairo Times.

Resident loungers, knowing that steamboat passengers feared for their personal safety, would describe in their presence horrible imaginary fights supposed to have taken place at a dance the night before, "Yes! real nice time four men killed. Helped bury 'em this morning. Put 'em all in a queensware crate and sunk 'em in Ohio. Stunk some," they would relate along with admiring comment upon the deftness of the knife work.

I saw the fight—most beautiful. Efe Larkin dropped his 'innards' the first rake he got from Eaf Noel's toothpick. He

flickered out laughing at the pretty lick. Ah! It was beautiful!
But that infernal butcher whose wizzen you clipped stabbed Mark's
carcass so awkwardly that I took it to be his first set to. Mark,
poor fellow, did his best, but of course he couldn't fight in close
quarters with a fence rail.

Then the two went for a drink.

Presently another traveler would be horrified by a conver-
sation between the same two natives; the one, rolling a barrel,
would be hailed by the inquiry, "Hank, what going do with
that?" "Coffin, Bill—boy dead," would be the sad reply.
Then Bill would implore Hank to get a box, be human, and
even proffer aid in the search of one, which would be forth-
coming. Hank would survey it and remark dubiously, "Too
short by a foot. But I will bury him decent. You see I can
just saw his legs off." Then the father in mock distress
would move off with the coffin on his back.

The editor supposed that Hank and Bill joined presently
for another drink.[91]

5. KEEPING HOME TIES

Jinglety Bang and the Water-Level Route

A journey on horseback from Carolina to Kentucky, runs
a reminiscence of Revolutionary times, "was a most Herculean
task." It was impracticable in the state of the roads to cross
the mountains with wagons. Everything that was brought
had to be packed on horseback. A steady old horse laden
with pots and kettles missed his footing and rolled from
the top to the bottom of the mountain. The pots were broken
but the horse, not seriously hurt, was always afterward called
"Jinglety Bang."[92]

The story of Jinglety Bang may stand for the comparative
ruggedness of the Uplanders' paths to the Northwest. Even
through central Kentucky, over the Wilderness Road marked
out by Daniel Boone in 1775, migration remained for twenty
years a "movement on foot." At the latter date the travelway
was declared by the legislature to be a wagon road; after

which it was "only a natural mountain road, worked and repaired, and furnished with bridges and ferries."[93]

Overland a return trip to the Uplands afoot, on horseback, or by vehicle was prolonged and tedious, not to say exhausting and dangerous. The discomfort of wagon travel is indicated by a woman who preferred to make the five-hundred-mile return to North Carolina from Indiana (the year was 1833) by horseback. And such conditions of land travel must have held until long after the Civil War. By water the return route was largely upstream, laborious and slow in hand-propelled craft, expensive and piecemeal if by steamer, with seasonal uncertainty as to water deep enough for navigation.

The experiences of a young Quaker, Addison Coffin, who made several traverses between North Carolina and Indiana, illustrate sundry points of detail. His first trip, begun afoot at New Garden in May, 1843, included what he called the Blue Mountain route, Peter's Mountain (in present West Virginia), New River gorge, Kanawha River falls, and the salt works at Malden. At Charleston he could not resist taking a steamer for Cincinnati, whence he continued into Ohio and Indiana afoot.

On his return to Carolina the next year, starting on foot, he traveled part way from Indianapolis to Madison by rail, by river steamer to Point Pleasant, then in Virginia, afoot up the Kanawha via the "Hawk's Nest" on New River, thence to Red Sulphur Springs and Peter's Mountain where he struck the route he had trudged in the opposite direction the year before. On his second going, alone, to Indiana at the beginning of February 1845, with horse and wagon, he ran into a snowstorm in crossing the Big Blue Mountains and was three days and nights without fire. He sometimes led the horse. He spent four days going fifty-five miles from the salt works, twelve miles above Charleston, to Point Pleasant where he shipped for Cincinnati. That he thought this the most exhausting and perilous journey of his life is understandable.

In October, 1851, Coffin went to North Carolina to fetch

his mother. From central Indiana he proceeded to Madison by rail, thence to Guyandotte, Virginia, by steamer, afoot to Charleston, by stage across the mountains, then afoot to New Garden. The return party consisted of Coffin, his mother, three girls, and two boys. Two old and inexpensive blind horses drew a light wagon full of provision, trunks, bales, and bundles. Only the mother rode in the wagon and she only part time. Two slept in the wagon, the others in a tent. In fording streams part of the company rode in the wagon, the remainder on horseback. At Malden, the party shipped for Madison, Indiana, arriving in central Indiana about May 5, a month after leaving New Garden.[94]

In contrast, the onset of the Yankee migration, which occurred several decades later than with the Uplanders, benefited from all the advances in the modes of transport. The open terrain from Albany to the Northwest (the "water-level route" as advertised by one of the great railway systems), the Great Lakes, the Erie and Welland canals, and after about 1850 several east-west railroads, all encouraged a two-way traffic between the Northwest and the Yankee East.[95] Canal, steamer, and rails shortened passage to the Northwest to a matter of days or hours even, whereas the journey from the farther Uplands continued for weeks or months.

Facility in transport early brought a sense of proximity between the Northeast and the Northwest of a sort not felt by the Uplands toward the latter. Indeed by the early 1820's Michigan was taking on the feel of nearness to the East. Said a notice in *Niles' Register*:

Michigan, this territory, so remote that we hardly heard of it once in three months before the late war, is so near to us now that we communicate with our friends at Detroit every week, and the time is about to arrive when a journey to that city will be a jaunt of pleasure, through the Erie Canal and a steamboat voyage on that lake . . . the water communication about to be opened will place the farmers of Michigan nearer to the market than most of their brethren in the old states are.[96]

A few years later a Yankee, contemplating the travel possibilities from the canals then building at the West, forecast: "We shall soon be able to sail, at the writing desk, or asleep, from New Orleans, Fort Mandan, or Prairie du Chien, through the interior forests to the beautiful bay of New York." And by the early 1850's, horizons still in retreat, and with a continuous iron track from their own door to Boston and New York, Michigan Yankees could return to their old homes in two days.[97]

Of the differing situations of the Yankees and Uplanders in the keeping of home ties none is more vital than the layout of railways around the year 1860, by which time a well-wrought system laced together the various portions of the North—to the point of "oversupply" in the Northwest, Professor Channing thought. But direct rail links between the Uplands and the region northward of the Ohio River were nonexistent, which lack Professor Channing charges to shortsightedness in southern leaders.[98] Such intersectional roads were of course discussed (one to connect Charleston with Cincinnati, for example), foreseen as freighting cereals and animal products southeastward against raw cotton which would make the Northwest so grand a success industrially that it would forget tariffs and become a true ally of the Southeast. But achievement was more difficult than the saying. Achievement was perhaps the less easy because Charleston and other southern ports were declining relatively as New York rose in importance. And it must be of symbolic importance at least that no railroad was built through Cumberland Gap until 1889.[99]

Whatever explains their nonexistence, a principal meaning of their absence was that the Uplanders never maintained as close contact in person and goods with their home region as did the Yankees with theirs. For a promising show of pre-railway traffic would have been the strongest inducement to laying the rails. In other words, there developed between the Northwest and the Uplands no persistent commerce of note (livestock driven southeastward against Kanawha salt, for example). Meanwhile the Northwest was increasingly attracted to the most favorable market on the continent, the North Atlantic seaports. By the 1850's much of the Northwest—perhaps the northerly three quarters—was oriented to this market.[100]

That these eastern outlets were realizable to the Northwest, Governors James B. Ray of Indiana and Shadrach Bond of Illinois (both southern-bred) were aware even before the Erie Canal was completed. To sense the East's magnetism, "the safest and best market in the United States," one may read their legislative messages.[101] To assess the potential of east-west watercourses and rails one may review a Buffalo newspaper of the 1840's, or hear the outgivings of Chicago editors when rail linkages with Atlantic tidewater were being made during the following decade. These rails, said the *Prairie Farmer,* had by the moment of their completion added 10 to 25 per cent to "every usable animal with four legs" and to every other saleable substance that animals produce, as well as to grass, grain, and land.[102]

To assign so heavy a benefit to these railroads may be in error, for the northern parts of the Northwest had for some years enjoyed, because of water outlets eastward, greater prosperity and more favorable prices than the southern parts.[103] But whether by water or by rail who could resist such a prospect? "They are putting the iron on the Railroad from lafaat to Indianapolis," wrote a Carolinian visiting in central Indiana the autumn of 1851, "and expect to be to thorntown from lafaat by Christmas which will bring the Newyork market lacking 4 cents within 3 miles of Nathan's barn."[104]

Unlike the Yankee whose continuing attachments to the East were in part commercial, the Uplander's trips by river craft to the New Orleans market did not mean a renewal but perhaps an alienation of home ties.[105] The Ohio River turned the interests of the lower Northwest toward new markets, away from the Valley of Virginia and the Southeast.[106] Nor did comparative poverty, rural living, and the stay-at-home inclination of farm people encourage travel back to old homes in the Uplands. Finally and importantly, even with transport equal to that which served the North the nonliterate ways of the Uplanders would have left them largely without the all-pervading force of the pen.

So between the Yankees' water-level route and that of Jinglety Bang to Virginia or Carolina the comparative difficulty of returning home inheres in the brag (from Wisconsin, 1839) that "I do not consider traveling from here to N. H. as anything"; while a Quaker woman late from Carolina (1829) must be content with assuring relatives of her continuing affection "notwithstanding there are many mountains between us. . . ."[107] A historian admirably summarizes the latter situation with the remark: "The Wilderness Road and the Kanawha River, for example, served people principally, not goods, and for a one-way journey," notwithstanding the "Seed Corn and irish tators" of William Calk.[108]

NOTES

[1] Quoted from the *Olive Branch,* in *Genius of Universal Emancipation* (Baltimore), II (December 23, 1826), 101.

[2] Stephen Rannay, Charlestown, Indiana, to William Plumer, Epping, New Hampshire, April 11, 1816, in *Indiana Magazine of History,* XXXV (June, 1939), 182; Reuben G. Thwaites (ed.), *Early Western Travels* . . . (32 volumes. Cleveland, 1904-7), IX, 235, quoting James Flint's *Letters from America* (Edinburgh, 1822).

[3] Karl Postel (Charles Sealsfield), *The Americans as They Are: Described in a Tour Through the Valley of the Mississippi* . . . (London, 1828), pp. 32-33; Indiana State Board of Agriculture, *Annual Report,* 1878 (Indianapolis, 1879), p. 381; Thomas Ford, *A History of Illinois* . . . *to 1847* (Chicago, 1854), pp. 69-70; *Home Missionary,* III (March, 1831), 318.

[4] See Chapter IV, Part 2, below.

[5] *Home Missionary,* XXXII (May, 1859), 15; Christina Holmes Tillson, *A Woman's Story of Pioneer Illinois,* edited by Milo M. Quaife (Chicago, 1919), p. 148; Nathan Hoskins, *Notes upon the Western Country* . . . (Greenfield, Mass., 1833), p. 72.

[6] This criterion was chosen because of ease of computation. If it had been $125, for example, Indiana's showing would have been much less favorable.

[7] Karl Postel (Charles Sealsfield), *Die Vereinigten Staaten von Nordamerika* . . . (2 volumes. Stuttgart and Tubingen, 1827), II, 64.

[8] See Chapter III below, Part 3.

[9] Milo Erwin, *The History of Williamson County, Illinois* . . . (Marion, Ill., 1876), pp. 26, 38, 71.

[10] *Genesee Farmer* (Rochester), II (June 9, 1832).

[11] *Ibid.,* III (May 18, 1833) ; *The Cultivator,* O. S. VII (October, 1840), 179. The latter article was initialed by Anthony Benezet Allen, well-known farmer-journalist, later editor of *The American Agriculturist.* See *Dictionary of American Biography,* I, 185.

[12] Ogdensburg (N. Y.) *St. Lawrence Republican,* May 14, 1833.

[13] Letters of Mrs. C. A. Moore, June 18, 1839 (Mrs. Moore had settled in Brown County, Illinois, in 1839), and Lucy Maynard, Fulton County, Illinois, to Mrs. Abel Piper, Phillipston, Massachusetts, December 3, 1835, both in MS collection on Illinois women, ILLSL; "Susan Short May," in *Journal of the Illinois State Historical Society,* VI (April, 1913), 122, 126. Albert L. Kohlmeier, in *The Old Northwest as the Keystone of the Arch of American Federal Union. A Study in Commerce and Politics* (Bloomington, Ind., 1938), p. 37, says that a large part of the goods shipped westward on the lakes and canals belonged to settlers coming to the interior.

[14] "Letter of George Churchill of Madison County, Illinois, to Mr. Swift Eldred, Warren, Connecticut, September 9, 1818," in *Journal of the Illinois State Historical Society,* XI, 66.

[15] Journal of the Travel of John Sedwick, p. 2, typed copy in ISL; David Abbot, Chillicothe, Ohio, to Senator Thomas Worthington, January 13, 1804, Comly Collection, OAHS.

[16] Cited in Thomas Speed, *The Wilderness Road* (*Filson Club Publications,* No. 2, Louisville, 1886), p. 35.

[17] *Journal and Letters of Col. John May, of Boston . . . in 1788 and '89* . . . (Cincinnati, 1873), pp. 40, 55, 67, 73, 89.

[18] Letter of J. V. Quarles, South Port, Wisconsin, to Isaac Thurston, Ossipee, New Hampshire, May 19, 1839, in *Wisconsin Magazine of History,* XVI (March, 1933), 315.

[19] "Julia," City Point, Indiana, to Mrs. Dezier Gallup, Agawam, Massachusetts, April 4, 1838, Gallup Collection, ISL.

[20] *Home Missionary,* XXVII (September, 1855), 226.

[21] Letters of James Crawford, Jefferson County, Indiana, May 1 and November 5, 1827, and Delphi, Indiana, December 12, 1832, AHMS; *Home Missionary,* XII (May, 1839), 8; also XIV (July, 1843), 49, and II (January, 1830), 144-45.

[22] *Southern Literary Messenger* (Richmond, Va.), I (November, 1834), 86.

[23] *New Englander,* VII (November, 1849), 594; *Boston Commercial Advertiser,* quoted in *The Argus of Western America* (Frankfort, Ky.), August 18, 1830.

[24] Wertenbaker, *The Old South,* pp. 3 ff.

[25] Channing, *A History of the United States,* I, 428-29; Dixon Ryan Fox, *Yankees and Yorkers* (New York, 1940), pp. 3-4; Frederick Jackson Turner, *The United States, 1830-1850* . . . (New York, 1935), p. 41.

[26] Wertenbaker, *The Old South,* Chapter V, "Tuckahoe and Cohee."

[27] See, for example, Armin K. Lobeck, *A Physiographic Diagram of the United States* (The Geographical Press, Morningside, New York, 1921).

[28] Church, *History of Rockford and Winnebago County, Illinois*, p. 253.

[29] Reverends B. C. Cressy, Salem, Indiana, November 8, 1830; Lewis McLeod, Harrison, Dearborn County, Indiana, March 15, 1826; J. R. Wheelock, Greensburg, Indiana, September 1, 1831; James Crawford, Jefferson County, Indiana, January 31, 1827, to Absalom Peters, AHMS.

[30] Prentiss, *The Union Theological Seminary*, p. 474; "The Illinois Farmer," in *The Chicago Magazine: The West as It Is* (Chicago), I (April 15, 1857), 140.

[31] Solon J. Buck (ed.), "Pioneer Letters of Gershom Flagg," in *Transactions of the Illinois State Historical Society*, 1910 (Springfield, Ill., 1912), p. 162, and *Illinois in 1818* (*Illinois Centennial Publications*, I, Springfield, 1917), p. 98; John D. Barnhart, "The Southern Element in the Leadership of the Old Northwest," in *Journal of Southern History*, I (May, 1935), 191.

[32] William Wilson to Mary Wilson, June 14, 1819, ILLSL; Robert W. Patterson, "Early Society in Southern Illinois," in *Fergus' Historical Series*, No. 14 (Chicago, 1881), p. 116; *Home Missionary*, XLI (April, 1869), 289.

[33] Frank L. and Harriet C. Owsley, "The Economic Basis of Society in the Late Ante-Bellum South," in *Journal of Southern History*, VI (February, 1940), 30.

[34] Timothy Flint, *A Condensed Geography and History of the Western States or the Mississippi Valley* (2 volumes. Cincinnati, 1826), II, 136-38.

[35] Letters of Reverends S. G. Lowery, Putnam County, Indiana, March 4, 1833; P. S. Cleland, Jeffersonville, Indiana, January 5, July 6, 1837; Robert I. Hall, Thorntown, Indiana, May 8, 1837; C. Young, Boone County, Indiana, March 8, 1833, AHMS.

[36] Reverend J. M. Ellis, Jacksonville, Illinois, July 30, 1828, AHMS.

[37] *New England Farmer*, XII (April 23, 1834), 322.

[38] Report of one J. Gould, in *ibid.*, XIX (July 15, 1840), 12.

[39] Tyler Dennett, *John Hay: From Poetry to Politics* (New York, 1933), p. 6.

[40] *New Englander*, XII (November, 1854), 522; *Home Missionary*, II (July, 1828), 50; letters of the Reverends James Crawford, Jefferson County, Indiana, January 24, 1828; J. R. Wheelock, Greensburg, Indiana, September 1, 1831; J. M. Dickey, Clark County, Indiana, January 23, 1832; William Sickels, Rushville, Indiana, November 13, 1828; E. Sharpe, Indianapolis, Indiana, April 9, 1827; and B. S. Cressy, Driftwood Church, Jackson County, Indiana [1834?], and of Allen Hamilton, Fort Wayne, Indiana, December 10, 1828, AHMS.

[41] Reverend A. St. Clair, Chicago, to Catharine M. Morse, February 12, 1848, MHC; John Humphries, Rockville, Parke County, Indiana, to Samuel Blackwood, Greenville, Augusta County, Virginia, January 7, 1836, ISL.

[42] Copy of letter of Timothy Flint, Cincinnati, to Reverend Abel Flint, Hartford, Connecticut, January 18, 1816, WHS.

[43] Reverend Leander Cobb, Charlestown, Indiana, to Absalom Peters, July 18, 1829, AHMS.

⁴⁴ John J. Hardin, Jacksonville, Illinois, to Robert W. Scott, Frankfort, Kentucky, July 29, 1830, Kentucky Historical Society, Frankfort.

⁴⁵ Quoted in George R. Wilson and Gayle Thornbrough, *The Buffalo Trace* (Indiana Historical Society *Publications*, XVI, number 2, Indianapolis, 1946), p. 191.

⁴⁶ Stephen S. Visher, "Indiana Regional Contrasts in Soil Erosion and Their Chief Causes," in Indiana Academy of Science *Proceedings*, 1936, XLVI (1937), 158; Charles O. Paullin, *Atlas of the Historical Geography of the United States*, edited by John K. Wright (Washington, D. C., and New York, 1932), Plate 5G.

Samuel Merrill, surveying the route of the Madison and Indianapolis Railroad, found that moving northward from Madison "the first 36 miles of the route is through poor and broken land for at least two thirds of the distance—that the 50 miles from thence to Indianapolis is through a level and very fertile country." Quoted in *Indiana History Bulletin*, XXX (June, 1953), p. 100.

⁴⁷ *Biographical and Historical Record of Putnam County, Indiana* (Chicago, 1887), p. 238. Among historians who minimize the Poor White "myth"—the assumption that southern society was composed of wealthy slaveholders and Poor Whites only—are Frank L. and Harriet C. Owsley, in "The Economic Basis of Society in the Late Ante-Bellum South," in *Journal of Southern History*, VI, 30, 43. These writers point out that at any time before 1860 the bulk of the farming population was land-owning yeomen, therefore middle class; and while there were both "economic" and "social" poor whites, the former were almost nonexistent. See also Lewis C. Gray, *History of Agriculture in the Southern United States to 1860* (2 volumes. Washington, D. C., 1933), I, 440, 487-88; Herbert Weaver, *Mississippi Farmers 1850-1860* (Nashville, 1945).

⁴⁸ A township trustee remarked at College Corner, Ohio, in 1926, "We have God's any number of Kentuckians." The apparent magnitude of the recent migration is reflected in the remark, to be heard in 1950, that "Kentucky took Indianapolis without firing a shot." Or that "Akron is the capital of West Virginia." For reference to a serious situation, involving an influx of tomato harvesters from Kentucky into central Indiana, see Indianapolis *Star*, August 16, 1939, with streamer headline: "Johnson County Wars on Migrants."

More recently Mary Heaton Vorse emphasizes the larger proportion in southern states of children under eighteen years: the southern states "pour out beautiful blonde children in an endless stream"; also the "bloodless conquest" of Ohio by Kentucky, and that Cincinnati and Toledo, Chicago and Peoria, for example, are all "full of Southerners." "The Child Reservoir of the South," in *Harper's Magazine* (New York), CCIII (July, 1951), pp. 55-61.

⁴⁹ Speed, *The Wilderness Road*, p. 43, and map at front; Frederick L. Paxson, *History of the American Frontier, 1763-1893* (Boston, 1924), p. 186.

⁵⁰ Percentages cited by Wood Gray, *The Hidden Civil War* (New York, 1942), p. 21.

[51] See Plate 76 in Paullin, *Atlas of the Historical Geography of the United States.*

[52] Arthur C. Boggess, *The Settlement of Illinois, 1778-1830* (*Chicago Historical Society's Collection,* V, Chicago, 1908), p. 93; also Speed, *The Wilderness Road,* p. 43.

[53] Esarey, *History of Indiana,* I, 163, 278, 296; Joseph Gillespie, "Recollections of Early Illinois," in *Fergus' Historical Series,* No. 13 (Chicago, 1880), p. 10; George R. Wilson, *Early Indiana Trails and Surveys* (Indiana Historical Society *Publications,* VI, number 3, Indianapolis, 1919), pp. 354, 358, 366, 413.

[54] Jarvis M. Morse, *The Rise of Liberalism in Connecticut, 1828-1850* (New Haven, 1933), p. 23.

[55] The motto appeared on a trade brochure of the Dietz Press. The paragraph by David Turner is quoted in *Bulletin* from Headquarters House, New York State Historical Society.

[56] *The Seventh Census of the United States . . .* (Washington, D. C., 1853), lxxxix.

[57] Calvin Fletcher, Indianapolis, to his parents, Ludlow, Vermont, February 22, 1823, and August 21, 1825, Calvin Fletcher letters, IHS; David Meade Massie, *Nathaniel Massie, A Pioneer of Ohio. A Sketch of His Life and Selections from his Correspondence* (Cincinnati, 1896), Preface, v.

[58] *Southern Literary Messenger,* I (November, 1834), 86.

[59] Owsley, "The Economic Basis of Society in the Late Ante-Bellum South," in *Journal of Southern History,* VI, 26.

[60] See the narrative of one J. Gould, "Wanderings in the West in 1839," reprinted from *New England Farmer* (1840), in *Indiana Magazine of History,* XXX (March, 1934), 71-72.

[61] "Letters of Richard Emerson Ela," in *Wisconsin Magazine of History,* XIX (June, 1936), 434.

[62] Buck (ed.), "Pioneer Letters of Gershom Flagg," in *Transactions of the Illinois State Historical Society,* 1910, p. 143; Bayrd Still and William Herrmann (eds.), "Abner Morse's Diary of Emigrant Travel, 1855-56," in *Wisconsin Magazine of History,* XXII (March, 1939), 335.

[63] See Chapter III, part 4, below, and part 5 of this chapter.

[64] *Southern Agriculturist* (Charleston), VI (February, 1833), 85; *Southern Literary Messenger,* N.S.IX (January, 1860), 48.

[65] Asher Edgerton, Quincy, Illinois, to Elisha Edgerton, Connecticut, May 28, 1842, ILLSL.

[66] John W. Brock, Seneca County, Ohio, to Moses Bowman, Timberville, Virginia, February 14, 1858, Wayland Papers, UV.

[67] Ruth Evans, Blissfield, Michigan Territory, to James Howell, Philadelphia, May 30, 1831, MHC.

[68] Lydia and Abel Griffith, Winchester, Ohio, to William Town, Canandaigua, New York, September 3, 1831, OAHS.

[69] Lemuel and Lydia Snow, Franklin County, Indiana, to relatives in Massachusetts, March 18, 1823, typed copy, ISL.

[70] Martin Coryell, Harrison, Ohio, to Moses Kelly, New Hope, Pennsylvania, November 22, 1836, photostat in IHS.

[71] James H. Smith, Elkhorn Grove, Illinois, to David Ports, Boonesborough, Maryland, December 29, 1839, ILLSL.

[72] Fox, *Yankees and Yorkers*, p. 2.

[73] Miller, *Sam Adams, Pioneer in Propaganda*, p. 315; Timothy Flint, *Recollections of the Last Ten Years* (New York, 1932), p. 8; *Niles' Weekly Register* (Baltimore), VI (May 21, 1814), 188.

[74] *Western Monthly Magazine* (Cincinnati), II (June, 1828), 12-15; *Church Record*, quoted in *Yankee Notions*, XI (September, 1862), 285; Bridgman, *New England in the Life of the World*, pp. 4-5.

[75] Bridgman, *New England in the Life of the World*, p. vii; Constance M. Rourke, *Trumpets of Jubilee* (New York, 1927), p. 122; Edwin D. Mead, "The Meaning of Massachusetts," in *New England Quarterly*, III (January, 1930), 31, 34, 35.

[76] *New England Farmer*, XIV (December 2, 1835), 16.

[77] *Ibid.*, XII (April 23, 1834), 322; letter of J. V. Quarles (Wisconsin), to Isaac Thurston, Ossipee, New Hampshire, March 11, 1839, in *Wisconsin Magazine of History*, XVI (March, 1933), 311; Ebenezer Welch, Monmouth, Illinois, to his parents, Monmouth, Maine, September 19, 1841, CHS.

[78] *Home Missionary*, XVI (July, 1841), 54.

[79] *New England Farmer*, XIV (December 2, 1835), 163.

[80] *Prairie Farmer*, VII (March, 1847), 94; *New England Farmer*, XII (April 23, 1834), 322; Richard Emerson Ela to Benjamin Ela, Lebanon, New Hampshire (ca. 1839), in *Wisconsin Magazine of History*, XIX (June, 1936), 448.

[81] James A. Atherton, Lexington, Kentucky, to C. H. Atherton, Amherst, New Hampshire, January 1, 1832, University of Kentucky Library; *Western Monthly Magazine*, II, 133; Nathaniel S. Shaler, *Kentucky* (Boston, 1888), p. 224.

[82] William T. Hutchinson, *Cyrus Hall McCormick* (2 volumes. New York, 1930, 1935), II, 37; A. H. Davidson, Indianapolis, to J. D. Davidson, Lexington, Virginia, December 27, 1859, McHC; Robert E. Cutler, Wilmington, Dearborn County, Indiana, to Robert C. Cutler, Lovingston, Nelson County, Virginia, November 7, 1838, Tucker-Coleman papers, Colonial Williamsburg, Inc. For a copy of the latter letter the author is indebted to Dr. Lester J. Cappon.

[83] Hutchinson, *Cyrus Hall McCormick*, II, 38.

[84] Matthias Bowman, Cicero, Indiana, to his brother, Rockingham County, Virginia, June 14, 1857, UV.

[85] See Chapter I, part 3, above.

[86] *The Cultivator*, N. S. I (April, 1844), 115; *ibid.*, N. S. IV (July, 1847), 210; O. S. IV (October, 1837), 135; and also *New England Farmer*, XVIII (September 11, 1839), 84.

[87] *The Cultivator*, quoted in *New England Farmer*, XVII (July 25, 1838).

[88] Flint, *Recollections of the Last Ten Years*, p. 19; *Home Missionary*,

XVI (January, 1844), 106-7; *ibid.*, XXIII (August, 1850), 87-88; XI (March, 1839), 248; XV (May, 1842), 14. See Chapter V, parts 2 and 5, below.

[89] Charles S. Sydnor, "The Southerner and the Laws," in *Journal of Southern History*, VI (February, 1940), 16.

[90] *The Chicago Magazine: The West as It Is,* I (April 15, 1857), 142.

[91] Adapted from *Yankee Notions,* VII (April, 1858), 119.

[92] "The Buchanans of Buchanan's Station," in *The Chicago Magazine: The West as It Is,* I (May 15, 1857), 222.

[93] Speed, *The Wilderness Road,* pp. 29, 30, 31, 44, 51.

[94] *Life and Travels of Addison Coffin Written by Himself,* pp. 27, 50 ff., 91-93, 103, 105. On his first journey Coffin had the company of a Carolina man; on the return young Milton Hadley went along to attend the Quaker school at New Garden, North Carolina.

[95] Lobeck, *A Physiographic Diagram of the United States.* The "water-level" railroad is the New York Central.

[96] *Niles' Weekly Register,* XXI (September 15, 1821), 48. See also Chapter V below, part 5.

[97] *The Western Monthly Review* (Cincinnati), I (October, 1827), 333 (this *Review* was edited by Timothy Flint) ; *Moore's Rural New Yorker* (Rochester), V (May 13, 1854), 153.

[98] Channing, *A History of the United States,* VI, 393. The map Channing reproduces, unlike maps in standard historical atlases, omits the road from Louisville to Nashville, a road which was in any case more a connection with the Deep South than with the Uplands.

[99] Kohlmeier, *The Old Northwest,* Chapter II, and pp. 17, 80; Jonathan T. Dorris, "Cumberland Gap," in *Dictionary of American History* (5 volumes + index. New York, 1940), II, 96.

[100] Channing, *A History of the United States,* VI, 378-79; Kohlmeier, *The Old Northwest,* pp. 36, 210-11.

[101] Ray's message to Indiana General Assembly, December 8, 1826, in Indiana *Senate Journal,* 1826-27, pp. 18 ff.; Bond's message in *Niles' Weekly Register,* XV (November 14, 1818), 192-93.

[102] Quoted in *The Country Gentleman,* I (June 23, 1853), 388.

[103] Kohlmeier, *The Old Northwest,* pp. 93-94, 112.

[104] Letter of James Woody, Boone County, Indiana, to John Russell, postmaster, New Garden, North Carolina, November 8, 1851, in "Stories about Indiana Quakers," in Genealogy Division, ISL.

[105] See Chapter V below, part 2; Kohlmeier, *The Old Northwest,* pp. 168-69.

[106] Van Bolt, "The Indiana Scene in the 1840's," in *Indiana Magazine of History,* XLVII, 338.

[107] Letter of J. V. Quarles, Southport, Wisconsin, February 14, 1839, in *Wisconsin Magazine of History,* XVI (March, 1933), 311; Luke and Avis Woodard, Wayne County, Indiana, to Elizabeth Stanton, Core Sound, North Carolina, April 10, 1829.

[108] Van Bolt, "The Indiana Scene in the 1840's," in *Indiana Magazine of History,* XLVII, 338.

Map showing areas of Eastern United States dependent upon Co-operative Drainage (Shaded areas indicate Wet Lands).

Chapter III

SOME GEOGRAPHY, PHYSICAL AND MORAL

1. DITCHWATER DESTINY

*"The Irishman with his spade was a necessity . . .
an angel of mercy. . . ."*

Accelerants to human migration such as gaps in mountains, watercourses, valleys, trails, and traces have seemingly been more emphasized by historians than have the natural conditions which retard and deflect man's dispersal. Such a natural deterrent to the settlement of the Old Northwest is suggested by a drainage map published as a part of the Federal census. This map shows large and sharply delineated areas which today are dependent upon co-operative drainage enterprise. At least three of these areas in the Old Northwest deserve our attention: the northwestern quarter of Ohio, the northern half of Indiana, the extensive but less compact spots in eastern Illinois.[1]

Scrutiny of this map alongside related data justifies the view that unusual and forbidding wetness of the soil faced the pioneers who settled in these areas. Because the effects of wetness were unevenly visited upon the Northwest, it is desirable to make a brief examination of how the various states were affected.

Wisconsin's originally wet stretches occurred, the drainage map indicates, in segregated spots and do not appear to have retarded much the general development of the state. But unlike Wisconsin, Michigan was for some years hampered by the swamps of northwestern Ohio which impeded land travel southward and eastward from Detroit.[2] It was presently discovered, however, that the wet and low-lying lands of southern Michigan were interspersed with hilly "oak openings."

By 1831 the *Genesee Farmer* of Rochester, paraphrasing Henry Rowe Schoolcraft, announced that the Yankees through "prying genius" had "threaded the intricate mazes of these damp lands," and opened to the sons of New England a country as fertile, and perhaps of easier clearing and tillage than old Genesee. The land westward of Detroit, believed by the French to be interminable swamp and scarcely worth surveying as military bounty lands, was in fact rolling, and assured good drainage and millsites (a condition which appears to be verified by the census drainage map). Happily Michigan would be "virtually an extension of our own state," settled principally with New Englanders and Yorkers. The spirit of her laws would be Yankee and every surplus article of produce from her fertile fields would pay a slight tax to eastern canals. Michigan's statehood was doubtless delayed but she had seen a vicious legend denounced in the eastern press and a flattering future prophesied.[3]

With Illinois the critical spot was Chicago. Its reputed swampiness of site as any schoolboy knows could scarcely have been more dismal. Yet the Chicago marshes amounted to no serious mental or physical hazard to Yankees. The lapping of the waves as the winds drove the waters of Lake Michigan into the Illinois River—with entire disregard for intervening streams—was echoed in 1820 in *Niles' Weekly Register*.[4] Indeed the *Cayuga Patriot* had reported four years earlier that "large boats" had passed from Lake Michigan to the Illinois River without removing their cargoes, "the waters of the Chicago and of the *Illinois* both heading in a pond, with two distinct outlets."[5] But the soundest reason for saying that nothing seriously curbed ingress of the Yankees to northern and central Illinois is the "Yankee invasion" itself.

Yet with eastern Illinois the story was a different one. Adjacent to the Indiana boundary lay a retarded tract variously described (the area might vary in size with rainfall) as extending from Lake Michigan to the Ohio River, "two or three counties in breadth and three hundred miles in length." Another estimate made it two hundred miles in length and a hundred in breadth.[6]   A president of the Illinois Central Railroad relates that when the road was built at midcentury the surveyors found southerly from Chicago "an almost unbroken wild, extending for over 130 miles," and that this part of the road offered little produce for shipment for a long time after the line was completed.[7]   Concerning the same railroad, Professor Gates notes that in ten prairie counties of eastern Illinois—Kankakee, Champaign, and Iroquois foremost among them—drainage was an acute problem which the managers tried to meet (around 1859) by experiments in costly artificial drainage; and later by reducing the sale price of its wet grant lands in the three counties just mentioned.[8]   Until around 1870, runs another statement, much of eastern Illinois (now the most desirable of farmland) was without rail service.   Communities lay as far as forty miles from a rail shipping point and entire townships and counties remained cut off from Chicago, their natural market.[9]

That the portions of eastern Illinois now under co-operative drainage are small in comparison with the total backward area of the 1850's bespeaks the telling location of the sodden barriers.   This was especially true of "the allmost impassible swamp of the Kankikee," so called by John Tipton who in 1821 surveyed the Illinois–Indiana boundary through this "most dreadfull swamp: . . . . after wadeing in this swamp four hours & a half many time to our waist and having allmost killed our horses and Drowned ourselve we made good our way Back to the plaice where we first entered the swamp." Tipton tells of another crossing of the swamp by his men and horses which required three hours and twenty minutes, the party "having waided about 5 miles in Travling 8." As if immersion, chill, peril, and exhaustion were not enough for his gloomy inventory Tipton included the "merciless attack of the muscheeter who almost Darken the air with their nos."[10]

Not strangely the Kankakee became a fixed symbol.   Its name, said Henry Ward Beecher who crossed the river (by bridge) a quarter century after Tipton ran the boundary, was as famous and significant of marshes and mud "as *Pontine* is in Europe," and of comparable significance as a barrier.[11] For this swamp made it impractical that settlers move southward in Illinois from Lake Michigan; while in Indiana the westward-curving sweep of the river—some eighty-five crow-flight miles—blocked off the northwestern corner of the state and would have reduced the value of even a good port at Michigan City. At the same time the upper Wabash Valley failed to funnel Yankees numerously through Toledo and into northern Indiana and eastern Illinois. This made for sparse population and hard going for missionaries from the East who, by the way, blamed their paltry achievement upon "the peculiar formation of the country as to drainage," as well as to absence of timber. (Surveyor Tipton also mentions where he crossed an arm of Illinois Grand Prairie extending into Indiana, "A grate want of Timber" along the upper part of his line.)[12] So, on the eve of the Civil War the missions men had made "scarcely a visible impression," they acknowledged.[13]

With Ohio, the darkened area of the drainage map is splashed over the entire northwestern quarter of the state, which is a matter of immediate interest because this great block of country came to be known as the "Black Swamp,"[14] though this name applied originally to a much smaller area, an elongated morass stretching through several present-day counties on the southern side of the Maumee River. These Black Swamps, lesser and greater, plagued the soldiery of the War of 1812[15] and, until the late 1830's at least, made of the Western Reserve and Maumee Road, the most important east–west highway in northern Ohio, "a vexation to travelers, a sticking-place for mails, and a standing disgrace to our State."[16] A pioneer of De Kalb County, Indiana, makes certain how travelers felt when he recalled his traverse from Dayton "by wagons through (not over) that horrible, *horrible* black swamp to Ft. Wayne."[17] And of more than usual interest are the troubles of one John Allen and family as they traveled from

Virginia to Michigan in 1824. The town of Ann Arbor is named for the wives of its proprietors, Ann Rumsey and Ann Allen, the latter a member of the Virginian family embarrassed by the swamps of Ohio.[18]

2. TOLEDO: A DESTINY SPOT

"Indians, muskrats and frogs"

Compared with the markings by nature, man's political boundaries are but faintly scored. Thus consideration of Indiana's wet lands trains the eye upon Toledo at the eastern gateway to the Maumee and Wabash valleys. Toledo illustrates how an unfavorable locale could delay the growth of a community and affect the cultural accent throughout a deep hinterland.

Jedediah Morse, the Yankee geographer, probably did the future Toledo no favor by telling in his books of the snakes "toward the western end" of Lake Erie, especially of the hissing snake: "When you approach it, it flattens itself for a moment, and its spots which are of various colours, become visibly brighter through rage; at the same time it blows from its mouth, with great force, a subtile wind, said to be a nauseous smell; and if drawn in with the breath . . . will infallibly bring on a decline that in a few months must prove mortal. No remedy has yet been found. . . ."[19]

Logically well located, Toledo appeared to some men certain to become the "great outlet" from the Great Lakes to the Ohio and Mississippi rivers. At Toledo, Lake Erie's waters penetrated deeply westward and, compared with the water distance to Chicago, the Maumee–Wabash route would save a thousand miles of dangerous navigation. Besides, Toledo was the nearest port for a territory as large as Massachusetts and Connecticut. "If I had millions," exclaimed the able John Law of Vincennes (1835), "at *present prices* I would not invest a dollar at *Chicago* or in its vicinity."[20]

But Toledo became soon after its founding a disappointment to its promoters and presently endured "a widespread and

almost universally-believed character for insalubrity."[21] Worse
still, its inhabitants scarcely rebutted these charges. Some of
the most improbable stories, got up by Toledans as a burlesque
on the current reports, were "swallowed, and . . . entered
into the general mind as facts not to be disputed."[22] Local
newspapers more than once printed self-disparaging verses
reciting the place's sorrows :[23]

> On Maumee, on Maumee,
>   Potatoes they grow small ;
> They roast them in the fire
>   And eat them—tops and all.
>
> On Maumee, on Maumee
> 'Tis Ague in the Fall ;
> The fit will shake them so,
>   It rocks the house and all.

The Wabash and Erie Canal, a portion of which was opened
in 1841, could not quickly overcome the effects of the hostile
palaver which had been carried on against Toledo by competing
lake cities.[24] Travelers were counseled to avoid the Maumee
because storms on Lake Erie were furious, navigation difficult,
harbors unsatisfactory, while at certain seasons of the year a
distressing green scum covered the Maumee's water. Dr. Drake
told of frogs which migrated countlessly through the streets of
Toledo and Maumee City. It is understandable that as late
as 1855 there was a movement to substitute "Grand Rapids"
for "Maumee" as the name of the river and valley.[25]

Toledo was in fact a destiny spot in the Old Northwest. If,
like Chicago, it had been from its early times a magnetic
entrepôt, the Maumee and Wabash valleys and even eastern
Illinois could well have become great Yankee colonies. But
upriver from Toledo there was other trouble. The difficulties
of transport made the name of Maumee a terror.

Almost every inch of the 220 miles from Toledo to
Indianapolis has been brought under organized drainage. There
was therefore no novelty when a traveler from New York to

Indiana in 1836 reported that westward of Toledo there was
no road for part of the distance and "we wended our way
through swamps."[26] A year earlier the Reverend Daniel Jones,
whose advisors in New York had been ignorant of travel
conditions westward of Toledo, admonished later comers not
to follow his sorry example but rather to approach northern
Indiana destinations from the northward, by way of the
St. Joseph River. "Dear bought experience" had proved the
overland trip from Toledo to Fort Wayne as costly for his
family and luggage as the trip from New York City to
Toledo; more "vexation and expense" than traveling a
thousand miles in another direction. To reach Fort Wayne
except by horseback was utterly impossible, he advised.[27]

Nor was land travel much more satisfactory southward
and westward from Fort Wayne. On the direct road from
Fort Wayne to Indianapolis there was in 1831 but one house
in a stretch of fifty miles, and on one road to Cincinnati but
one house in a certain twenty-four miles. John Morrill, a
minister who removed from southeastern to northwestern
Indiana in 1834 (from Connersville to La Porte), proceeded
by a roundabout course touching Greenville and St. Marys
in Ohio and Niles, Michigan. The hazards of travel by a
more direct route Morrill considered too great.[28]

Other typical references to northern and central Indiana
are in accord. A description in 1844 of Randolph County,
which lies some sixty miles south of Fort Wayne and contains
the point of highest elevation in the state, depicts the country
as "almost a dead level. In some places the water lies on the
surface of the earth the greater part of the year."[29] A pas-
senger by train from Chicago to Indianapolis in 1861 disposed
of the country as "about the poorest I ever saw anywhere, until
you get nearly to Lafayette. For forty or fifty miles it is so
low and wet you could almost run a flatboat over. No farms,
no houses, or fences, and population to match. . . ." Early
road builders complained that "no depth of drainage would
make the track dry in many parts of the north, as for instance

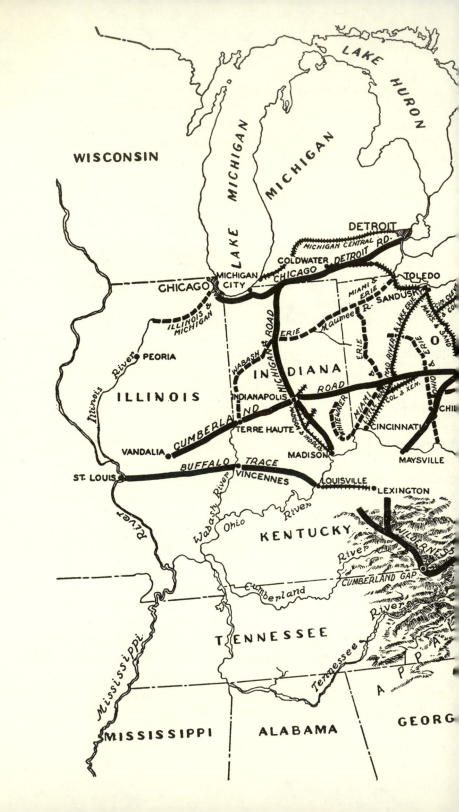

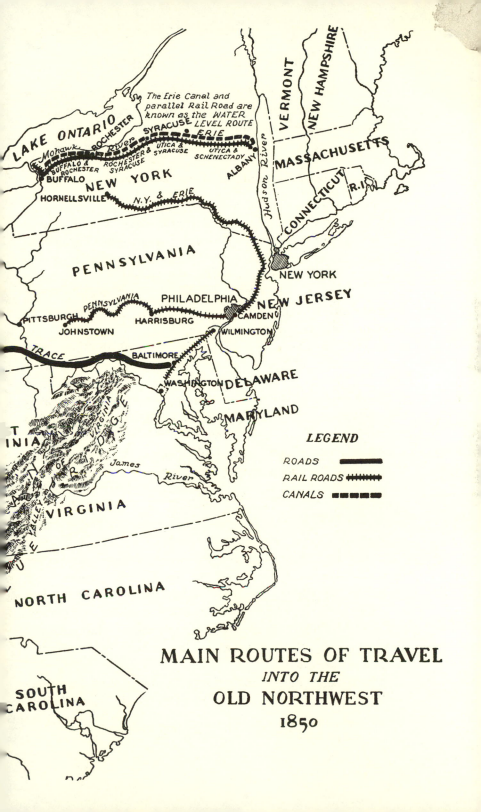

MAIN ROUTES OF TRAVEL
INTO THE
OLD NORTHWEST
1850

along the Michigan road." Statements like these emphasize a geographer's conclusion that "perhaps no state owes more to artificial drainage" than does Indiana.[30]

3. INDIANA PARADOX

"never fully explored; much less cultivated"

Some of the more noticeable consequences of wet lands in the Old Northwest were comparatively late exploration, delayed settlement, and insulation of certain great areas against the Yankee "invasion." There was general public ignorance of the area. Witness the upper Wabash Valley.

Said the Hon. Henry L. Ellsworth, superintendent of the United States Patent Office and a farming enthusiast with a promoter's interest in the valley, in 1837: "Very little is yet known of the valley of the Wabash. Although the fertility of the soil is unequalled, few have ever seen this country. . . . Five thousand people [a figure which sounds large] left Buffalo in one day to go up the lake, and yet not one went into the valley of the Wabash."[31] A correspondent in the *Ohio Farmer* who visited Logansport in 1855 wrote favorably of the country but was clearly doubtful whether Ohio readers would know anything of the Wabash country. Indeed, in 1844 the *Home Missionary* published a map of Indiana along with an elaborate description of "The Wabash Country." Similar accounts, with maps, of Wisconsin and Iowa—areas much "younger" than Indiana—had been published, one in 1839, the other in 1841. Nor was the upper Wabash the only obscure portion of Indiana. The year the report on the Wabash country was published, the missionary organization, after seventeen years of effort there, carefully resurveyed the southern portions of Indiana and Illinois—a country the field men found especially difficult. This area, they said, had "never been fully explored; much less cultivated."[32]

The paradox of Indiana's insularity, in spite of its prominence on the map, was felt by Easterners who blamed their small influence in Indiana upon the peculiarities of its position and settlement. Elaborated, this meant that "the great thoroughfares led around rather than *through* the state. . . ."[33] Until recently, another explained, "It has had no channel by which the stream of emigration could flow into it; while the facilities for transportation around the lakes and down the Ohio river, have caused those who were seeking a western home to pass around and beyond it."[34]

And Henry W. Ellsworth, son of Henry L. Ellsworth, wrote:

The cause which has hitherto prevented the true advantages of this delightful valley from being known, is found in the extreme difficulty of gaining access to it. . . . A journey to the Upper Wabash, from the Ohio river, by land, owing to the extreme roughness of the roads; the difficulty of obtaining suitable vehicles and accommodations and withal the distance, was one of extreme fatigue. . . . The single pioneer and hardy hunter could indeed press through these obstacles; but the emigrant, with his family, could travel only the more convenient routes along the borders of the State.[35]

So while Indiana lay in the path of westward-moving thousands, thousands moved westward and never saw it. Northeasterners could in fact reach a half-dozen preferred destinations in the Northwest and never see, much less halt within this sequestered portion. This point was not lost upon all contemporary Hoosiers. Dr. Ryland T. Brown, a physician and scientist with intimate knowledge of the state, deplored in the 1850's the "wave of immigration" rolling past to find homes elsewhere, while Indiana was not what it should have been "even as an agricultural State."[36] Colloquially phrased by a Wabash Valley historian, the pioneers from New England and Pennsylvania, "like a huge flock of blackbirds, arose and soared across the state and settled in the prairies of the West. Only a few of the hardier ones, of the Daniel Boone type, dropped down into the fertile valleys of the Wabash and tributary streams."[37]

Maps compiled by a scholar some forty years ago indicate

that Yankees settled most thickly in the southern parts of
Michigan and Wisconsin, northern Ohio, northern Illinois, and
extreme northern Indiana, while most of Indiana and southern
Illinois were left preponderantly to non-Yankees. Indiana, the
scholar specified, "was never a favorite stopping-place for the
New England, for the Southern element was so strong
here. . . ."[38]

There is indeed a sort of correctness in this view. But this
explanation is secondary to the difficulties of land transport in
northern Indiana and adjacent Ohio, to the unfavorable repute
of Toledo, and to Indiana's forlorn prospect of a lake port
at Michigan City. These circumstances allowed Indiana to
remain largely a vacuum so far as Yankees were concerned.
Men of southern breeding were winners in default of effective opposition.

4. THE BUBBLE REPUTATION

Michigan and Wisconsin: *"New York's Daughter States"*
Ohio: *"the most enlightened state. . . ."*
"Elanoy": *"the mellifluous name. . . ."*
Indiana: *"the lash of neglect"*

"The idea is so prevalent," wrote David Thomas of York
State after visiting the West in 1816, "that we say it is natural
to look for new people in a new state."[39] Surely the American
people have derived much satisfaction from attributing traits
real and imaginary to states and localities, a practice which
sometimes tinged the fortunes of such places. For reputation
depended upon chance as well as upon popular talent of the
population in generating publicity favorable to their community and in parrying whatever was unfavorable.

Central New York, according to a recent statement, was
by 1800 "almost as Yankee in population as Connecticut
itself." This fact helps to explain why Michigan and Wisconsin, dutiful and legitimate daughters of York State, seem
almost always to receive unequivocal praise from Yankeedom.[40]

Ohio took prestige from her greater age, and wealth which made the Ohioans seem like God's people.[41]   The eastern press teemed with flattering references.   Within a generation after entering the Union, Ohio was called "The Yankee State," indicating her ties to the Northeast.   The great valleys of southern Ohio had attracted Southerners the Yankees could approve because of their immense cornfields and generally good farming.   Rated as "the most enlightened State of the West," with a larger proportion of those inclined to become students, artisans, and professionals, Ohio was credited with the "northern propensity" to form villages and concentrate population; also with having more than other western states, "settled" ministers in the New England sense of that term.[42]

With meaning for literacy and urbanity, readers will recall that in the year 1860, 5 per cent of Ohio's populace had been born in slave states, while with Indiana and Illinois the proportion was twice as large.[43]   At the same date farmers made up 34.5 per cent of all men employed in Ohio; in Illinois the percentage was 39, while in Indiana was the highest of the three, a percentage of 47.[44]

Ohio became widely famed for her early progressiveness. Cincinnati alone was perhaps sufficient to make the name of Ohio great.   Travelers reserved their superlatives for it.   Men of science and letters such as Caleb Atwater, historian, the renowned physician Daniel Drake, Timothy Flint, and James Hall, erstwhile of Illinois, embellished Ohio and her Queen City.[45]   The Black Swamp quarter of Ohio was boggy, to be sure, but was of least strategic meaning to the state.   Ohio was in any case ruggedly able to endure some adversity.

Long before Illinois became a state of the Union the name bore good repute.   Gilbert Imlay, quoting Thomas Hutchins, wrote that the Illinois country with its fine oak, hickory, cedar, and mulberry trees, its dye roots, medicinal plants, hops, and wild grapes, was "in general of a superior soil of any part of North America I have seen."   Jervis Cutler, Hezekiah Niles, and Timothy Flint are examples of writers who praised Illinois in the pitch set by Hutchins and Imlay.[46]

In James Hall, who published the *Illinois Monthly Magazine* at Vandalia beginning in 1830, the state had an unusual advocate. Hall believed his depictions had lured many to the "beautiful Prairies of Illinois": "We have done something for Illinois—the home of our adoption, and the land in which our affections are centered." The assuring effect of Hall's short-lived magazine upon cultivated Easterners is certain even from turgid verses by one "Cora" of Stockbridge, Massachusetts. Following is the final stanza of several she composed upon receiving a copy of the magazine from her sister in St. Louis.

> There came a voice! it spake of wealth, and of the
> kindling rays
> Of science and religion, that bright begin to blaze;
> That voice, that spake of many things I dreamed not,
> nor have seen,
> Was—shall I tell?—the Illinois, the Monthly Magazine![47]

Illinois, like any other state, contended with drawbacks, if only from the failure of the shiftless and unprepared. But Egypt was neatly tucked away. The great Illinois River Valley and the northern counties, said to be rolling and well drained, abounding in millsites and streams in which speckled trout swam, were largely exempt from the clogging effects of wetness. By 1837 Chicago was proclaimed "without doubt, the greatest wonder in this wonderful country. Four years ago the savage Indian there built his little wigwam—the noble stag there saw undismayed his own image reflected in the polished mirror of the glassy lake."[48] Illinois, like Ohio, possessed an urban symbol of greatness.

So if one were minded to make an anthology of ecstacies over Illinois he would readily find sample entries. "Illinois is, in truth, a *fairy land*. The very word itself possesses such a rich, smooth, flowing sound that one can almost fancy himself in an Elysium, as he pronounces this blandest of all Indian names."[49] A minister to his sister-in-law in Boston:

"Should you come in June, you will see such fields of grain as never blessed the sight of your eyes. Such endless fields of flowers also, as mock the feebleness of art, and as it never entered into the heart of an Eastern yankee to conceive. It will be in the commencement of summers beauty. . . ."[50]

Less orthographic, but equal in poetic feeling, is a floral tribute by a Marylander: "The prararies in the summer present one vast natural garden of delights spreding before the aye sush a butiful and varagated senery decked with flowers of evry shape, sise, and hugh, that he that could not admire them must be destitute of a sence of beauty and elegance."[51]

There may well have been tears of joy in the eyes of the one who intoned:

Oh what has God wrought for it? He has given it favor in the sight of a large portion of the intelligent and pious. He has raised it up friends and patrons in the east. A thousand eyes look this way; a thousand hearts beat for its welfare & a thousand hands are opened for its help.[52]

The year was 1850. The editor of *The Western Journal,* a monthly review of commerce published at St. Louis, had been trying to compile an article on the progress of improvements in the West. Unable to obtain a firsthand report from Indiana he had to be satisfied with copying an article from a railroad publication. Surprised and pleased at the achievement indicated by the article (which, he suspected, some Hoosier had released in an unguarded moment), the editor commented: "Truly the State of Indiana is getting on rapidly." "They certainly do more and say less about it than any other people we have heard of."[53]

From the beginning Indiana was weakly publicized. Timothy Flint was aware of this before the state was ten years old: Indiana had been "silently" populated, he said, mostly by young men, unmarried or without families; while Illinois and Missouri received early migration "with a certain degree of eclat," including men of "name and standing," with four- and six-horse wagons.[54]

Guidebooks, letters, newspaper matter, and agricultural journals substantiate this view.[55] Public men chafed because Indiana's rise had been "noiseless and unnoticed." "There is less known abroad, this day, of Indiana, in her great elements of wealth," declared Governor Joseph A. Wright in 1851, "than any other State in the Union of her age and position." Governor Oliver P. Morton reiterated the point a dozen years later.[56] Thus could Hoosiers sympathize when the Nantucket *Inquirer* complained that communities as well as individuals "not infrequently have to smart under the lash of neglect."[57]

The few Yankee-Hoosiers who should have been among Indiana's readiest and strongest defenders were uncommonly objective about their adopted commonwealth. Solon Robinson, tireless agricultural writer, was loyal enough to northern Indiana where he settled for a time, but toward the rest of the state, "richer in soil than anything else," he was cool and disparaging. In 1841 he traveled southward to Logansport on the Wabash to be disappointed because that place gave but twenty subscriptions to the Albany *Cultivator,* to which he was a contributor. Onward toward Indianapolis he saw improvement in the grass and livestock, which was offset when he recalled the dormant condition of the state agricultural society. And when it came to mind that the editor of the *Indiana Farmer* had futilely "sunk his own small fortune in the attempt to do good to his fellow creatures," he wailed, "Oh, Indiana! when will she arouse from her lethargy?" All of which, along with almost intemperate praise of Kentucky and Ohio and their peoples, was broadcast by the influential *Cultivator.*[58]

Henry Ward Beecher, another Hoosier by temporary adoption and sometime editor of the *Indiana Farmer and Gardener,* also looked at Indiana objectively in the 1840's: "As it is, we have a great State, of incomparable resources, with little capital, little reputation, a vast and accumulating public debt, distracted in council by almost equally balanced parties, more vigilant, (it has seemed to us), of each other, than of schools, mechanic arts, agriculture, and the actual commonwealth."[59] Contrast James Hall's affections and labor for Illinois!

Indiana was also at a disadvantage because she failed to fire the imagination of eastern churchmen. Numerous and detailed were complaints that she received narrow sympathy at the East.[60]

While persuing an agency in New England, I have been beyond measure astonished at the want of information concerning Indiana. Some intelligent, giving men never heard anything of its wants or of its character. Says one, "is it not a great deal further off than Illinois? How long has it been settled? Do the people even go to meeting?" While attending associations and other public places I have often heard of the destitutions of Missouri, Illinois, Michigan, Ohio, & c., but only once has Indiana been alluded to in my hearing.

"Now I want the people of the eastern states to know that *there is such a place as Indiana . . .*," declared the writer at the crest of his irritation.[61]

Another, feeling that Indiana was slighted by the *Home Missionary,* examined the nine annual volumes to find that "about sixty-six pages have been devoted to Indiana and about one hundred and fifty to Illinois." Circumstances had thrown Indiana much into the background, he acknowledged, but others "must of course conclude that you regard Illinois more important than Indiana."[62]

This sensitiveness of Indiana's friends became a delicate matter for the executives and editors. Absalom Peters, the corresponding secretary, was reproached for having seen on his round in the mid-1830's more of Illinois' "beautiful prairies & its white waving fields than of Indiana"; also his references in general had been "perhaps too often descriptions of Illinois. . . ." The remarks referring to Indiana which he published were truly unenthusiastic and clipped: "How vast the territory! How rapid the increase of its population! How wide its destitution, and how appalling the causes which are combining to keep it so!"[63]

On their part, the editors sometimes found it politic to

temper or delete overwrought praise of Illinois before field reports were printed. Charged with negligence and bias, they replied that Indiana brethren had been less vocal than others in making their wants known. They also shifted blame to the inaccessibility which had kept this "interesting portion of the Great Western Valley comparatively out of notice."[64]

What has gone before makes clear Indiana's discomfort from being overshadowed. "In the seminaries most of the talk was about Illinois," wrote a worker who rejoiced that he had not "passed over Indiana with neglect." The attention of New England Christians, another explained, "has been turned to Illinois as almost a terrestrial paradise. . . . Illinois is riveted in their minds . . . !"[65] While they nursed injured feelings, spokesmen for Indiana denounced effort for worldly ends: "We who are upon the ground, have chosen rather to have the State stand upon its own merits, than to extol it in poetic strains as *our river begirt realm.*"[66] A like disdain was expressed by another: "These brethren have been labouring, not to have the world know that Indiana was the place to lay up wealth,—'the most beautiful and rich and fertile part of the West.' Their desire has been to build up her waste places. . . ."[67] It is practical to suggest that the workers who went to a reputedly difficult field would labor faithfully and not become public-relations men. But self-effacement was leanly rewarded when editors reiterated their failure to be "direct and importunate" in their appeals.[68]

The possibilities of promotional activity by religious workers were enormous. Aware of their responsibility churchmen sometimes toned down their language; such was the case with one who feared he might overstress the beauties of Iowa. Others were, as we have seen, uninhibited.[69] Fuel was added to the sizzling boilers during the 1850's when the Illinois Central Railroad, with grant lands to sell, began advertising in scores of publications in the older states and distributing widely hundreds of thousands of pamphlets which depicted the practical and aesthetic glories of Illinois.[70]

It was predictable that the "mellifluous name" would be sounded too often, and that Illinois with soil so rich it could be cropped for centuries (it was said) and remain no less fertile, would be overpromoted. It was also probable that ears other than Hoosier ones would ring from the shrill praises of Illinois. Thus a guidebook of 1838 insisted that parts of the West including Illinois had been "cracked up" beyond what they ever were and thousands disappointed, especially from New England.[71] The agricultural press eventually condemned the "agricultural departments" in the religious papers as "infinitely mischievous." During a protracted altercation, Orange Judd, editor of the *American Agriculturist,* accused the religious editors of "bloviating"—telling "whoppers"— about Illinois farming, and insisted that they confine themselves to appropriate subjects rather than lead eastern farmers astray by means of "Munchausen stories."[72]

The land merchants of the Illinois Central also overshot the mark. Intending that the dryness of the earlier pamphlets and circulars give way to vividness and appeal, the composers of these materials "piled it on thick." A president of the railroad acknowledged that the land department had possibly exaggerated the profits of Illinois farming, but apparently failed to implement his regret by having the company's land literature more nearly accord with the facts. Years later a writer in a Chicago newspaper thought it would have been difficult for prospective settlers to doubt that "the real scene of Adam and Eve's interview with the apple lay anywhere else than down about Kankakee. . . ."[73] In other words, when the "Garden State" was mentioned people knew it meant the Garden of Eden and the state of "Elanoy," as a songwriter called it.[74]

5. "MORAL GEOGRAPHY" AND LEGEND MAKING

"huddled, 'snouts out,' on the defensive"

One could too readily accept the pronouncements of earnest men from the East that specific communities in Bartholomew, Jefferson, Putnam, and Ripley counties, Indiana, for example, could vie with any similar areas in Christendom for "ignorance, dissipation and isms," to use a typical phrase.[75] Their calling was to seek out places "in this new fertile world where ignorance, prejudice, pride, little party feeling, and poverty all dwell together in unity." Their writings abound in terms such as "waste places of Zion," "dry and parched lands of error and sin," and "error and delusion which are rolling over like a mighty wave."[76]

Yet one would duly expect tidings of improvement. An important report from territorial Wisconsin described progress of religious institutions without parallel in respect to early establishment, rapid advancement, harmony, and success. A similarly welcome report from Calhoun County, Michigan, included the words: "What a mighty change has nine years produced!" But with Indiana, "always . . . the hardest field to cultivate," improvement was slow. During his three-months resurvey of southern Indiana–Illinois in 1844 the Reverend J. M. Dickey uncovered little but "advancing desolation." While a Congregational churchman deplored failure to plant a single organization of that sect in a southwestern Indiana area the size of Connecticut.[77]

Sometimes the question, "often . . . asked by *eastern* people," was put bluntly: "Why is it that southern and southwestern Indiana is so far behind northern Indiana, Illinois, Wisconsin, and Iowa" when many parts of the former were settled long before them? And bluntly answered: "It is because the inhabitants of southern Indiana have no *enterprise,* no good *society,* no *intelligence."* With no effort to ease a harsh judgment, "a hundred times repeated," the writer blamed poverty and a "poor class" of eastern people who had moved into the region twenty or twenty-five years before, and "not being able to mould *western minds* easily," had done nothing to improve the country.[78]

Nor can we overlook New Harmony, the "center of infidelity at the West," "where Satan's seat is."[79] Dozens of references to infidelity from Indiana in the 1830's suggest that mere association did its damage.[80]   Years later, 1849, the Reverend Albert Barnes was still insisting in a widely circulated sermon that "infidelity never found a place more favorable for developing its nature, than New Harmony, (Ind.)." Even the urbane Dr. Drake thought that Mr. Owen's *"savans"* "knew much more of the physical than of the moral world."[81]

For it was under the heading "infidelity," also in the year 1849, that Puritan faultfinding with Indiana reached its highwater mark.   Forty among the two hundred heads of families of an unspecified community had been reported openly infidel.   To which the editors rejoined in exasperated sympathy: "There *may be* fields in heathen lands less desirable than this, as places of comfortable labor, but they cannot be many.   Nor do we know of any circumstances in which a missionary has a better right to regard himself as making a sacrifice for the sake of doing good. . . ."[82]

Over the years wry accounts continued to appear in print which, because they were often anonymous and did not designate localities, could be vaguely assumed by readers to apply to Indiana generally.

"Moral geography" had also its political uses.   With the Kansas excitement of 1854 and the Frémont campaign two years later Republican writers slurred the Uplanders because of their "African" or Democratic voting preference.   "Egypt can furnish as many Democratic votes as may be required," assured the St. Louis *Intelligencer*.[83]   "We have an Egypt in Indiana as well as Illinois," echoed an Indianapolis paper, linking the heaviest "African" majorities to places where illiteracy was most prevalent.[84]   (Literacy figures from the Census of 1850 had made more rods for the whipping boy.) The *Independent* of Columbus, Ohio, berated the entire Hoosier populace; with a larger proportion of nonliterates it was no wonder the Republican party was there more heavily voted down than in any other northern state.   "In fact," ran the summary, "just in proportion as a State, county or even a village is civilized, enterprising, virtuous and intelligent, Frémont's majority is increased."[85]

It becomes apparent that the general repute of Indiana and that of the some twenty or thirty southernmost counties of Illinois bear more resemblance than is the case with the two states at large. Indiana appeared more often and vividly upon the record but southern Illinois fared much the same in effect: "Slave state people," lacking Bibles, and noted for "intemperance, profanity, and *fisticuffs* on all public days. . . ." Egypt was also stereotyped as "so long shunned by capital and education, so long given over to ignorance and wickedness."[86]

Thus Egypt–Hoosierdom remained an obstacle to faith that the West would yield to the "plastic hand." Even California was cited as improving quickly by comparison. A petitioner, acknowledging the "enduring hardness" of that "old" field, based his appeal for Indiana, over the new and romantic states touching the Pacific, upon the stern adage "the greater the cross the greater the crown."[87] So modest withal are claims of achievement that it appears the Yankee–Puritans, overtaken by the cataclysm of war and by an ebb in evangelistic effort, quietly lifted the siege.

But there is fortunately no need to turn our backs on Egypt–Hoosierdom as they stand gravely impeached. Whatever its causes—the "moral power" of railroads, the telegraph, agricultural societies, or what someone calls the regenerative power of the frontier—a literature of self-respect, self-exertion, and rebuttal was ready to appear.[88] Its argument is easy to surmise. Southern Illinois professed delight in the name Egypt. Its people were "noble descendants of worthy sires." The light of truth was breaking forth, a brighter day dawning. Misrepresentation was rebuked. "The telegraph wires and the iron horse have flashed the news and thundered the truth abroad, and intelligent, moral, industrious citizens are pouring in on us by thousands from eastern and northern states."[89] No longer must Illinois acknowledge an "unseemly waste in her domain." From Bond County came a corrective

protest that Egypt was not, as many supposed, "a frog pond."
Rather the whole of southern Illinois was high, rolling, and
heavily timbered.[90]

Moreover, several circumstances meliorate the degraded
hopelessness assigned to southern Indiana–Illinois. Most of
the observers upon whom we rely watched at the busiest
grooves of migration where humanity showed its worst. Many
a man who resembled the "poor whites" must have been in
fact a real farmer, "stable and home-loving, thrifty and
laborious, and migratory only to better his condition."[91] Also,
as an elderly Methodist minister cautioned, incidents of apos-
tacy, immorality, infidelity, and violence were surface ripples
which did not represent the character of the people.[92]. Meanwhile, a research published in 1936 by the late Professor
James A. Woodburn would itself go a way toward refuting
charges of total depravity in early southern Indiana. While
he acknowledges two distinct skeins or qualities of population,
he has no trouble naming scores of native notables: college
teachers and presidents, men of letters, scientists, diplomatists,
lawyers, travelers, explorers, and journalists, many of them
of the highest order. Not a bad showing for a people who
stood during most of a century (Professor Woodburn's
metaphor) "huddled, 'snouts out,' on the defensive."[93] As
John Hay's father remarked, there must have been "some
leven of a better character."

While the pious lamented, a pack of writers dealt irre-
sponsibly with southern folkways of the Northwest. This was
especially prominent in the monthly *Yankee Notions* which ran
through some fifteen annual volumes after its appearance in
New York in 1852. Intended to epitomize the Yankee genius
of humor, *Yankee Notions* used the Hoosier folk type as a
means of lampooning a contrasting culture. There were four
references to "Hoosier" in the opening number and during the
following decade dozens more.[94] A sort of clearinghouse for
Hoosier–Egypt quips and stories, *Yankee Notions* doubtless
encouraged the general press to traffic in such matter.

Egypt was pictured as a land of "rich sile, an' big swamps, of tall corn and snortin' muskeeters, of human men and big turnips, of wild oxen and all-fired gals." "They didn't go in an' dig wells, an' build barns, an' split rails, an' clear up the land, an' cultivate the sile, an' raise stock, like white people do now-a-days, but they just squatted on the land."[95] Something of the lightness with which Easterners carried their knowledge of Indiana's terrain and natural history shows in the following piece, said to be a New England girl's impression of the Wabash Country:

> Great Western waste of bottom land
> Flat as a pancake, rich as grease;
> Where gnats are full as big as toads,
> And 'skeeters are as big as geese.
>
> Oh, lonesome, windy, grassy place,
> Where buffaloes and snakes prevail;
> The first with dreadful looking face,
> The last with dreadful sounding tail.
>
> I'd rather live on a camel's rump,
> And be a Yankee Doodle beggar,
> Than where they never see a stump,
> And shake to death with fever 'n ager.[96]

And so the legend makers—or, perhaps better, legend fixers—got in their work. "Hoosier" and "Egypt" remain today indelible bits of American folklore.

NOTES

[1] *Fifteenth Census of the United States, Drainage of Agricultural Lands* (Washington, D. C., 1932), map facing p. 1. The quotation in the title of this section is from Rolland Lewis Whitson (ed.), *Centennial History of Grant County, Indiana 1812-1912* (Chicago, 1914), p. 85.

[2] A. C. McLaughlin, "Influence of Governor Cass on the Development of the Northwest," in American Historical Association, *Papers,* III (New York, 1888), 315, 316, 317. See also George Fuller, *Economic and Social Beginnings of Michigan* (Lansing, 1916), Chapter II; James Westfall Thompson, *History of Livestock Raising in the United States, 1607-1860* (Washington, 1942), p. 101.

[3] *Genesee Farmer,* I (May 21, 1831), 158.

[4] *Niles' Weekly Register,* XVII (January 8, 1820), 309. Parenthetically,

the early "important discovery" of continuous navigation from "Lake Erie to the Rivers," near Fort Wayne, never attracted any such migration of Easterners to the Wabash Valley as went to the Valley of the Illinois. *Ibid.,* XV (September 19, 1818), 64.

[5] Cited in *ibid.,* X (August 24, 1816), 427.

[6] *Home Missionary,* XXII (June, 1850), 42; XXIV (April, 1852), 261.

[7] W. K. Ackerman, "Early Illinois Railroads," in *Fergus' Historical Series,* No. 23 (Chicago, 1884), p. 42.

[8] Paul W. Gates, *The Illinois Central Railroad and Its Colonization Work (Harvard Economic Studies,* XLII, Cambridge, 1934), pp. 239, 240, 291, 292. The other seven poorly drained counties were Will, Livingston, Ford, McLean, DeWitt, Macon, Piatt.

[9] H. W. Beckwith, *History of Vermillion County [Illinois]* . . . (Chicago, 1879), p. 353; *The History of Edgar County, Illinois* (Chicago, 1879), pp. 538-39.

[10] *John Tipton Papers,* edited by Nellie A. Robertson and Dorothy Riker (3 volumes. *Indiana Historical Collections,* Volumes XXIV, XXV, XXVI, Indianapolis, 1942), I, 261, 262, 268, 272, 273.

[11] *Indiana Farmer and Gardener* (Indianapolis), I (November 8, 1845), 353.

[12] *John Tipton Papers,* I, 268.

[13] *Home Missionary,* XXXI (May, 1859), 14; XXIII (June, 1850), 42.

[14] Ohio State Board of Agriculture, *Annual Report,* 1870, p. 397.

[15] Richard Lyle Power, "Wet Lands and the Hoosier Stereotype," in *Mississippi Valley Historical Review,* XXII (June, 1935), 38-39. ". . . on the 20th of Jany 1813 I saw Gen. Harrison ride into Gen. Winchester's camp on the north side of the Maumee river, near the foot of the rapids, having hastened from Sandusky across the black Swamp at great personal risk and exposure, the snow being some two feet deep and the river frozen over." Leslie Combs (who served as a scout in the war) to Sanitary Committee, Cleveland, Ohio, January 20, 1864, printed in *Indiana History Bulletin,* XXVIII (September, 1951), 147-48.

[16] "Ohio in 1838," in *The Hesperian: or, Western Monthly Magazine* (Columbus, Ohio), I (May, 1838), 13.

[17] *History of De Kalb County, Indiana* . . . (Chicago, 1885), p. 272; W. B. Moore, Cincinnati, to Dr. E. H. Porter, Saratoga Springs, New York, November 10, 1829, Porter–Gardner collection, OAHS.

[18] "John Allen and His Family," in *Michigan Alumnus* (Ann Arbor), XLIV (December 4, 1937), 17-22.

[19] *The American Universal Geography* . . . (2 volumes. Boston, 1805), I, 180-81.

[20] John Law, Vincennes, Indiana, to his brother William, August 13, 1835 (letter incomplete), ISL; also J. W. Scott, "The City of Toledo, Ohio," in *Merchants' Magazine and Commercial Review,* edited by Freeman Hunt (New York), XVII (November, 1847), 489, 493.

[21] Horace S. Knapp, *History of the Maumee Valley* (Toledo, 1872), p. 543.

[22] Scott, "The City of Toledo, Ohio," in *Merchants' Magazine and Commercial Review*, XVII, 493.

[23] Clark Waggoner, *History of Toledo and Lucas County, Ohio* (New York, 1888), p. 31, quoting Maumee City *Express*, June 24, 1837.

[24] Knapp, *History of the Maumee Valley*, 543; J. Richard Beste, *The Wabash: or Adventures of an English Gentleman's Family in the Interior of America* (2 volumes. London, 1855), II, 154-55. Dr. Jacob Clark left Canton, St. Lawrence County, New York, in April, 1834, for Toledo. At Cleveland he was told he must go first to Detroit; there was no boat from Cleveland to the Maumee River, because there was not at Toledo sufficient water or trade to justify the connection, the town being in the midst of a great marsh and its inhabitants Indians, muskrats, and frogs. He reached Toledo by way of Detroit. At the latter place he got the same reports of Toledo as at Cleveland. Waggoner, *History of Toledo and Lucas County, Ohio*, p. 666.

[25] Waggoner, *History of Toledo and Lucas County, Ohio*, pp. 22, 33, 666; Almon E. Parkins, *The Historical Geography of Detroit* (Lansing, 1918), p. 193; Daniel Drake, *A Systematic Treatise . . . on the Principal Diseases of the Interior Valley of North America* (2 volumes. Cincinnati, 1850), I, 364.

[26] Indiana State Board of Agriculture, *Annual Report*, 1878, p. 512.

[27] Reverend Daniel Jones, Fort Wayne, Indiana, to Absalom Peters, October 29, 1835, AHMS; see also *Home Missionary*, XVI (May, 1843), 18; XXXI (June, 1858), 27.

[28] Reverend James Chute to Peters, December 12, 1831, and Reverend John Morrill, La Porte, Indiana, to Peters, January 20, 1834, AHMS; see also Power, "Wet Lands and the Hoosier Stereotype," in *Mississippi Valley Historical Review*, XXII, 37-42.

[29] *Home Missionary*, XVII (July, 1844), 66. See also *ibid.*, XXXIII (May, 1860), 3, for condition of roads, mail service, etc., at Logansport, Indiana, in 1829.

[30] Jordan (ed.), *Letters of Eliab Parker Mackintire to William Salter, 1845-1863*, p. 131; Indiana State Board of Agriculture, *Annual Report*, 1851 (Indianapolis, 1851), p. 278; Charles Redway Dryer, "Geographical Influences in the Development of Indiana," in *Journal of Geography*, XI (1910), 19.

[31] Quoted in Abner D. Jones, *Illinois and the West*, pp. 183-84.

[32] *Ohio Farmer* (Cleveland), June 23, 1855; *Home Missionary*, XVII (August, 1844), 73-75; XII (November, 1839); XIV (May, 1841); XVII (May, 1844), 19-21; XVII (December, 1845).

[33] *Home Missionary*, XXXVII (December, 1864), 182; XXV (May, 1852), 14.

[34] *Ibid.*, XVII (August, 1844), 74; XXIX (June, 1856), 41; see also photostat clipping from *The Independent* (New York), October 9, 1862, ISL.

[35] *The Valley of the Upper Wabash . . .* (New York, 1837), pp. 2-3.

[36] Indiana State Board of Agriculture, *Annual Report*, 1856 (Indianap-

olis, 1858), p. 492. For the same view, see a letter written from Indianapolis in *Genesee Farmer*, VII (October 15, 1836), 330-31.

[37] E. B. Heiney, in *Biographical Memoirs of Huntington County, Indiana* (Chicago, 1901), p. 239.

[38] Mathews, *The Expansion of New England*, p. 254, and *passim*.

[39] *A Tour Through the West in the Summer of 1816* (Auburn, N. Y., 1819), p. 108.

[40] David M. Ellis, "The Yankee Invasion of New York, 1783-1850," in *New York History*, XXXII (January, 1951), 8.

[41] Chapter II above, part 1.

[42] Flint, *Recollections of the Last Ten Years*, p. 45; *History of the Formation of the Ladies' Society for the Promotion of Education at the West* . . . (Boston, 1846), p. 14; "The Religious Character of the Western People," in *Western Monthly Review* (Cincinnati), I (September, 1827), 269; "The Western Country," in *ibid.*, I (October, 1827), 331-32.

[43] Cited by Wood Gray, *The Hidden Civil War*, p. 21; see above, p. 38.

[44] Cited by Harvey L. Carter, "Rural Indiana in Transition 1850-1860," in *Agricultural History*, XX (April, 1946), 118. Wisconsin's percentage was 40, Michigan's 37.5.

[45] See *Niles' Weekly Register*, V (September 4, 1813), 3; *The Plough Boy* (Albany), III (November 24, 1821), 207; *American Agriculturist*, IV (December, 1845), 371-72; VII (April 4, 1848), 112-13; *Home Missionary*, II (February, 1830), 157; (March, 1830), 171-72. Absalom Peters who wrote so discouragingly of Indiana was entranced by the "already great and powerful *state of Ohio*." Caleb Atwater, *The General Character, Present and Future Prospects of the State of Ohio* . . . (Columbus, 1826), and Daniel Drake, *Pioneer Life in Kentucky* (Cincinnati, 1870), p. xxi. Southeastern Ohio, while poor, was promising and did not offer the same problems to the missionaries that southern Indiana did. *Home Missionary*, XXIV (March, 1852), 264; XXI (October, 1848), 122.

[46] Imlay, *Topographical Description of the Western Territory of North America* (London, 1793), p. 21; Cutler, *A Topographical Description of the State of Ohio, Indiana Territory, and Louisiana* . . . (Boston, 1812), p. 63; Flint, *Recollections of the Last Ten Years*, p. 43, and *A Condensed Geography*, II, 121; *Niles' Weekly Register*, XV (November 14, 1818), 195; (January 30, 1819), 432.

[47] *Illinois Monthly Magazine*, II (December, 1831), 105; *Western Monthly Magazine*, I (January, 1833), 10; IV (January, 1836). Hall was successively editor of both of these.

[48] Springfield *Sangamo Journal*, February 2, 1832, p. 2; S. Augustus Mitchell (comp.), *Illinois in 1837* . . . (Philadelphia, 1838), p. 133.

[49] Springfield *Sangamo Journal*, December 2, 1837, p. 1.

[50] Reverend A. St. Clair [Illinois? no place or date], to Catharine M. Morse, Boston, Massachusetts, MHC.

[51] James H. Smith, Elkhorn Grove, Illinois, to David Ports, Boonesborough, Maryland, April 16, 1839, ILLSL.

[52] Reverend John G. Bergen, Springfield, Illinois, January 22, 1830, to Peters, AHMS.

[53] *The Western Journal* (St. Louis), III (January, 1850), 248-52.

[54] Flint, *A Condensed Geography*, II, 136-38.

[55] James M. Peck, *A New Guide to the West* (Cincinnati, 1848), p. 255; photostat of clipping from Cincinnati *Journal*, July 8, 1831, ISL; letter from Lima, La Grange County, Indiana, in *Moore's Rural New Yorker*, IX (June 5, 1858), 182.

Nearest resembling an early publicity boom for Indiana in the eastern press is a series of favorable mentions in *Niles' Register* during the years from 1815 to 1826: IX, 171, 186; X, 112, 234; XI, 95, 208; XII, 224; XIV, 440; XV, 64; XX, 129; XXX, 338, 437.

[56] Indiana State Board of Agriculture, *Annual Report*, 1851, p. 255; Lafayette (Ind.) *Journal*, January 10, 1863.

[57] Quoted in *New England Farmer*, XI (1833), 272.

[58] Kellar (ed.), *Solon Robinson, Pioneer Agriculturist*, I, 242-47.

[59] *Indiana Farmer and Gardener*, I (November 15, 1845), 370.

[60] Letters to Absalom Peters from the Reverends Cobb, August 11, 1828; Cressy, June 6, 1831; Kent, April 17, 1833; Post, June 26, 1833; Lowry, August 20, 1835; Wilder, April 3, 1837; Messrs. Bliss and Bennett, November 26, 1834, AHMS; and *Home Missionary*, XVII (August, 1844), 73, and XVIII (January, 1846), 210.

[61] *Home Missionary*, VIII (August, 1835), 67-68.

[62] *Ibid.*, IX (September, 1836), 90.

[63] Reverend Moses H. Wilder, Fairfield, Indiana, to Absalom Peters, February 8, 1836, AHMS; *Home Missionary*, V (January, 1833), 142.

[64] See, for example, Reverend Moses H. Wilder, Fairfield, Indiana, to Peters, February 8, 1836, AHMS; *Home Missionary*, IX (April, 1837), 211; VIII (August, 1835), 67; XVII (August, 1844), 74; XVI (February, 1844), 226. See also Part III of this chapter.

[65] *Home Missionary*, IX (September, 1836), 90; VII (August, 1835), 67.

[66] Reverend B. C. Cressy, Salem, Washington County, Indiana, to Absalom Peters, June 6, 1831, AHMS.

[67] *Home Missionary*, IX (April, 1837), 211.

[68] *Ibid.*, XVII (August, 1844), 75.

[69] *Ibid.*, XIV (May, 1841), 4; Reverend Calvin W. Babbit, Jacksonville, Illinois, to Absalom Peters, December 4, 1830, AHMS, is a good example.

[70] Gates, *The Illinois Central Railroad*, p. 225 and Chapter IX.

[71] *New Englander*, XII (November, 1854), 510; *Wisconsin Farmer* (Racine and Madison), XII (January, 1861), 7; Abner D. Jones, *Illinois and the West*, pp. 147-48.

[72] *American Agriculturist*, XV (July, 1856), 225-26; also XVII, 38, 364.

[73] Gates, *The Illinois Central Railroad*, 175-77.

[74] Carl Sandburg, *The American Song Bag* (New York, 1927).

[75] Reverends M. A. Remley, Columbus, Indiana, November 28, 1833; M. H. Wilder, Jefferson County, Indiana, February 3, 1834; S. G. Lowry, Putnam County, Indiana, August 27, 1833; and Samuel Gregg, Ripley County, Indiana, September 4, 1835, to Absalom Peters, AHMS.

[76] Reverend James Crawford, Jefferson County, Indiana, May 30, 1827, and Reverend Lucius Alden, Lawrenceburg, Indiana, July 17, 1827, to Peters, AHMS; *Home Missionary,* XVII (May, 1844), 19.

[77] *Home Missionary,* XVII (June, 1844), 39-40; XVI (July, 1843), 49; XVII (October, 1844), 140; IX (April, 1837), 210; XVII (May, 1844), 19-21; XVII (December, 1844), 187. See Chapter III, part 3, note 5, above.

[78] *Ibid.,* XVII (December, 1844), 187.

[79] George B. Lockwood, *The New Harmony Movement* (New York, 1905), p. 101; "Extracts of correspondence of Mrs. Abby Soper relative to New Harmony, Indiana, 1831-1835," 1831 file, AHMS; Reverend Calvin Butler, Evansville, Indiana, February 14, 1832, to Peters, AHMS.

[80] Reverend Ulric Maynard, Liberty, Indiana, May 8, 1829, Church elders, Evansville, Indiana, December 16, 1833, Reverends James Chute, Fort Wayne, Indiana, March 12, 1832, and B. H. Cressy, Salem, Indiana, March 14, 1832, to Peters, AHMS; *Home Missionary,* XXIV (March, 1852), 262.

[81] *Home Missionary,* XXII (November, 1849), 160; Drake, *A Systematic Treatise . . . on the Principal Diseases of the Interior Valley of North America,* I, 315.

[82] *Home Missionary,* XXII (October, 1849), 151.

[83] Quoted in Brookville (Ind.) *American,* November 28, 1856.

[84] Quoted in New Albany (Ind.) *Ledger,* November 19, 1856.

[85] Quoted in New Albany (Ind.) *Daily Tribune,* November 17, 1856; Gates, *The Illinois Central Railroad,* pp. 244-45.

[86] *Home Missionary,* XXXI (October, 1858), 146; XXIX (June, 1856), 42.

[87] *Ibid.,* XII (March, 1840), 246; XXVII (November, 1854), 162; XXV (May, 1852), 14.

[88] *Ohio Farmer* (March 6, 1858); V (March 22, August 16, 1856); VI (June 20, 1857).

[89] For comment on this more fortunate sort of migrant see Aaron Wood, D.D., *Sketches of Things and People in Indiana* (Indianapolis, 1883), pp. 15, 35-36; Arthur C. Cole, *The Era of the Civil War, 1848-1870 (Centennial History of Illinois,* Volume III, Chicago, 1919), p. 15.

[90] *Spirit of the Times* (New York), IV (June 12, 1858), 226; *Home Missionary,* XXIII (February, 1851), 243; Illinois State Agricultural Society, *Transactions,* I, 1853-54 (Springfield, 1855), p. 522; II, 1856-57 (Springfield, 1857), pp. 56, 442.

[91] Lewis C. Gray, *History of Agriculture in the Southern United States to 1860* (2 volumes. Washington, D. C., 1933), I, 440. For a description of the Uplander see I, 487-88. Also see Chapter II, above, part 3.

[92] Wood, *Sketches of Things and People in Indiana,* p. 38.

[93] James A. Woodburn, "Pioneer Folk of Early Southern Indiana," in *Indiana University Alumni Quarterly,* XXIII (Fall, 1936), 401-11; also his *History of Indiana University* (Volume I, Bloomington, 1940), p. 70.

[94] *Yankee Notions,* I (January, 1852), 11, 17, 22, 25.

[95] *Ibid.,* VI (March, 1857), 84-85.

[96] *Ibid.,* X (1861), 317.

Chapter IV

LIVING SIDE BY SIDE

1. FARMWAYS

"Even the horses made cultural adjustment"

Certain remarks of Connecticut-bred Solon Robinson, busy and provocative writer on agriculture, epitomize Easterners' views of western agriculture. Of a New England settlement at Bunker Hill, Illinois, he wrote in 1845:

There is more grass, more fruit trees, more barns, more good houses, more scholars at school, and more readers of agricultural papers in this eight year old settlement, than there is in some of the oldest settlements in the State, where the population is double.

To offset such perfection Robinson described a farmer of southern origin living near Auburn, Illinois,

upon a farm upon which he keep 100 head of cattle, and a "right smart chance" of hogs, but they are dying with the kidney worm, and he made a "bad crap; it was so powerful wet in the spring that the crap got right smartly in the grass! and then again it got dreadful dry," and so with all these misfortunes, he felt too poor to subscribe for a paper.[1]

Many were the sermons preached by Yankees as if from Robinson's texts, and the pronouncement, "they are poor farmers," runs like a refrain through their comments.[2]

No criticism was more recurrent than that southern-bred men lacked the industry and neatness to bring their operations up to Yankee standards. The people of Illinois Territory were said to do the least work of any people in the world. Half the farmers of one Illinois community had no aspiration above a "hog and hominy" existence, and were willing to have the

"shakes" half of the year to enjoy the other half. "Yankee
energy and enterprise do not enter into the composition of
their character," was a verdict from southwestern Indiana.[3] If
Westerners rejoined that Yankees labored "severely," the
latter insisted they never hurried except at harvest—the secret:
they did not waste their time; which recalls Charles S. Sydnor's
remark that the Southerner, lacking the New Englander's zeal
for improvement and reform, could enjoy rest with a clear
conscience and was perhaps the only American of any generation to whom leisure was not a sin.[4]

The feeling that western farming was on too large and
careless a scale was aggravated by reports that corn gathering
in Illinois was not finished until January or later (though it
was heartening that Illinois farmers shucked corn into the
wagon and didn't "throw it on the ground at all,"[5] which
latter was a southern practice), and that a corn crop could be
made in the West without a hoe ever being used. "I do not
believe 100 hoes are sold yearly in the county, and only for
gardens," wrote a correspondent from Lafayette, Indiana—
disturbing men bred to the spirit of Bronson Alcott's jingle:

> Soul and muscle
> In mundane tussle—
> I deem sodding
> A sternest godding.[6]

Proof of shiftlessness was complete when Yankees learned
that in the West townspeople paid seventy-five cents a load
to have manure hauled away.[7]

If down-east frugality need demonstration it is supplied
from the "farm wisdom" of Ezekiel Rich of Troy, New
Hampshire. Avowing the use of "children's labor to save that
of men," Rich told farmers to "allow" a few couplets for the
boys to sing while harvesting. He submitted specimens:

> In harvest, be saving,
> Or farewell to thriving.
> Save every potato,
> Nor slight a tomato;

An apple or pumpkin
Is surely worth something;
Even acorn or nut
Should ne'er be forgot.

He that won't stoop for bean or pea,
Is not a man or boy for me.
Who slights a small ear of corn
Is not to wealth or honor born.
The man who cares not for saving,
Must soon beg or else be starving.
It is always foolish to crave,
When idle or careless to starve.

From worker morale Farmer Rich's "thrift lecture" shifted to the soil. "You could cause every hog to work enough in making manure to pay all his expenses! Then don't allow him to be idle." Prose failing him at this point, Rich concluded:

You can treble your manure,
By means now in your own power.[8]

Perhaps as significant in its own way as the Mayflower Compact is the counsel a Yankee urged upon his brother who was about to go on a land claim not distant from Chicago.

If you do go on I beseech you to take up with my advice and sell your Caty dear as she may be to you and purchase another horse cheap and serviceable that can live without Oats and lay out the overplus money in provisions and tools and go on your claim immediately go right onto the ground and Mary with you as soon as you can get the things comfortable. You want rails go at them—the oak of the forest will yield to continued blows and after persevering for a while, you will find labour sweet and only regret that you had not acquired industrious habits before—Be sure to rise early and get the start of the day. You will want plowing—link in with Brown or some of them, even if you have to turn one of your horses into a yoke of Oxen learn to *contrive* and to *economize* George. Go in there. Give the grove your name. Get the young Andrus in with you in some way that will save you your board. Let 'Yankee Fixings' go to the Deuce at some convenient Season when you may perhaps raise some provisions by them—Make a claim as I told you of More Timber and

some prairie down this side—consider it your right and talk ac-
cordingly if anyone qu[e]ries. and sell this claim for as much as
you can. If you cant do better you can give it away to some good
fellow and thereby perhaps make a friend. These are the words
of truth and soberness—consider them and don't be headstrong
against your own convictions.[9]

Small wonder if neighbors of the "go day, come day" sort
stood their distance.

Few practices have greater effect upon farms and farmers
than the culture of hay and grass. Visiting New England,
where haying lasted through the better part of summer, a
Virginian was struck with the "universality of *hay* crops" on
hills as well as in meadows. How anyone could ignore pastures
and meadows was a mystery to Yankees who early carried
hayseeds to the West and boasted that upon the "second- or
third-rate" lands between Toledo and Chicago growing villages
and clover fields showed what could be done by close economy
and perseverance.[10]

Southern Indiana was a fine country for grain and grass,
a man wrote to his father in Massachusetts, but its people were
not inclined to practice grazing. Another reported from Illinois
(near St. Louis, 1818), that most of the people there "cut no
hay for their cattle & horses but this is a foolish way of
theirs. . . ." It meant a rotation of "corn, weeds, hogs, mud
and corn," and the cry was "no money" in spite of raising
more and bigger corn than all the rest of creation, "Old
Kaintuck" included. Generalizing, Robinson noted that "where
the most corn is fed and little else, there I find 'scrub breed' in
the highest state of scrubbiness."[11]

Signs from below the Ohio River, where men sometimes
contended that corn blades excelled hay as winter forage
(though the dwarfish skin-and-bones livestock, somebody said,
would have voted otherwise), clarify western reluctance to
make hay. The neighborhood of Lexington, one man noted,
was about the only place in Kentucky where hay was grown;
livestock wintered on corn fodder; at every house one saw

TABLE II—(Based on 1850 Census)
COMPARATIVE PRODUCTION OF HAY AND ORCHARD
PRODUCTS

States	Tons of hay harvested 1849	Value of orchard products 1849
Maine	755,000	$342,000
New Hampshire	598,000	248,000
Vermont	866,000	315,000
Massachusetts	651,000	463,000
Rhode Island	74,000	63,000
Connecticut	516,000	175,000
New York	3,728,000	1,761,000
Maryland	157,000	164,000
Virginia (including W. Virginia)	369,000	177,000
N. Carolina	145,000	34,000
S. Carolina	20,000	35,000
Tennessee	74,000	52,000
Kentucky	113,000	106,000

stacks of it. From Tennessee, 1854: "Hay is not known." It is interesting, too, that Yankee and Southerner did not call some of the common grasses by the same names. What was herd's grass to a Southerner was timothy to a Yankee; a New Englander's red top was a Southerner's herd's grass, someone noted.[12]

The same year, one of his salesmen assured Cyrus H. McCormick that New England would be "worth a dozen" North Carolinas, whence he wrote, as a market for mowing machinery:

As for *mowing* here it is all out of the question—they raise no grass for hay—What I mowed at this place was on a lawn in front . . . kept as a sort of curiosity—turkeys retreat & c—He don't know what to do with the hay—but talked yesterday of having it "toted" to the pasture grounds for his cattle & mules to pick over—[13]

Indeed, for several years preceding 1853 hay had been shipped from New England to Atlanta and Dalton (Georgia), for example. Thus, among our customary upland states only Virginia reported more hay in 1850 (369,098 tons) than did

Oneida County, New York, alone (167,047 tons). Eight New York counties (Chautauqua, Chenango, Delaware, Jefferson, Oneida, Otsego, St. Lawrence, Steuben) reported almost one-fourth more tons (1,013,000) than the six Southern states (878,000 tons). Vermont alone produced nearly as much hay in 1850 (866,000 tons) as did the six southern states.[14]

The same western farmers who had been "enemies of the grasses" (in a Southerner's phrase) were condemned for not having a fruit tree in the world. " 'And why don't you set an orchard.' 'Well, I reckon may be I will some day—did set out a few trees once, and they grew powerfully, but the cattle soon destroyed 'em.' And no wonder, for they were set in 'the big field,' the eternal corn field."[15]

Some of the earliest correspondence from the Northwest Territory shows concern of Yankees for fruit culture in the new land. Letters often mention fruit and nursery stock as well as exemplary farmers who profitably cultivated fruit.[16] At Tremont in the Illinois county of Tazewell, for example, the Yankees had "departed from the fashion of this country," by providing multitudes of shade and fruit trees. Yankees claimed credit for establishing systematic culture of fruit in southern Illinois, where "Brahmin or Northern" incomers, in addition to building factories, roads, and a better sort of house, had "in short . . . made it a large fruit-raising community."[17]

Culture of fruit was not a strong part of the Uplander's breeding, nor suited to his casual ways; whereas at midcentury it appeared that every eastern farmer was planting an orchard. The seven Yankee states reported orchard products valued at about six times that of the six states which supplied Upland population to the Northwest. This gives pertinence to Jefferson's remark that even the wealthy people of eighteenth-century Virginia were very little attentive to the raising of fruits.[18]

"If I had a good wife," wrote Joseph V. Quarles (father of the United States Senator from Wisconsin), "I would make me a farm and keep a dairy."[19] "Cow-milking Yankee Puritans" early distinguished themselves in the Northwest. A

Vermonter found in Ohio that "Some Milk 30 or 40 cows these are New England people. The country people never make any Cheese which makes cheese the same price as Butter." The next year (1818) he remarked that very little cheese was available in Madison County, Illinois. None was made except by eastern people. Eight years later the Vermont man was milking eleven cows and made a cheese daily.[20]

Yankees seem to have made of dairying a special means for laying toll upon western grass and grain. At the same time it satisfied hunger for their own make of butter and cheese. Thus a woman near Quincy, Illinois, included a milk room when she built a comfortable framed dwelling. It was commonplace that a family or two that understood butter- or cheesemaking would do well in some certain locality. Wistful of again tasting cheese, Mary Mace wrote of southern Indiana: "This will be a good country in a few years if the people would clear up their land and go to raising stock and have some dairys

TABLE III—(Based on 1850 Census)
COMPARATIVE PRODUCTION OF DAIRY PRODUCTS

	Number of persons per milch cow	Approx. lbs. butter per capita 1849	Average lbs. butter per milch cow 1849	Lbs. cheese produced
Northeastern States				
Maine	4.4	16	70	2,434,454
New Hampshire	3.4	22	74	3,196,563
Vermont	2.1	20	83	8,720,834
Massachusetts	7.6	8.1	67	7,088,142
Rhode Island	5.25	17.5	36	316,508
Connecticut	4.3	17.5	76	5,563,277
New York	3.3	25.7	85	49,741,413
Average	4.33	20.9	70	. . .
Southern States				
Maryland	6.8	6.5	44	3,974
Virginia (including W. Virginia)	4.5	8	35	436,292
N. Carolina	3.9	5	19	95,921
S. Carolina	3.4	4.5	15	4,970
Tennessee	4	10	33	177,681
Kentucky	4	8	40	213,954
Average	4.3	7	31	. . .

but now there is no cheese made in these parts as I know of and but little butter." True to her upbringing, Mary Mace was going "to learn my girle" to make cheese.[21]

Yankees talked as though they held a sort of franchise upon proper dairying. Cow milking had penetrated them deeply. Even the stage Yankee expresses preference for a farm girl over a stylish lady because the former could "milk cows, set up the butter, make cheese, and darn me, if they ain't what I call raal downright feminine accomplishments." Yankees sometimes showed a testy impatience with the dairying of the western people, who had come to the Northwest with "but little stock."[22]

On his way to the Indiana University commencement in 1845 Editor Henry Ward Beecher thought he had found the origin of some of the "unutterably dirty" butter which came to Indiana markets.[23] New Englanders were pleased to sell their surplus at 15 cents a pound while others got only 12 1/2 cents: "A Yankee woman can make better butter than succers. . . ." A storekeeper in Illinois told a western buttermaker that "if you had left a little more buttermilk in it I could have squeezed out a good drink." Yankee disapproval also extended to nomenclature. The same man recalled his disgust in "this land of strange customs" at seeing people "eating loppered milk, calling it bonnyclapper, when at my Grandfather's I had seen it used as pigs' food only."[24] Perhaps he illustrated what James Hall called "veriest trifles" which sometimes nourished dissension.

Two principal inferences appear to be justified: strikingly different management and uses of dairy products; and a lesser efficiency of southern dairy livestock. Interestingly there were in 1850 4.33 persons for each milch cow in New York–New England, while, in our six southeastern states the number was almost the same, 4.43. But from there on similarity dwindles. For the seven Yankee states, pounds of butter reported per person was 20.9; for the usual southern states, 7 pounds. The same northern cows were credited each with 70 pounds of butter annually (in addition to a large make of cheese), while southern cows averaged 31 pounds.[25] Such differences would affect the basic living of the two peoples, their eating habits and nutrition, and farmways in general.

C. K. Laird was born in Vermont, removed at early age to Indiana where he learned farming, and returned to Vermont. He soon found himself considered "an ignorant fellow who had come from a Country where the people did not know how to make hay or even to raise corn and that I was in the way. . . ."[26]

Laird's experience means that there were practical differences by the score which at least provoked remark. "Worm" or Virginia-style rail fences were long the rule in southern Illinois to the exclusion of the "straight board fences" to which the New Englanders were accustomed. The Yankee was disdainful of southern-western handicraft—"miserable" oxbows, yokes, and carts. Considerable planters in Rowan County, North Carolina, were said to make use (around 1820) of grapevines and hickory withes, instead of iron traces on their harness. The Yankee noted the inconvenience of narrow-tread eastern carriages running unevenly on the wider-tracked roads of the Illinois prairies. The wider track had been gnawed out by primitive vehicles such as "Carolina" carts and wagons, made entirely of wood (except perhaps a wagon's linchpin). The wheels were discs cross-sawed from a suitable log, and though lubricated by soft soap, the noise made by such vehicles is described as terrific.[27]

Then the southern method of driving a team, even a four-horse one, with a single line attached to the near (left) lead horse, the teamster astride one of the horses, was queerly different. This mode of driving was said to be universal at the South, while the Yankees drove their teams with double reins known as check lines, the driver riding on the wagon. And Yankee check lines were destined to prevail largely. When Mr. Pigg, who was among the first in Sullivan County (southwestern Indiana) to do so, adopted double-rein driving, his neighbors helped him break his horses into that "new

fangled mode of horse-tailoring."[28]   Even the western horses
did not escape cultural adjustment.

Interestingly for us, the nation's race horses and race horse-
men were sectionalized. In the Northeast, and especially in
New England, harness racing, with the horses hitched to a
vehicle, was dominant. In the West and South, running races,
with riders up, prevailed. A democratic and informal part of
the latter was the quarter race, held on a quarter-mile straight-
away.   Such bouts are said to have been held almost every
Saturday during the 1840's, on West Street in Indianapolis,
for example. This was the equivalent of the "brushing" that
took place between harness trotters on the "Race Streets" in
northern cities. Following the Revolution, running races were
tried in New England but failed to catch necessary support.
Later, legislation attempted to prohibit horse racing, but the
courts took the view that a horse could not achieve his maxi-
mum speed hitched to a vehicle, hence the harness race was not
in fact racing. But running races were banned, and the entire
field in the Northeast was left to the harness men and their
trotters. Perhaps the suppression of running races, improved
roads, snow and ice tracks in winter, wealthy patrons, and agricultural fairs all helped to make of New England a "hotbed" of
harness horse affairs. At any rate, New England defended
and propagated harness racing, which by 1840 was organized
in an arc of cities extending from Boston to Baltimore. As the
guardian and protector of the harness cause the New Englanders evidently could think of no favor greater than sharing
with others the delights of this form of sport. Hence in the
winter of 1857 men from Providence and Boston went with
their horses to New Orleans. A note from Providence in
Porter's Spirit of the Times reads: "We are gratified to learn
that eastern turfmen are inclined to do all within their power
to assist their southern brethren to establish trotting races at
the South." At the same moment other race lovers were talking of a Central National Course in Washington. If secession

and rebellion had been left to the racemen, we should probably still be waiting for them to come about.[29]

An interesting explanation of the irregular shape of farms in Virginia and western Pennsylvania is that in staking claims farmers were guided mainly by the tops of surrounding ridges. They located their buildings on the lower ground enclosed by the ridges. Hence the farms were amphitheaters and everything came to the house downhill. At any rate, Southerners carried to the Northwest an indifference to rectangular layout. Someone noted that the Hoosiers kept their farms and clearings as far as possible from being square.[30] Southerners also brought the practice of locating their buildings back from the highway near the center of the farm, while the Yankees located theirs near the road. An aggravated case of isolation due to farm layout was reported by a Yankee trader who mingled freely with the very early settlers near Connersville, Indiana, chiefly southern people. They built "small log cabins with the door the back side of the house, the house the back side of the fields, & the fields frequently in the back side of their farms." Perhaps the South Carolinians inclined to the unusual in the layout of earth tracts and the orientation of buildings. An early visitor said of Charleston: "Houses stand sidewaies backward into their yard and only endwaies, with their gables toward the Street."[31]

2. SHELTER

"for Horses very bad"

In his *Notes on the State of Virginia,* Thomas Jefferson describes huts of logs laid horizontally in pens, the interstices stopped with mud.[32] Such buildings could be cited as proto-types of western dwellings "hastily erected and hastily abandoned" by a people more of the pastoral than of the agricultural character. Other testimony affords additional not-too-flattering detail. A German traveler of the 1820's suggested that the wandering spirit of the western men had "still to contend with the principle of steadiness in the very construction of their buildings." A Virginian slave mistress spoke of houses "none too good for stables" in Illinois to the westward of Vincennes. Another, referring to southern Illinois, remarked "little old miserable dwellings," furnished, as another described, with "an empty packing-box for a table, while two or three old chairs and disabled stools graced the reception room the dark walls of which were further ornamented by a display of dirty tinware and an article or two." Some of the farmhouses near Chicago (mostly one-room affairs) were no larger than ten by twelve feet, and with low head clearance. In such undersize log-built dwellings "they do all their work all lodge, & all stay contentedly. 'To be content's their natural desire.' "[33]

Friends back East were therefore briefed to expect at the West buildings smaller and cheaper than at home. Those who had money preferred to speculate or to buy land instead of laying it out for a "great house." Houses of the better sort were confined to the towns. A woman who traveled the hundred miles between the Illinois villages of Shawneetown and Carlyle around 1822 saw no framed houses except at the terminal points. Savanna in the same state was said to have (1838) thirty-five houses, mostly "genteel frames." But even these "genteel frames," in keeping with the size of building lots, were comparatively small in western towns. One who spent his boyhood at Lafayette, Indiana, was astonished when he first went East at the extraordinary number of stairways he was expected to climb—outside the public square back home there were scarce any houses of more than one story.[34]

The observation that western houses were built before they were planned, whereas among eastern people they were first planned, then built, appears borne up by Yankees who expected to live as soon as possible in comfortable framed houses. For some townish Yankees the best was none too good. This was the case with Calvin Fletcher, a young Vermont-born attorney. Writing in 1834 from Indianapolis where he had settled, to his wife who was visiting in Urbana, Ohio, he asked her to look out for "the very best modal for a house gardens & other improvements   There are none save in Springfield & Dayton worthy of imitation," he added.[35]

As to weather worthiness and comfort of western dwellings some of our best clues come from New England via the South. A Virginian who had visited New England approved, among lesser things, "closed doors . . . *rumfordized* fire-places [and] *seasoned* wood. . . ."[36]   Another Southerner after a turn there ventured to name "seven wonders" of New England. Third in his list was that all firewood was dry, sawed to size, and stored in shelter.[37]   By a sort of cultural triangulation we are prepared for a Yankee's surprise at finding western chimneys "turned outdoors" (which spent heat needful to comfort in winter); and for the complaint that the western cold would not be felt so much if the country and the houses were not so "generly open."[38]   The latter point was taken up by a Virginian in Illinois:

You wanted to know why the people didden have better stable if the ground [is] so good.   the peopl is neglectful and lazy   they doant care chist so they can live hur in the timber   in the praries the building is a heeptiter than what they are in the timber.[39]

It should be redundant to say that the Uplanders relied upon the timber to supplement man-made shelter, while Yankees, willing to risk living on treeless prairies, relied upon construction a "heeptiter."[40]

New Englanders also found novelty in corncribs made of rails as a Yankee would "build a Cobhouse,"[41] and in the western "cellar," excavated when a cabin-house was built, the dirt affording mud for chinking and for the chimney.   Accessible by way of loose boards in the floor, this type of cellar provided storage for potatoes and the like, but its capacity was not one tenth enough to please one Yankee woman.[42]   At least one New Englander was surprised to find western houses roofed with shakes or clapboards, presumably in place of shingles.[43]

To barn-loving Yankees lack of barns or inadequate ones was the most distressing feature of western shelter arrangements—though certainly not all Yankees went so far as the

Above. New England-style House, Bristol, Indiana. Built c. 1840.
Below. Southern Federal-style House, Newburgh, Indiana. Built 1834.

Connecticut man who told his father: "I shall mortgage my land, if I can, to raise $300, to build a barn." Even if the western man provided a "suckerbarn," a temporary shed and stable built of rails and straw, Yankees thought it little short of barbarous. The readiest explanation of differing practices in the sheltering of livestock is that the Uplanders had come from where average January temperatures range from about 35° to 45° F., while January temperatures in New England– New York range from 20° to 30°.[44]

But neither sort of man was entirely blameless. It is notable that at the same moment the Yankees were scolding the Uplanders, barns were reported few in the Yankee parts of Illinois and Indiana; near Peoria and Chicago, and in the northern-tier Indiana counties of La Grange and St. Joseph. Still more surprising is the admonition of the Watertown, Wisconsin, *Chronicle* that near-by farmers build barns. Many farmers had none. They should postpone new houses, plaster up the old log house and make it do, but they should build barns.[45]

Meanwhile Yankees did not fail to trace back South the character of western husbandry. One boasted that in Illinois he could take his bearings from the presence or absence of barns and other "Yankee fixings," which if absent indicated that "corn-growing, hog-feeding, corn-bread and bacon-eating southerners" were in a majority in that latitude. That a physician in Illinois had no shelter for his two horses was tied in with his "brought'n up" in a section of the United States "that 'I reckon' you will not wish me to tell you lies south of the celebrated line of Mason and Dixon." Perhaps this "really good man," as his critic acknowledged him to be, was a descendant of the North Carolinians who, around 1765, offered to travelers accommodation "very middling, and for Horses very bad. . . ."[46]

3. COOKING AND EATING

*"What'll ye take: wheat bread and chicken fixens,
or corn-bread and common doins?"*

On the authority of a Methodist clergyman who throughout
his life "boarded around" and who reckoned that he had slept
in more than eight hundred houses in the state of Indiana
alone, the Virginians and Marylanders were polished, hospitable, and skilful in preparing dinner and entertaining guests.
So were the *South* Carolinians, said the minister with calculated
emphasis. The *North* Carolinians, Tennesseeans, and mountain
Kentuckians were poor cooks, but the New Jerseyans could
make the best appearance on small means, and the Yankees
the most fuss.[47]

As one would expect, cooking and eating share the anec-
dotage of adjustment. Yankees were eloquent when they won
the confidence of a feckless squatter in Iowa by introducing
him to mince pie.[48] An eastern schoolmistress relates that
whenever bread-and-milk was requested, a plate of bread and
a glass of milk were brought on. Western hospitality expected
the visitor would munch the bread and drink the milk, instead
of spooning up immersed broken bread. (The Yankee girl
had "begged the privilege" of the latter method.) Sour milk, in
the same girl's experience, was so much used that the visitor
was always asked which he preferred, sweet or sour. Such
preferences, which illustrate difference in the management
and use of dairy products, were deep-rooted. A Southerner
who saw New England in the 1830's could not forgive their
bringing no buttermilk to the table. The natives seemed
wholly ignorant how pleasant and wholesome a food it was
for man, and gave it to their pigs.[49]

Both Southerners and Yankees brought preferences or
staples with them to the Northwest. "Dined on Codfish &
potatoes," a Muskingum settler wrote, July 20, 1788. "O how
I long for one of Mothers Good Cheese—I would readily give
a Barrel of Super fine flour for one of them." It needs no

remarking that this longing originated with a Yankee. Uplanders continued to take satisfaction from dock and polk
greens. A Marylander at Buffalo Grove, Illinois, heard many
regret that no sassafras grew there. All believed it would
thrive if introduced. At least one Quaker couple from tidal
Carolina felt the loss of seafood. We may be sure too that
the Yankees carried with them a true affection for the apple.
"The juice of the apple seems native to our New England
constitutions . . .," wrote Alcott in his journal. The same
woman who hungered for New England cheese and fish also
felt the lack in southern Indiana of "cyder" and apples which
she thought might cure her ague and shortness of breath and
palpitation. An elderly man demurred at leaving the Bay
State for Ohio, afraid, a relative explained, "that he shall
not get cyder enough if he goes there. . . ."[50]

Travelers sometimes found that their reputed choices and
dislikes had reached the western woods before them. A Maine
youth recalled concerning his first Hoosier meal, in 1832, that
"At the table I was a little amused at having a saucer of molasses set before me to eat either with my bread or pork, the old
man by his inquiries having ascertained that I was a Yankee."[51]

Certain of the novelties that impressed a Virginia-born
schoolboy in Connecticut somewhat over a century ago are
paralleled in the Northwest.

One or two mornings . . . they have had hominy for breakfast
which although it was yellow instead of white was very good.
Every Northerner eats it with molasses and every Southerner
without. It seemed very strange to me to see them eat molasses
at breakfast, as well as cider and pickle, when I first came here.
Here at dinner when they have pickles they do not give you a
piece of cucumber as we would do, but they give you a whole
one at once.[52]

Southern-bred people down to the present generation express distaste for meal not the grist of white corn. Any person
of middle age can recall how Midwest farmers would vary the
annual planting of yellow corn to include a small field, or part

of a larger field, in white corn for household meal and for lye hominy. Yellow corn, perhaps recalling the "hard Yellow Flinty Corn of New England," was out of the question for household uses. Meanwhile yellow corn was said to fetch about four cents more on the bushel than white corn at Boston and New York.[53]

As to cookery proper, a Massachusetts woman described carefully the southern style practiced in Illinois by neighbors principally from Indiana and Kentucky:

but everything is so different . . . for instance, they think that a boiled dish as we boil it is not fit to eat; it is true they boil their food but each separate it won't do to boil cabbage or turnips or beets carrots or parsnips in their meat nor potatoes without drain- ing and the water that the meat is boiled in must be all boiled down so that there is nothing left but the fat and a very little of the water and that is taken up in the dish with the meat and answers for gravy; this is well enough—I speak of it because it is so different.[54]

The preceding quotation was read without any preliminary explanation to a man who was brought up in the South, and he at once remarked that it was nothing other than a Yankee's reaction to southern cooking. "With a little more accurate statement about gravy," he said, "that was the way my mother and grandmother cooked; that is the way Southerners cook now. And they have a pretty low estimate of the sickly hash that a New Englander calls a 'boiled dinner.' "

From Chicago a southern woman gave her opinion of Yankee cooking: "The people here cook very differently from what they do in Virginia. Here they live on tea, cold meat and bread, crackers and cheese, pastry and cakes, and Irish potatoes for supper and breakfast. They never have a single meal without potatoes."[55]

The most frequent comment on western eating was the heavy use of corn-hog products and other animal food—"whole hog bacon, corn meal dogger & mush & milck," as one Yankee spelled it out.[56] Remarks of Thomas Jefferson forecast such characteristics. The eighteenth-century wealthy Virginians, he wrote, were "attentive to the raising of vegetables, but very little so to fruits. The poorer people attend to neither, living principally on milk and animal diet." This emphasis upon animal diet remained a fixed part of expanding southern culture. Daniel Drake, outstanding physician of his age, observed in the Great Valley an unusual dependence upon "animal food." A gazetteer-maker confidently noted that Illinois families ate more meat in proportion to numbers than was consumed in the older states.[57]

What lop-sided food resources meant to a dietitian-in-the-woods was set down by an Ohio pioneer who after supper made meal for the johnnycake for breakfast; after breakfast she made meal for the pone for dinner; and after dinner meal for the mush for supper. The same captive of monotony could have written, "You had hog for breakfast, pig for dinner, and pork for supper." A Yankee youth reported from northern Indiana a family of twelve who consumed in a year twenty-five swine, a record impressive in numbers at least, though more significant if the weight and quality of the carcasses were known.[58]

In explaining why the Yankees made, in the words of Aaron Wood, "the most fuss," several points may be mentioned. They had brought from the East knowledge, if not the invariable practice, of setting their tables in a more elaborate way, known as Yankee, or down-east, style.[59] They felt their foodways superior in quality and variety. Also they appear to have provided themselves with cookstoves before their Midwest neighbors did so. A vein of stovemongery runs through their writings. One man, from La Grange County, northern Indiana, mentioned "our fine stove," and added that in migrating from York State he was sacrificing few comforts. One was having a stove forwarded from New York City by way of New Orleans to Quincy, Illinois. Another insisted, *"I must have a stove,"* which with pipe and other fixings would cost about $15 in Madison, Wisconsin—cheaper than in New York state.[60]

While these are not clearly designated as cookstoves, even

a heating-stove would eliminate need for a fuel-devouring fireplace, and thus encourage or necessitate stove cooking. Some of the stoves, such as the Franklin Alterable Cooking Stove, were built for dual service, cooking and space heating. At any rate a wide prevalence of cookstoves by the latter 1850's is certain from the remark of a North State man that Illinois women, having cookstoves, could get breakfast before North Carolina women could get a fire started.[61]

But back of anecdote and incident, habits and preferences were of a pattern geographically large and long in duration. The point is illustrated by potatoes and sweet potatoes. One will recall the remark of the Virginia woman—the year was 1838—that at Chicago they never had a single meal without potatoes. Further back in time and territory (Vermont, 1820) a young man explained that because pork, corn, wheat, and bacon were high in price, "the poor people lived almost solely on potatoes, particularly during the winter." At the same moment one young Burton from Brownsville, Illinois, was telling his sister in Vermont, that sweet potatoes, "a rarity of the North," were common there. While a few years earlier, 1817, Yorker Samuel Whedon sent word from southern Indiana that Carolinian neighbors used sweet potatoes as a substitute for bread.[62]

These various items relate to the dependence of the seven Yankee states upon potatoes and the similarly heavy dependence of the six southern states under consideration upon sweet potatoes. Indeed from the greater South only 10 per cent of the nation's potatoes, but 94 per cent of its sweet potatoes, were reported in 1859.[63] Excepting Connecticut, which reported eighty bushels, the Census of 1850 shows no sweet potatoes grown in New England, while New York is credited with only 5,629 bushels of sweet potatoes against fifteen million bushels of potatoes. The six southern states combined produced in 1849 less than five million bushels of potatoes and something over fifteen million bushels of sweet potatoes. (See Table IV.)

The uneven distribution of at least two other staples should

TABLE IV—(Based on 1850 Census)
COMPARATIVE PRODUCTION OF POTATOES AND SWEET POTATOES
Comparative Production of Potatoes and Sweet Potatoes

State	Irish Potatoes (bushels)	Sweet Potatoes (bushels)
Maine	3,436,040	....
New Hampshire	4,304,419	....
Vermont	4,951,014	....
Massachusetts	3,585,384	....
Rhode Island	651,029	....
Connecticut	2,689,725	80
New York	15,398,368	5,629
Maryland	764,939	208,993
Virginia (including W. Virginia)	1,316,993	1,813,634
North Carolina	620,318	5,095,709
South Carolina	136,494	4,337,469
Tennessee	1,067,844	2,777,716
Kentucky	1,492,487	998,179

be mentioned: first, the considerable prevalence of Indian corn almost all over the South, as compared with its relatively slight occurrence in New York–New England.[64] This is not to say that the Yankee did not know his johnnycake, dodger, and pone, though he was probably more a wheat-eating man than was the Uplander. By 1840 Bay State Yankees had almost banished dark bread from their tables, said an official report, and the poorest family was not satisfied without wheat bread. For while New England was receiving wheat inexpensively from the West, the men to the southward of the Old National Road in Ohio–Indiana–Illinois appear to have been selling off a substantial fraction (half of eight million bushels, 1849) of the wheat they grew. The result was that the area's populace, southern bred for the most part, ate corn bread and mush in place of light bread the wheat would have afforded.[65] One could almost say the Yankees demanded wheaten bread and that the corn-eating Westerners were pleased they should have it. At any rate, southerly emphasis upon corn, along with sparse cultivation of wheat,[66] accounts for the unending references by Yankees to the "power of coarse cornbread" in southern and western diet, although they might concede wheat flour for "biscuit every Sunday morning."

Finally, and with no attempt to prove anything: When Sergeant Orville Mullins, a released prisoner of the Korean war, was returning to his home in Covington, Kentucky, in April, 1953, his mother was interviewed by Mr. Peter Grant of radio station WLW. Presently the talk turned to food: What did Orville like, pie? Pie Orville liked, Mrs. M. said, and he should have it, and then added touchingly, "But what Orville really wants is cornbread."

4. THE LANGUAGE OF THE PEOPLE

"it would please you much to hear them converse"

"They *will* not, or they *cannot* read. They are not generally a reading people, but a thinking and a talking people. They are accustomed to catch the glance of the living eye, and to be instructed and animated by the counsels and persuasions of the living voice."[67] With these words a churchman estimated the singular importance with western folk of the spoken word.

"Preacher" was the universal title of the clergy in Iowa, the young William Salter wrote with apparent impatience to his fiancée back East: "He must preach." When a native of South Carolina was considering service among southern people at Rushville, Illinois, a churchly superior approved: He has been 'raised' among them—knows all their peculiarities—understands their dialect . . . this disarms prejudice. . . ." Another complained against "a frothy & turgid kind of ready eloquence . . ." characteristic of every class of western public speakers. A western lawyer was therefore compelled to become a great advocate or public speaker, a young attorney explained in a letter back East, while "in your country any man can be a great lawyer without saying a word."[68]

Barred from discussing the finer shadings of difference most lay critics of western speech confined themselves to

terminology, usage, and other novelties, or cleared the subject
by a remark such as "I think it would please you much to hear
them converse. I expect it would be very difficult for you to
understand them at first. . . ."[69] But the expressive Timothy
Flint included in his analysis difference in dialect, enunciation,
colloquy, figures, illustrations, and frequency of profanity and
strange curses.[70] Indeed the usages of the two peoples were so
far apart as to be sometimes mutually unintelligible. This is
apparent from a Yankee's description of a runaway team: "It
run into the bush and run astride astraddle, and broke the
neap, reach and evener." Rendered in Hoosierish the account
was: "The horses got skeert and run astraddle of a saplin
and broke the tongue, double-tree and couplin pole."[71] The
story goes, that during the Kansas excitement of 1854 Border
Ruffians, wishing to stop immigration of Yankees, stationed
guards at the Missouri River crossing and instructed them to
ask every traveler to utter the single word "cow." If anyone
said "keow," he was to be turned back. The plan worked it is
said. History records a victory for the slavery party in Kansas
that year. It was also a victory for the spoken word.[72]

After explaining that in Illinois a wedge was called a *glut,* a
hill a *bluff,* a stream a *slew,* that *prote* was the name applied to
wheat bread and that *reckon* was used when a Yankee would say
guess, the writer asked his brother in Maine to translate a "western" sentence: "On Friday week (a week from Friday) I took
the *gluts,* passed over *yon slew,* by the side of *yon* bluff, & found
a *right smart chance* for splitting a *heap of rails.* I felt *powerful weak* so I returned home." The word *heap,* he explained,
was used to denote amount or degree of rain, of mud, of wind,
business, of hot weather "& a heap of everything else."[73]

In extreme northern Indiana, a harrow was called a *drag*
and a drag was a *stone boat.* They *geared* their horses instead
of harnessing them, said *hit* for it, *Aprile* for April, *cheer* for
chair, *shet* for rid: a pupil said to his teacher, "I have had the
ague but have got *shet* of *hit.*" They referred to *tame* grass
and fruit, while a Yankee spoke of tame animals only. The

names of many trees were different. Rock maple was *sugar tree,* basswood was *linn,* butternut was *white walnut,* whitewood was *sycamore,* and poplar was *quaking asp.* *Chance, smart chance,* and *right smart chance* were used as positive, comparative, and superlative. Division of the day into "morning" and "evening" was curious; likewise a man's reference to his bride of sixteen as "my old woman," or mention of his ill wife as "powerful sick today." The cry "Books, books," as a signal that school was about to take up, was as strange to the Yankee boy as the companion announcement "School's broke."[74]

At least one Yankee ventured to correct the speech of his western flock. At Greensburg in southeastern Indiana the Reverend J. R. Wheelock was at first much pleased with the community, where as many as two thirds of the inhabitants were from Kentucky. He presently advised his eastern sponsors that his wife had opened a school of twenty or thirty scholars in which she would use "the most approved N. E. school books," to be obtained by a local merchant from Philadelphia. "She makes defining a distinct branch of study and this gives her a very favorable oppy. of correcting the children & thro' them, the parents, of 'a heap' of Kentuckyisms." Fifteen months later things were a-tangle for the Wheelocks. There is no reason to doubt the pastor's sincerity in believing that his "New England divinity" had caused the trouble. One suspects, however, that too many parents had been corrected "of 'a heap' of Kentuckyisms."[75]

A visitor in North Carolina during the early 1900's followed in the Charlotte *Observer* a series of articles on expressions long in use in the Carolinas. There was included not a word or expression, he noted, which he had not heard as a boy in Indiana: "And language and dialect is always proof of kinship."[76] This view harmonizes with the findings of a wide-scale survey of speech geography in the Old Northwest undertaken during the latter 1930's.

If nothing else were known about the region, studies in linguistic geography would point to southern culture origins over great areas of the Old Northwest. For example, it was found that the term currently used by the indigenous population for wheat bread in loaves is "light bread," which is the southern term, used predominantly throughout Indiana and the southern half of Illinois. Another example involves the pronunciation of "greasy" (whether with an "s" or a "z" sound). The survey found the "z" pronunciation (the southern) prevailing in southern Illinois, all of Indiana except the most northerly portion, and in the southern part of Ohio.[77] Thus, in the Old Northwest as elsewhere, survival of early speech characteristics helps to identify originally dominant culture within the area.

From preceding passages one notes the tendency of Yankees to quote with interest, amusement, or scorn the speechways carried by the Southerners to the Northwest. However quaint or faulty southern speech may have been, it is a large misfortune that, because the Uplanders generally lacked the habit of writing, their ideas of Yankee folk-speech, itself so vulnerable to caricature, went so nearly unrecorded.[78]

5. CLERGY AND LAYMEN

"Preachers and coon dogs were in about equal demand. . . ."

Southern religious organizations, whether Baptist, Methodist, Presbyterian, or Quaker, was, as we might expect, important in fostering cultural similarities between the Uplands and the Northwest. The point is illustrated by the Western Methodist Episcopal Conference which from 1800 to 1811 extended from New Orleans to Detroit, the Mississippi River its western boundary. Three fourths of its ministers, notes a scholar citing official records, began their work in the South or were working there in 1800. Less than one fourth of them began their work north of the Ohio River, and seven eighths of them preached part time in the South. Probably three fourths of them had southern antecedents. "If the people of the South had any peculiar culture, this organization must have been a very efficient instrument in transferring it north of the Ohio."[79]

The chief religious contrasts between Yankees and South-

erners in the Northwest boil down to different standards of
ministerial training, duty, and support; contrasting behavior in
the place of worship; a suspicion on the part of Westerners that
eastern men might subvert the principle of "a free church in a
free state"; and doubt as to the efficacy of each other's gospel.

Ministers with fervent readiness of speech and pen were
prominent on both sides. Sometimes there were name calling
and disparagements. If a Yankee pronounced the western
gospel "shorter than a man can stretch himself thereon, and
narrower than a man can wrap himself therein,"[80] a pioneer
clergyman replied that New England, largely lacking the
warming truths of Methodism and having accepted too much
of Unitarianism and Universalism, had "well-nigh . . . dis-
mantled her glory . . . civil, literary and religious."[81]

The eastern preacher in the West, the experienced Theron
Baldwin warned, "is often the very 'antipodes' of his audience,"
looked upon as a "mysterious, suspicious being from another
hemisphere or another planet."[82] The carefully prepared, sometimes hand-written, sermons of the college-trained New England preacher contrasted sharply with the "seesaw, hum and
spit" kind of preaching often heard at the West, by preachers
who might intend to exhort on the next Sunday provided
'twere not a good bee day—if it were, the preacher would
go bee-hunting instead.[83]

To zealous eastern clerics the swarms of "preaching
vagrants" only heightened the need for trained workers in
the West. Until better were provided the vagrants would
"*feed* the people; and if they have no fine flour, they take
corn; and if this be not ground, they pound it in a mortar."[84]
But poetic idiom was lacking from the description one Yankee
gave of the type of minister likely to succeed where he had
not: "I think . . . that a stout southerner about seven feet
and a half high, with a voice like Stentor, and who could live
through the week on the wind that he had preached out on the
Sabbath would suit them, be his principles and practices almost
what they would."[85]

Case histories exemplify the clash between eastern preachers and western hearers. The Reverend Moody Chase, a missionary at Orleans, southern Indiana, owned that he had criticized his parishioners in a "pretty severe" manner: "They are afraid of the reports of a Presbyterian preacher; especially if he be an *Eastern* man." Thirteen months later he wrote from near-by Paoli: "I could not keep a S. School in operation. And some of our people had heard that I was a new-school man and under the . . . [Home Missionary Society] away off to the East *there*. And it seem to me that it was not best to fish where there were so few fish and they among so many rocks."[86]

Reverend John Morrill, with charges at Connersville, Liberty, and Brownsville (southeastern Indiana) in 1833, attributed the fix he was in to those who learned that he "was from N. E., & acting on the principle that 'no good can come from thence,' with much apparent kindness warned the good people of this place of their danger." Upon removal to La Porte (northwestern Indiana), Morrill hoped he might escape such troubles: "They seem to be more acquainted with N. E. people, & consequently not to be afraid of them."[87]

Western churchgoers could hardly be expected to warm to leaders who, as a Moravian minister noted, described an angry Jehovah in fearful manner. The love of Jesus was mentioned only incidentally, continued the Moravian, who had heard the sermons of New England Presbyterian missionaries at Madison, Indiana. In one instance a New England pastor reported that the professors of religion in one Indiana county would, almost to a man, be excommunicated from an eastern church. Westerners evidently returned blows worthily, for at a later date those requesting workers from the East promised: "We shall not persecute them *even* if they come from Western New York or east of the Hudson River."[88]

In the interval between the sermons of two Methodist preachers at one service in Illinois in the early 1820's, an eastern laywoman noted the children rushed to the fire to roast eggs in the ashes, and straightway devoured the eggs.

Mothers who had suckled babes during the preceding part of
the service now lighted pipes and looked happy as the smoke
curled from under their sunbonnets, while the men moved one
by one toward a water pail with its gourd dipper in a rear
corner of the room. Each thoughtfully removed his quid
while another was drinking; then taking the gourd in the
hand not hindered by the quid, rinsed his mouth, spat the water
on the floor, took a drink of water, and was ready to chat.[89]

Yankee ministers, uncomfortably aware that the free
church manners of the West would throw "a deep shade of
influence" over their own, sought to correct their charges.
Thus a young Easterner censured Illinoisans for entering
church with their hats on, "the mark of an ignorant, vulgar
people. . . ."[90] Even to a sympathetic Yankee one Hoosier
congregation appeared to act lost in church:

When I rose to commence the service by prayer, nearly all kept
their seats, staring at me as though wondering what I meant. During the sermon, two or three children, just beginning to walk, were
running about the house, and some of the grown people were
frequently passing out and in. This was not from any intention to
disturb the meeting, but because they knew no better.[91]

"These are hard sayings of mine and should not be published. . . ," wrote a missionary explaining that "the younger
baptists who . . . often mingle in our assemblies . . . have
never been taught to keep their feet still even when they go
to the house of God. . . ."[92]

Yankee ministers were also distrusted as tools of politics.
Westerners possessed an arsenal of epithets—"clerical arrogance," "domineering priesthood," "church and state"—with
which to combat supposed political designs.[93] Of this phase
of opposition an uneasy field man wrote, "The loud note of
Chh & State echoes along the base of either side of the
Alleganies, but it reverberates, not in dying accents, but with
deepened strains through the broad valley of the West."[94]

The New England practice of providing a minister's entire
support, assuming that he would not derive income from any

secular undertaking of his own, did not prevail in the West. Sons of the Puritans failed to understand that the "farmer preacher" was natural to a rural people with little or no money. They were shocked to learn that in certain Ohio Presbyteries more than three fourths of the ministers were farmers. But they were perhaps too optimistic over a report from Indiana that "one brother after another confessed the sin of farming, until the whole meeting was melted together; and they determined to rid themselves of it without delay."[95]

Since Westerners appeared to shun direct and adequate money contributions, Yankees taunted them with willingness to hear a "larned" preacher "provided it costs them nothing." The Reverend William Salter thought it "singular to build a house by eating" when the women of his congregation in Burlington, Iowa, raised money by giving a public dinner. "Isn't this the West," he exclaimed, "But there seems to be no other way of raising money!"[96]

Objectively viewed, both groups were evangelical Christians and neither could safely be called more or less religious than the other. The Census of 1850 shows the value of church property per capita in New York–New England as $6.64; for the six southern states it was $2.80. But what is evidently indicated is difference in wealth and physical outlay rather than interest in religion. Of more significance perhaps are the ratios of population to church-seating accommodations (1850) which were almost identical (1.4 northeastern, 1.5 southern) in the two groups of states. Also the average number of persons per congregation (637 northeastern, 552 southern) would tend to the conclusion that the southern area was almost as thoroughly "churched" as was the northeastern.[97] This also enhances credibility of the statement of an Easterner who named as his "one great difficulty" that nearly all of the aged or middle-aged belonged to the church in some denomination, and since the children were difficult to reach by teaching, there was "but little timber to work upon."[98]

TABLE V—(Based on 1850 Census)
COMPARISON OF CHURCHES AND CONGREGATIONS

	Value of church property per capita	Ratio of persons per church seating accom'dations	Average size of church congregations
Northeastern States			
Maine	$2.96	1.8	667
New Hampshire	4.43	1.3	508
Vermont	3.87	1.3	521
Massachusetts	10.26	1.4	674
Rhode Island	8.53	1.47	647
Connecticut	9.61	1.2	691
New York	6.82	1.6	749
Average	6.64	1.4	637
Southern States			
Maryland	$6.77	1.5	641
Virginia (including W. Virginia)	2.00	1.6	597
N. Carolina	1.41	1.5	484
S. Carolina	3.25	1.4	565
Tennessee	2.21	1.6	497
Kentucky	1.21	1.4	532
Average	2.80	1.5	552

It was therefore not a case of religion against irreligion, of truth against falsehood, or enlightenment against darkness, but cultural differences. The following mellow acknowledgment shows that Yankees sometimes saw the true situation:

One devoted, intelligent Baptist Missionary could do more to save the west than a dozen presbyterians, other things being equal. They could unlock bolts that we must file off. They could turn the current that now sets so strong against even enlightened effort to promote an intelligent piety;—while we must stem it until it spends its force.[99]

6. MINGLING, ORDINARY AND POLITE

". . . but little rancor or malignity. . . ."

In the first place we should recall that it was the poor, fast-breeding, and uneasily settled Uplander who distressed the Yankees, and not the enviable Virginia or Kentucky planter type. "Were I not a Yankee, I would be a Kentuckian," wrote a Yankee grandly parodying Alexander.[100] Nor was the contest always a simple two-sided affair. From Urbana, Ohio, where the harvest was carried on with exchange of labor and much whiskey drunk, it was reported that "the Kentuckyons & Virginians frequently have a pitched battle between each other."[101] While at Salem, southern Indiana (1829), where sectional prejudice ran "very high," there were three physicians to share the patronage of the community on the basis of their geographical origins, Connecticut, North Carolina, and Kentucky. Even so the Yankee doctor after ten years got small practice because he was "stiff-necked, that is, does not bow often enough."[102]

The name of Stark County, Illinois, represents a victory of Vermonters over Tennesseans who would have named the county for General Coffee. But in a contest over locating the post office, and over winning control of the county offices, Wyoming, or Spoon River, men, comprised of Yankees, Pennamites, and some newcomers from England and Scotland, were victors over so-called Essex men from Ohio, Virginia, Kentucky, and Tennessee. There was high spirit but little rancor or malignity in elections, a local historian adds.[103]

An eastern man at the West is soon discovered by this one fact, said a New Hampshire man: "They admit here that every man works for a profit & he that gets the most is the best fellow." Perhaps the face of Yankee character least in need of demonstration is his commercial acuteness, ranging from the genius of the Boston merchant, viewed by many with almost religious reverence, to the doings of the common peddler. Even a South Carolinian owned that the Yankees did business "cheap and well," and urged his fellows to copy Yankee methods and "out-compete" them.[104]

Naturally many Yankees of enterprising persuasion were attracted to western towns. The eminent prosperity of Cincinnati was attributed to the "calculating genius" of New England so abundantly present in that city. "It requires Yankees to build up these cities," was a claim with practical meaning for a place such as Rockford, Illinois, whose seven thousand persons included a large proportion of *"young men,* from 18 to 35 years of age, most of them keen, *trading* Yankees, full of great *projects* and *hopes.* . . .*"*[105]

A Virginian accustomed to more leisurely ways was therefore impressed by the speed with which workmen at Chicago cleared the smouldering ruins of a grain warehouse for the erection of a new building, as boys posted signs in English and German offering for sale the damaged grain. That, the Virginian called Yankee "go-ahead a-tiveness." By comparison the "foolish and incoherent" transactions reported from southern lubberland could only excite laughter : a book-store in Wilmington, North Carolina, forced to close because people had borrowed and forgotten to return the books; the exhausting journey of a Tarheel who traveled thirty-five miles to dispose of five bushels of oysters, paid two bushels for food and shelter on a two-days' journey, and sold the remainder of his stock for a gallon of molasses.[106]

Writing of the southern-born settlers of Sangamon County, Illinois, a native of Tennessee recalled that all business was done on the confidence principle. Notes, receipts, mortgages, or bonds, were scarcely ever given in those days; and afterward, when the Yankees, as we called them, came among them and sought to introduce their system of accounts, written notes and obligations, they were looked upon with great suspicion and distrust, and their mode of doing business regarded as a great and unwarrantable innovation upon established usages.[107] To the Southerner his own way of doing business affirmed confidence and personal honor. To the Yankee it was a lack of proper system, a sinful inefficiency. What to one was sound business practice indicated to the other a mean and suspicious spirit.

Curiosity and comment about manners at the West came from both sides : "You want to know the manners and customs of the people in this state [Ohio] they appear to be verry civil the manners are somewhat different of that of virginia but not in dressing." An Easterner's view was that manners at Cincinnati bore "a great resemblance to that of the Yankees."

A Yankee farmer, recorded one who spent a lifetime planting
Methodism in the West, entertaining a traveling preacher,
would soon begin to talk of his work and go at his chores, and
if one did not know that this was to show Yankee smartness,
would feel that he had come at the wrong time. Differences
were likewise felt within polite circles. A young Virginian
who visited the Leander McCormicks in Chicago in the latter
1850's was shocked by a Mrs. Hill, "a real Yankee," who
was a member of an informal group playing whist at the
McCormicks': "She invited herself there—after a while
said to Mrs. McC.—send your compliments up to Mr. Hill
and ask him to come down. It was the most impudent trick
a Virginian can conceive of."[108]

From early times in western communities an elite strove
to express itself. At Indianapolis, newly gouged into the
woods, Sarah Fletcher (herself Kentucky born, and wed to
a rising Yankee-born lawyer) noted that she had attended a
quilting where there were "several ladys who were formaly
from Kentucky & I think in their descorse a mong the Females
they use a gradeal of vulgarity."[109] At Chicago, a half decade
old, stratification was even more clearly at work as shown by
a letter of Mrs. Leander McCormick dated December 10, 1838.

A Great many Yankees here. Mrs. Hamilton [who was from
Kentucky] does not like them much. She says that we must have
a Southern society and let the Yankees, Germans, Irish and French
all alone. The people here seem to be from all quarters of the
globe. We will soon have as many acquaintances as we want, and
of the best in the city.[110]

Though the Yankees might look upon the upland men
with sly amusement they were quick to bespeak the simple
good will of the latter, generally "clever and friendly,"
though sometimes an "ignorant indolent set." Thus Lucy
Maynard, writing from Hancock County, Illinois, 1836:

we have very many neighbors. they appear very friendly; they
were principally from Indiana and Kentucky some from Virginia
all friendly but very different from our people in their manners
and language and every other way, but are very likable people.[111]

Within three weeks of the arrival in southern Indiana of a New Hampshire family, poor Kentucky neighbors had given them sixty hens, and a committee from Vernon (settled "entirely" by Kentuckians), ten miles distant, having heard of her unusually broad schooling, came to secure the mother to teach a school.[112]

We should of course expect contrast in dress, the western women wearing, according to a typical report, sunbonnets made from calico, calico caps, and striped linen frocks to meeting, while eastern folk dressed much as they did back home. Western men at labor wore homemade garments of coarse cloth which might be Kentucky jeans. But at Indianapolis plainness in men's dress carried upward into the professional class: "come and see me in my log house," a New Hampshire man invited his brother, "and let me advise you a little that is come in plain clothes dont dress too fine in the west you will gain nothing by it and might be set down as fops." Again, "you would save much in clothing were you here. Our first men wear homemade cloth and nothing else."[113]

If a Yankee thought the Uplanders slovenish in their work and cared little about improvements, the latter were apt to feel that the Yankees were extravagant in living, building, and dress. The Uplanders thought it queer that Yankee women should paint about the house.[114] There was much comment too about western women riding horseback, sometimes sharing the horse with a second rider. Thus Solon Robinson sneered at the upland women as they rode astride, with attendant offspring, to new homes, "a good deal 'sorter like' the coarse filling with which the great western web of wilderness is woven."[115]

Differences also settle around burial of the dead. Compared with New England where it was custom to bury all the town dead in a common graveyard, the Uplanders—understandably, considering their mobility—tended to "scatter" their dead in single graves or in family burying plots.[116] The mode of interment followed by southern folk near South Bend around 1835 was plain in the extreme. Clad in everyday attire, the mourners came with a plain coffin covered with a white sheet, drawn in a lumber wagon. The interment was made without religious service, which, to a Yankee who associated with burial the pall, the hearse, badges of mourning, the gospel minister, Scripture reading, prayer, words of consolation and warning, seemed "perfectly heathenish."[117]

General statements about the course and character of social adjustment are difficult, so various was the experience with different persons, places, and times. The author of a guidebook to the West might be clumsily insulted because he was a Yankee; while a Bay State schoolmistress was astonished at the indulgent treatment she received. At Adrian, Michigan, dress was in as good taste and manners as refined as in any New England village; while an Ohio River county of Indiana afforded "lazy worthless scum in abundance," "poor *Devils* not worth a picayune apiece. . . ."[118]

Someone ventures that friction was greatest before 1825, and greatest in rural places. Indeed *The Yankee,* a popular weekly issued at Portland, Maine, beginning 1828, remarks in its salutatory that the name it carried no longer bore opprobrium. Yet to designate the year 1825 as the peak of animosity brings surprise that the onset of prejudice had been so early and thorough. It suggests that the Yankee peddler and his like rather than the nineteenth-century reform movements carried the virus. Moreover, it is often difficult to judge how seriously denunciation was intended, although reports of signs on trees offering "so much for the *skin* of a Yankee" may be at once relegated to folklore.[119]

Novelty soon dissolves into familiarity. Much unlikeness could disappear during a single generation, particularly if all sorts attended public schools together. Acquisition of new interests and prosperity from Corn Belt soil would lessen the prejudice. Memories of factions in early county politics dulled and were seldom recalled in the county histories.[120] Meanwhile more Yankees learned the lessons of patience and tact—like Catharine Beecher who supplied Yankee girl teachers for the West, "so instructed in the notions and habits of the country where they go, as to avoid all manners and measures that will awake jealousy or prejudice."[121]

The men held jointly as part of their general heritage the Bible, British-American constitutional experience, and the common law. Also a hair-trigger sense of the rights of the individual. Actually they were not far apart in basic ideas and feeling as suggested by the following venture in self-appraisal from southern Indiana.

Conservatism in money affairs, veracity in statements, honesty of purpose, the love of home, respect for law and order, abhorrence of a debt, sincerity in religious matters, outspoken in political affiliations, respect for a promise once made, and industry, in particular, are the general characteristics of the citizens of Dubois county.[122]

With some emphasis on general schooling added this might very well have flowed from the pen of a self-examining Yankee.

Eyewitness versions of "The Heterogenious Mingling of the Diversified Elements of Society"[123] have a practical interest for blending. A southern man in Illinois at first looked upon the Yankees as "selfish, small-dealing and narrow-contracted," but "after a few years . . . these prejudices in some degree wore off, and a general good feeling prevailed." The Southerner came to hold Yankees among his best friends.[124] Another contemporary remembers that at first the Southerners in Illinois thought the New Englanders "penurious and heartless" but "by degrees, the Eastern people became more frank and open in their manners, and the Western people somewhat more reserved in their intercourse with comparative strangers."[125]

Looking at the larger scene, Professor Turner noted that in the midst of "more or less antagonism between 'bowie knife Southerners,' 'cow-milking Yankee Puritans,' 'beer-drinking Germans' and 'wild Irishmen,' " all of them adjusted to Middle Western conditions while an educational give-and-take was at work.[126] There appears then to be large truth in the view that on reaching the Valley the feelings of all groups soon moderated and many of their sectional antipathies became extinct.[127]

NOTES

[1] Kellar (ed.), *Solon Robinson, Pioneer Agriculturist*, I, 420-21, 425.

[2] Diary of Enoch Honeywell, p. 57, typed copy in ISL.

[3] Buck (ed.), "Pioneer Letters of Gershom Flagg," in *Transactions of the Illinois State Historical Society*, 1910, p. 162; Kellar (ed.), *Solon Robinson, Pioneer Agriculturist*, I, 427; *Ohio Farmer*, V, August 16, 1856.

[4] *The Luminary*, VIII, October 5, 1831; Sydnor, "The Southerner and the Laws," in *Journal of Southern History*, VI, 6.

[5] Letter of B. H. Frank, Buck Horn P. O., Illinois, to Alexander Frank, Cedar Bush, North Carolina, November 27, 1857, DU; Paul M. Angle (ed.), "The Story of an Ordinary Man," in *Journal of the Illinois State Historical Society*, XXXIII (June, 1940), 223.

[6] Odell Shepard, *Pedlar's Progress* (Boston, 1937), p. 391.

[7] *The Cultivator*, O.S. IV (October, 1837), 135; *New England Farmer*, XVIII (September 11, 1839), 84.

[8] *The Cultivator*, N.S. II (February, 1845), 62-63.

[9] Richard Ela to George Ela, February 29, 1835 [1836?], in *Wisconsin Magazine of History*, XIX, 437.

[10] *Southern Literary Messenger*, I (November, 1834), 85; *Ohio Farmer*, October 27, 1855.

[11] Letter from Jefferson County, Indiana, April 23, 1825, ISL; Buck (ed.), "Letters of Gershom Flagg," in *Transactions of the Illinois State Historical Society*, 1910, pp. 158, 162; Kellar (ed.), *Solon Robinson, Pioneer Agriculturist*, I, 419, 420, 443.

[12] *Southern Agriculturist*, VI (May, 1833), 229, article signed "A Highlander"; James H. Atherton, Lexington, Kentucky, to C. H. Atherton, Amherst, New Hampshire, January 1, 1832, Kentucky University Library; *The Country Gentleman*, III (April 27, 1854), 263. Northern hay was selling at $30.00 per ton in Columbia, South Carolina. *The Farmer and Planter* (Columbia, S. C.), XI (April, 1860), 111.

[13] Letter of A. D. Hager, Halifax County, North Carolina, June 13, 1854, McHC.

[14] *Southern Cultivator* (Augusta, Ga.), XI (July, 1853), 203, quoting Athens (Tenn.) *Post*. The article also discusses the hay trade from East Tennessee to Atlanta. *The Seventh Census of the United States* [1850], Table XI under the various states.

[15] *The Cultivator*, O.S. VIII (September, 1841), 155; *The Ninth Census of the United States*, 1870, volume III, *Wealth and Industry* (Washington, D. C., 1872), p. 217; map in Percy W. Bidwell and John I. Falconer, *History of Agriculture in the Northern United States, 1620-1860* (Washington, D. C., 1925), p. 372; Kellar (ed.), *Solon Robinson, Pioneer Agriculturist*, I, 414, 428.

[16] Woodbridge–Gallaher collection, dating from the late 1780's, for example, OAHS; letter of George Churchill, Madison County, Illinois, September 9, 1818, in *Journal of the Illinois State Historical Society*, XI, 66; Buck (ed.), "Pioneer Letters of Gershom Flagg," in *Transactions of the*

Illinois State Historical Society, 1910, p. 177; letter of Abigail B. Deming, *circa* 1837, Deming collection, Illinois Historical Survey, Urbana.

[17] Kellar (ed.), *Solon Robinson, Pioneer Agriculturist,* I, 414, 428; *Home Missionary,* XLI (April, 1869), 289.

[18] Bidwell and Falconer, *History of Agriculture,* p. 380; Thomas Jefferson, *Notes on the State of Virginia* (New York, 1801), p. 225.

[19] Letter of Joseph V. Quarles, Southport, Wisconsin, September 29, 1838, in *Wisconsin Magazine of History,* XVI, 303.

[20] Buck (ed.), "Pioneer Letters of Gershom Flagg," in *Transactions of the Illinois State Historical Society,* 1910, pp. 148, 162, 182.

[21] Mary Mace, New Lexington, Indiana, to Benjamin and Rebecca Mace, Tewksbury, Massachusetts, November 10, 1820, ISL; also letter of Lucy Maynard, February 29, 1836, ILLSL; letter of Minor Deming, St. Marys, Hancock County, Illinois, April 11, 1838, Deming collection, Illinois Historical Survey, Urbana; *Rhode Island History,* I (October, 1942), 128: Alma M. Stevens, Quincy, Illinois, to Miss Lucia Birdsey, Middletown, Connecticut, February 7, 1836, CHS.

[22] Richard M. Dorson, "The Yankee on the Stage—A Folk Hero of American Drama," in *New England Quarterly,* XII (September, 1940), 485; Memoir by Reverend Isaac Reed, November 28, 1921, in First Presbyterian Church, Indianapolis, *Centennial Memorial* (1925), p. 399.

[23] *Indiana Farmer and Gardener,* I (October, 1845), 290.

[24] Angle (ed.), "The Story of an Ordinary Man," in *Journal of the Illinois State Historical Society,* XXXIII, 221; Samuel Willard, "Personal Reminiscences of Life in Illinois, 1830 to 1850," in *Transactions of the Illinois State Historical Society,* 1906 (Springfield, 1906), p. 79.

[25] See maps of distribution of dairy cows and butter production 1850 and 1860 in Bidwell and Falconer, *History of Agriculture,* pp. 431-33.

[26] Diary of C. K. Laird, p. 53, IHS.

[27] Kellar (ed.), *Solon Robinson, Pioneer Agriculturist,* I, 416, 444, 446; Wilson, *History of Dubois County,* p. 136; Patterson, "Early Society in Southern Illinois," in *Fergus' Historical Series,* No. 14, p. 107; Indiana State Board of Agriculture, *Annual Report,* 1878 (Indianapolis, 1879), p. 381; Cornelius O. Cathey, "Agricultural Implements in North Carolina, 1783-1860," in *Agricultural History,* XXV (July, 1951), 129.

[28] Harris, *Some Recollections of My Boyhood,* p. 54; Berry Sulgrove, *History of Indianapolis and Marion County, Indiana* (Philadelphia, 1884), p. 73; *Kentucky Farmer* (Frankfort), III (February 15, 1861), 119; Kellar (ed.), *Solon Robinson, Pioneer Agriculturist,* I, 416; *History of Greene and Sullivan Counties, Indiana* (Chicago, 1884), p. 692.

[29] John Hervey, *The American Trotter* (New York, 1947), pp. 24, 25, 27; Margaret C. Self, *The Horseman's Encyclopedia* (New York, 1946), pp. 157, 182, 325; Sulgrove, *History of Indianapolis and Marion County,* pp. 75-76; *Porter's Spirit of the Times,* I (February 21, 1857), 401; III (September 19, 1859), 40.

[30] Samuel Kercheval, *A History of the Valley of Virginia* (Woodstock, Va., 1850), p. 216.

[31] Letter of John Baird, Wabash, Indiana, January 7, 1860, in *Indiana*

Magazine of History, XXXI (March, 1935), 64-65; Diary of Enoch Honeywell, p. 52, typed copy in ISL; *South Carolina. A Guide to the Palmetto State*
(New York, 1941), p. 186.

³² *Notes on the State of Virginia* (1801), p. 225.

³³ James Hall, *Legends of the West* (Philadelphia, 1832), pp. 4, 8, and
Statistics of the West . . . 1836 (Cincinnati, 1836), p. 63; Sealsfield, *The
Americans as They Are,* p. 35; Diary of Sarah Ann Quarles Chandler, p. 11,
ISL; *Yankee Notions,* X (April, 1861), 118; Still and Herrmann (eds.),
"Abner Morse's Diary of Immigrant Travel, 1855-1856," in *Wisconsin
Magazine of History,* XXII (March, 1939), 331; Ebenezer Welch, Mon-
mouth, Illinois, to his parents, Monmouth, Maine, September 19, 1841, CHS.

³⁴ Angle (ed.), "The Story of an Ordinary Man," in *Journal of the
Illinois State Historical Society,* XXXIII, 222; Tillson, *A Woman's Story
of Pioneer Illinois,* p. 70; James H. Smith, Savanna, Illinois, to David Ports,
Boonesborough, Maryland, May 27, 1838, ILLSL; *St. John's Church,
Lafayette, Indiana, Sermon and Addresses . . . 50th Anniversary . . .
March 27, 1887,* p. 11; *Prairie Farmer,* X (August, 1850), 238; Hayes, "Let-
ters from the West, 1845," in *Iowa Journal of History and Politics,* XX, 35.

³⁵ "Reminiscences of Solomon Ashley Dwinnell," South Bend, Indiana,
circa 1835, WHS; Calvin Fletcher, Indianapolis, to his wife, Urbana, Ohio,
June 15, 1834, IHS.

³⁶ *Southern Literary Messenger,* I (April, 1835), 425-26. The writer
also expressed liking for public schools, township government, courts of
"probat," and *"cold light-bread."*

³⁷ *The Plough, The Loom, and The Anvil* (Philadelphia), I (August,
1848), 81. The other six wonders were: every house looked as though it
had been painted white as snow within the past week; all houses wooden,
fences stone; carefully managed manure and compost; universal attention
to fruit; absence of poor or superfluous livestock; but where were their
staple crops?

³⁸ Dwinnell's Reminiscences, WHS; James H. Smith, Elkhorn Grove,
Illinois, to David Ports, Boonesborough, Maryland, December 24, 1839,
ILLSL.

³⁹ William and Christina Boss, Versailles, Illinois, to relatives in Virginia, May 2, 1858, DU.

⁴⁰ Gates, *The Illinois Central Railroad and Its Colonization Work,* p. 11.

⁴¹ Angle (ed.), "The Story of an Ordinary Man," in *Journal of the
Illinois State Historical Society,* XXXIII, 214.

⁴² Letter of Lucy Maynard, Fulton County, Illinois, December 3, 1835,
ILLSL.

⁴³ Dwinnell's Reminiscences, WHS.

⁴⁴ Letter of Minor Deming, Cincinnati, Ohio, April 11, 1838, in Illinois
Historical Survey, Urbana; Paullin, *Atlas of the Historical Geography of
the United States,* Plate 5.

⁴⁵ *Boston Cultivator,* November 27, 1852, March 12, 1853; Buck (ed.),
"Pioneer Letters of Gershom Flagg," in *Transactions of the Illinois State
Historical Society,* 1910, p. 162; Angle (ed.), "The Story of an Ordinary

Man," in *Journal of the Illinois State Historical Society*, XXXIII, 214; Still and Herrmann (eds.), Abner Morse's Travel Diary, in *Wisconsin Magazine of History*, XXII, 331; Dwinnell's Reminiscences, WHS; *Prairie Farmer*, XI (January, 1851), 13.

[46] Kellar (ed.), *Solon Robinson, Pioneer Agriculturist*, I, 416, 424; Journal of Lord Adam Gordon, 1764-1765, in Newton D. Mereness (ed.), *Travels in the American Colonies* . . . (New York, 1916), p. 402.

[47] Wood, *Sketches of Things and People in Indiana*, p. 38. For the quotation used at the opening of this part see M. M. Mathews (ed.), *A Dictionary of Americanisms on Historical Principles* (2 volumes. Chicago, 1951), I, 399, quoting from Edmund Flagg, *The Far West* . . . (2 volumes. New York, 1838), II, 72.

[48] *Home Missionary*, XXXIX (February, 1867), 248.

[49] M. I. Bradley, Covington, Indiana, to Jesse Bradley, Lee, Massachusetts, August 12, 1841, IHS; *Southern Literary Messenger*, I (December, 1834), 168.

[50] Journals of James Backus, entry for July 13, 1788, OAHS; C. E. Eaton, Dresden, Ohio, to his parents, Candia Turnpike, New Hampshire, October 23, 1837, Eaton letters, OAHS; Erwin, *History of Williamson County, Illinois*, p. 41; James H. Smith, Buffalo Grove, Illinois, to David Ports, Boonesborough, Maryland, January 28, 1840, ILLSL; Luke and Avis Woodard, Wayne County, Indiana, to Elizabeth Stanton, Core Sound, North Carolina, April 10, 1829, IHS; Odell Shepard, *The Journal of Bronson Alcott* (Boston, 1938), p. 360; Mary Mace, New Lexington, Indiana, to Benjamin and Rebecca Mace, Tewksbury, Massachusetts, November, 1820, ISL; "Diary of a Journey from Massachusetts to the Ohio Country in 1798 . . .," in *The New England Historical and Genealogical Register* (Boston), LXXXVI (January, 1932), 34.

[51] "Journal of Ebenezer Mattoon Chamberlain 1832-5," in *Indiana Magazine of History*, XV (September, 1919), 240.

[52] Mrs. Kirkland Ruffin (ed.), "School-Boy Letters of Edmund Ruffin, jr., 1828-1829," in *North Carolina Historical Review*, X (October, 1933), 301-2.

[53] *The Dollar Farmer* (Louisville), II (January, 1844), 101; Gray, *History of Agriculture in the Southern United States to 1860*, II, 815.

At a small social gathering a year or so back someone suggested that white corn meal had disappeared from commerce; to which the homemakers present rejoined in a single voice, "You have to watch closely or you will get it any time here in Indianapolis."

[54] Lucy Maynard, Fulton County, Illinois, December 3, 1835, to Mrs. Abel Piper, Phillipston, Massachusetts, ILLSL.

[55] *Chicago Yesterdays*, garnered by Caroline Kirkland (Chicago, 1919), p. 39, from a letter of Mrs. Leander McCormick, December 10, 1838.

[56] Ebenezer Welch, Monmouth, Illinois, to his parents, Monmouth, Maine, September 19, 1841, CHS.

[57] Jefferson, *Notes on the State of Virginia* (1801), p. 225; Drake, *A Systematic Treatise* . . . *on the Principal Diseases of the Interior Valley*

of North America, pp. 644-50; James M. Peck, *A Gazetteer of Illinois* (Jacksonville, Ill., 1834), p. 43.

[58] Henry Howe, *Historical Collections of Ohio in Two Volumes* (Newark, Ohio, 1896), I, 243; *The Chicago Magazine: The West as It Is,* I (June 15, 1857), 319; Dwinnell's Reminiscences, WHS.

[59] Ebenezer Welch, Monmouth, Illinois, to his parents, Monmouth, Maine, September 19, 1841, CHS.

[60] Mills Averill, Lima [present town of Howe], Indiana, to N. H. Raymond, Strykersville, New York, December 8, 1836, IHS; C. I. Swartwout, Quincy, Illinois, to Gen. Robert Swartwout, New York City, May 22, 1837, CHS; and "Silas J. Seymour Letters," in *Wisconsin Magazine of History,* XXXII (December, 1948), 195.

[61] B. H. Frank, Buck Horn P. O., Brown County, Illinois, to Alexander Frank, Cedar Bush, North Carolina, November 27, 1857, DU; G. W. H. Kemper (ed.), *A Medical History of the State of Indiana* (Chicago, 1911).

[62] Diary of C. K. Laird, p. 17, IHS; Letter of one Burton, Brownsville, Illinois, to Miss Achsah Burton, Andover, Vermont, December 13, 1820, ILLSL. Also see maps of potato production 1839, 1849, 1859, in Bidwell and Falconer, *History of Agriculture,* pp. 373, 377, 378; Samuel Whedon, Brownstown, Jackson County, Indiana, to his brother, Seneca Township, Ontario County, New York, June 27, 1817, IHS.

[63] Gray, *History of Agriculture in the Southern United States to 1860,* II, 811.

[64] For colored maps showing distribution of corn, hay, and dairy production, see *The Ninth Census of the United States,* III, *Wealth and Industry,* pp. 121, 217, 369.

[65] Turner, *The United States 1830-1850,* p. 45; Kohlmeier, *The Old Northwest,* pp. 94-95.

[66] See maps of distribution of wheat production 1839, 1849, 1859, in Bidwell and Falconer, *History of Agriculture,* pp. 321, 322, 332.

[67] *Home Missionary,* VI (March, 1833), 17, letter to Absalom Peters from Jacksonville, Illinois.

[68] Philip D. Jordan (ed.), "William Salter's Letters to Mary Ann Mackintire, 1845-1846," in *Annals of Iowa,* XIX (July, 1934), 376; Reverend Theron Baldwin, Vandalia, Illinois, to Absalom Peters, August 16, 1830, AHMS; Timothy Flint, St. Louis, Missouri, to Reverend Abel Flint, Hartford, Connecticut, July 2, 1816, WHS; Calvin Fletcher, Indianapolis, to Michael Fletcher, Staatsburg, New York, February 23, 1823, IHS.

[69] Alma M. Stevens, Quincy, Illinois, to Miss Lucia C. Birdsey, Middletown, Connecticut, February 7, 1836, CHS.

[70] "National Character of Western People," in *Western Monthly Review,* I (July, 1827), 135.

[71] Weston A. Goodspeed and Charles Blanchard, *Counties of Porter and Lake, Indiana* (Chicago, 1882), p. 550; David Thomas, *A Tour Through the Western Country in the Summer of 1816,* p. 230.

[72] Frank Luther Mott, "A Word List from Pioneer Iowa and an Inquiry into Iowa Dialect Origins," in *Philological Quarterly,* I (July, 1922), 202.

[73] Ebenezer Welch, Monmouth, Illinois, to relatives in Monmouth, Maine, September 19, 1841, CHS.

[74] Dwinnell's Reminiscences, *circa* 1835, WHS; Willard, "Personal Reminiscences of Life in Illinois, 1830 to 1850," in *Transactions of the Illinois State Historical Society*, 1906, pp. 74-75.

[75] J. R. Wheelock, January 31, 1831, May 20, 1831, August 27, 1832, and May 9, 1833, AHMS; *Great Republic Monthly* (New York), I (June, 1859), 635.

[76] Adolph Rogers, "North Carolina and Indiana: A Tie that Binds," in *Indiana Magazine of History*, V (June, 1909), 55.

[77] Albert H. Marckwardt, "Folk Speech in Indiana and Adjacent States," in *Indiana History Bulletin*, XVII (February, 1940), 120-40. Also, Marckwardt, "Middle English ŏ in American English of the Great Lakes Area," in *Papers of the Michigan Academy of Science, Arts, and Letters*, XXVI, 1940 (1941).

But the neat boundaries indicated by these two terms may be misleading. Out of 588 terms or usages investigated in Indiana and Michigan, 398 did not show sharp regional variation; 116 showed possible regional variation; only 74 showed definite regional variation. "Indiana Hoosierisms," Preliminary data sheet, Table III, clipping file, Indiana Division, ISL.

[78] However, the southern influence was predominant in the spoken language. As far west as Iowa, Frank Luther Mott, investigating the origins of words in use in that state between 1833 and 1846, found that among 198 terms, 62 were of Yankee origin and 136 southern. *Philological Quarterly*, I (July, 1922), 220-21.

[79] Barnhart, "The Southern Element in the Leadership of the Old Northwest," in *Journal of Southern History*, I (May, 1935), 192-95.

[80] Reverend Solomon Hardy, Greenville, Illinois, to Absalom Peters, December 20, 1830, AHMS.

[81] Allen Wiley, "Early Methodism in Southeastern Indiana," in *Indiana Magazine of History*, XXIII (June, 1927), 135.

[82] Reverend Theron Baldwin, Vandalia, Illinois, to Absalom Peters, August 16, 1830, AHMS.

[83] Patterson, "Early Society in Southern Illinois," in *Fergus' Historical Series*, No. 14, p. 106. One explanation of why ministers became so migratory was that they studied so little and became "preached out." William Dean, *Ministerial Support. A Sermon* . . . (Indianapolis, 1857), p. 13.

[84] *Home Missionary*, XVI (July, 1843), 54.

[85] Reverend Solomon Hardy, Greenville, Illinois, to Absalom Peters, December 20, 1830, AHMS.

[86] Letter from Moody Chase, July 8, 1833, August 11, 1834, AHMS.

[87] John Morrill, September 18, 1833, January 20, 1834. Also see experience of Reverend J. R. Wheelock, above, 114.

[88] Adolph Gerber (trans.), *The Journey of Lewis David von Schweinitz to Goshen, Bartholomew County, in 1831* (Indiana Historical Society *Publications*, VIII, number 5, Indianapolis, 1927), p. 229; Samuel Gregg, Ripley County, Indiana, to Absalom Peters, September 4, 1835, AHMS, and

Samuel K. Snead, New Albany, Indiana, to Milton Badger, New York City, June 5, 1839, AHMS.

[89] Tillson, *A Woman's Story of Pioneer Illinois,* p. 79.

[90] James Hall, Vandalia, Illinois, to Absalom Peters, August, 20, 1831, AHMS.

[91] *Home Missionary,* XXXI (October, 1858), 149.

[92] James Crawford, Jefferson County, Indiana, May 30, 1827, AHMS.

[93] *The Reformer,* I (November, 1820), 245. On this topic see this periodical, volumes I-IV, *passim.,* and Chapter I, above, Part 1.

[94] Reverend B. C. Cressy, Salem, Indiana, to Absalom Peters, November 8, 1830, AHMS; Colin B. Goodykoontz, *Home Missions on the American Frontier* (Caldwell, Idaho, 1939), pp. 92-96, and *passim.*

[95] *Home Missionary,* VIII (September, 1835), 77-78.

[96] *Ibid.,* XXIV (June, 1851), 49; Jordan (ed.), "William Salter's Letters to Mary Ann Mackintire, 1845-1846," in *Annals of Iowa,* XIX (June, 1934), 465.

[97] See Table V.

[98] Jeremiah Hill, Owen County, Indiana, to Absalom Peters, February 22, 1831, AHMS.

[99] Reverend J. W. Parsons, China, Jefferson County, Indiana, to Absalom Peters, February 20, 1833. A recent survey indicates that religious characteristics today in the Upland South are not too different from those of a hundred years ago. *Economic and Social Conditions of the Southern Appalachians* (U. S. Department of Agriculture, *Misc. Pub. 205,* Washington, D. C., 1935), pp. 168-82.
Also see Chapter III, above, Part 5.

[100] *New England Magazine,* II (March, 1832), 236. See also Jedidiah Morse, *The American Geography* (London, 1792), p. 406; *Home Missionary,* II (April, 1830), 189; Samuel R. Brown, *The Western Gazetteer; or, Emigrant's Directory* . . . (Auburn, N. Y., 1817), pp. 113-14; Flint, *Recollections of the Last Ten Years,* pp. 65, 70; N. P. Willis in *St. Lawrence Republican* (Ogdensburg, N. Y.), November 11, 1834.

[101] Calvin Fletcher, Urbana, Ohio, to Jesse Fletcher, Ludlow, Vermont, July 25, 1818, IHS.

[102] Dennett, *John Hay, From Poetry to Politics,* p. 5.

[103] Mrs. E. H. Shellenberger, *Stark County [Illinois] and its Pioneers* (Cambridge, Ill., 1876), pp. 44, 46, 47, 51.

[104] "Letters of Joseph V. Quarles," in *Wisconsin Magazine of History,* XVI (March, 1933), 314; *Southern Agriculturist,* II (May, 1835), 204-5.

[105] Michel Chevalier, *Society, Manners and Politics in the United States* . . ., translated by Thomas G. Bradford (Boston, 1839), p. 202; Hayes, "Letters from the West in 1845," in *Iowa Journal of History and Politics,* XX, 32; William S. Brown, Rockford, Illinois, to friends at Dansville, New York, February 5, 1856, ILLSL.

[106] Diary of Greenlee Davidson of Lexington, Virginia, 1857, pp. 35-36, McHA; Robert J. Parker, "A Yankee in North Carolina: Observations of

Thomas Oliver Larkin," in *North Carolina Historical Review*, XIV (1937), 329, 334.

[107] Daniel M. Parkinson, "Pioneer Life in Wisconsin," in *Wisconsin Historical Collections*, II (Madison, 1856), 327; Dwinnell's Reminiscences, WHS. A. D. Jones, in his *Illinois and the West*, p. 156, warns Yankees "against imbibing the—it must be confessed—too slovenly spirit of the west in the management of their business; let him adhere to the economical, industrious habits to which he has been trained. . . ."

[108] Elisha Lawler, Franklin County, Ohio, to Joseph Lawler, Warrenton, Virginia, February 13, 1833, DU; E. Stanley, Cincinnati, Ohio, to Henry Watson, East Windsor, Connecticut, June 29, 1812, DU; Wood, *People and Things in Indiana*, p. 39; Diary of Greenlee Davidson, p. 31, McHC.

[109] Journal of Calvin and Sarah Fletcher, January 29, 1822, IHS.

[110] *Chicago Yesterdays*, garnered by Caroline Kirkland, p. 38.

[111] Diary of Enoch Honeywell, p. 51, ISL; letter of Lucy Maynard, Hancock County, Illinois, February 29, 1836, ILLSL; also Ebenezer Welch, Monmouth, Illinois, to his parents, Monmouth, Maine, September 19, 1841, CHS.

[112] Diary of C. K. Laird, pp. 37, 38, 40, IHS.

[113] Alma M. Stevens, Quincy, Illinois, to Miss Lucia Birdsey, Middletown, Connecticut, February 7, 1836, CHS; Dwinnell's Reminiscences, WHS; T. V. Denny, Indianapolis, to C. O. Denny, Keene, New Hampshire, February 6, 1841, ISL.

[114] Alice Felt Tyler, "A New England Family on the Illinois Frontier," in *Papers in Illinois History . . . 1942* (Springfield, 1944), p. 75. See letter of Ebenezer Welch, Monmouth, Illinois, to his parents, Monmouth, Maine, September 19, 1841, CHS, and Dwinnell's Reminiscenses, WHS.

[115] Kellar (ed.), *Solon Robinson, Pioneer Agriculturist*, I, 444.

[116] *Southern Literary Messenger*, I (January, 1835), 217; *The Farmer and Planter*, X (February, 1859), 59. On the plantation where this notice was written were nine burial plots, five for whites, four for blacks. "How different from New England . . . is the system of sepulture in the plantation states," exclaimed the writer.

[117] Dwinnell's Reminiscences, WHS. Louella I. B. Case, Patriot, Indiana, in a letter to Dr. Levi S. Bartlett, Kingston, New Hampshire, June 2, 1847, notes that recently at a funeral of a young girl they carried the bier on the shoulders and almost all the people walked in procession. IHS.

[118] Thomas, *Travels through the Western Country in the Summer of 1816*, pp. 236-37; M. I. Bradley, Covington, Indiana, to Jesse Bradley, Lee, Massachusetts, August 12, 1841, IHS; Hayes, "Letters from the West in 1845," in *Iowa Journal of History and Politics*, XX, 60; letter of George C. Leavitt, Leavenworth, Indiana, to his parents, Chichester, New Hampshire, February 23, 1847, in possession of Dr. Paul W. Gates, Cornell University.

[119] Patterson, "Early Society in Southern Illinois," in *Fergus' Historical Series*, No. 14, p. 131; *The Yankee*, I (January 1, 1828), 1; Hayes, "Letters from the West in 1845," in *Iowa Journal of History and Politics*, XX, 29.

Hayes says that ill feeling had declined by 1845, and though "Yankee" was still a term of reproach, the term "New Englander" was significant of honor.

[120] See, for example, *The County of Ross* [*Ohio*] (Madison, Wis., 1902), p. 76; Shellenberger, *Stark County* [*Illinois*], *and its Pioneers*, pp. 44, 46, 47, 51.

[121] *Prairie Farmer*, VII (June, 1847), 194.

[122] Wilson, *History of Dubois County, Indiana*, p. 395.

[123] *History of Wabash County, Indiana* (Chicago, 1884), p. 99.

[124] Parkinson, "Pioneer Life in Wisconsin," in *Wisconsin Historical Collections*, II, 328.

[125] Patterson, "Early Society in Southern Illinois," in *Fergus' Historical Series*, No. 14, p. 114.

[126] Frederick Jackson Turner, *The Frontier in American History* (New York, 1920), p. 349.

[127] Drake, *A Systematic Treatise . . . on the Principal Diseases of the Interior Valley of North America*, p. 646.

Chapter V

TOWARD UNDERSTANDING THE OUTCOME

1. Blending

*"The Heterogenious Mingling of the Diversified
Elements of Society"*

Fortunately certain nineteenth-century onlookers recorded their views on cultural blending in the West. Concerning this transmutation James Hall remarked: "The Yankee or Virginian, taken away from his harpoon, snug cottage, blooming garden or tasteful grounds, soon becomes a different man. . . ." Michel Chevalier believed that rivalry would impart a singular vigor to American life and that fusion would yield a superior third type of American. With more detail Dr. Drake ascribed the new western society to intermarriage, climate, "fuller diet," to different political, social, and moral conditions, and to "such a commingling of races" as the world had never seen. Meanwhile, popular interest in the topic is apparent from midcentury headlines reading: "The Three American Races, viz. the Yankee, the Virginian and the Western-Man."[1]

Twentieth-century scholars have added little except awareness that fusion was more complicated than their predecessors believed. Interested in northern unity during the Rebellion, Professor Channing cautiously mentions "something akin to a changing mental outlook and mode of living" which by 1861 caused the people of the Northwest to look eastward instead of southward. To Professor Turner the outcome represented "a new type, which was neither the sum of all its elements, nor a complete fusion in a melting pot."[2] Professor Wertenbaker serves the cause well when he writes:

But the Virginian and the Yankee could no more remain a Virginian and a Yankee than their ancestors had remained Englishmen in Virginia or in Massachusetts. The West gripped them, changed their economy, modified their political institutions, affected deeply the form if not the substance of their religions, influenced their architectures. They found themselves, also, in contact with other groups of settlers from other parts of America or from Europe, and so were subject to the operation of the melting-pot. There was a merging of Congregationalism and Presbyterianism, a mingling of dialects—eastern Virginian, Scotch-Irish, New England, Pennsylvanian; Southern agricultural methods were modified by the thrifty habits of the Connecticut farmer or the English immigrant; the son of a North Carolinian might marry the daughter of a New Yorker, and their daughter in turn, mate with an Ulsterman from western Pennsylvania.[3]

Professor Wertenbaker leaves no doubt as to the multiphased nature of the adjustment. It is significant that his paragraph on cultural coalescence uses sundry verbs and locutions. It therefore appears that a common denominator term may as well be an ordinary word such as "adjustment," "fusion," or "blending."

Blending of cultures in the northwest is manifest in numerous ways and is not confined to persons directly. The dent corns of the Corn Belt and the later hybrid strains are, appropriately, the result of crossbreeding, accidental and intentional, of yellow "flints" of the North Atlantic states and the rough white "gourdseeds" of the South. "Most maize breeders," writes one authority, "have not understood that the hybrid vigor they now capitalize is largely the dispersed heterosis of the flint-dent mongrels."[4] Has the same superior quality been attained by the blending of the two peoples? is an interesting question for speculation.

The merging of arts, crafts, and forms in pioneer furniture and furnishings within newer states has recently been pointed to: the coalescence in Ohio, for example, of New England, Pennsylvania, and Maryland forms.[5]

The vernacular architectures of Virginia–Kentucky and New England met about midway in Illinois, with the old

National Road through Terre Haute, Vandalia, and St. Louis
dividing them.[6] We are free to suppose there was a belt of
overlapping where each style influenced the other.

The geography of farm neatness in Illinois—clean fence
corners, absence of weeds, everything in its place—resembled
that of architecture. One appraiser says the Illinois farmer
occupied a mean position between New England tidiness and
southern slovenliness.[7] Yet a fortunate reminder of the ruling
hotchpotch is a sentence from Henry Ward Beecher's *Indiana
Farmer and Gardener*: "A man must come to the West to see
a little of every sort of farming that ever existed; and some
sorts, we will affirm, never had an existence before anywhere
else—the purely indigenous farming of the great valley."[8]

At Cincinnati early in the last century Timothy Flint noted
that "the language of the bar was in many instances an amusing compound of Yankee dialect, Southern peculiarity, and
Irish blarney."[9]

The trend or outcome of cultural adjustment is sometimes
predictable. Thus John Webster Spargo of Northwestern
University, said in 1947 that Midwestern or "general American," speech used by ninety millions, may in time cause twenty-
six millions of Southerners to lose their drawl. Other varia-
tions may disappear along with the nasal twang of ten or eleven
millions of Easterners. General American, one of whose main
characteristics is that the *r* sound is pronounced wherever it is
spelled, is expected to prevail, Professor Spargo said, because
the area between the mountain ranges has the greatest concentration of population in the nation. These ninety or more
millions go in great numbers to other parts of the country on
business, to take up residence or on vacation and "impose" on
others their own type of speech.[10]

The evolution of at least one popular folk type during the
nineteenth century parallels other examples of blending: the
submergence of the perennial stage Yankee in his later phases,
"within a more general character, a sort of grown up Huck

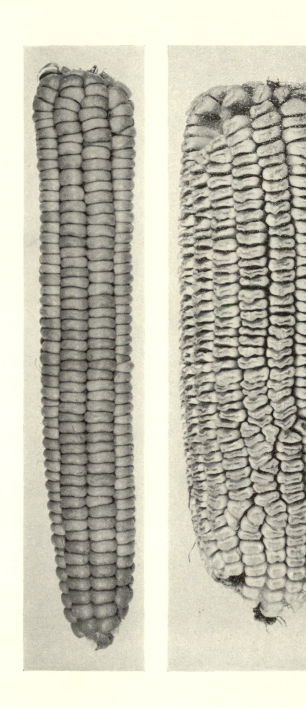

Northern Flint (above) and Southern Gourdseed (below).

Finn," who hailed from a cosmopolitan America rather than rural New England.[11]

The formula above seems tailored to the career of Virginia-born Cal Stewart, creator of "Uncle Josh," Yankee farmer. Stewart, whose phonographic recordings of Uncle Josh made millions familiar with his voice, traveled over the entire United States and studied all American rural sorts. "Out in Indiana I found every type; some characters had part of them all in one. Out there you can hear 'I reckon,' 'I calculate,' 'I suppose,' and all the other expressions of the farmer."[12]

The founding of Union College in 1795 by Congregationalists, Presbyterians, and Dutch Reformists jointly—there were many colleges jointly sponsored—has implication for blending. Located at the junction of two of York State's valley thoroughfares, the college would draw students from all quarters, and no single denomination would be permitted a majority of the trustees.[13]

Those tabbed "Kentucky" men or "Whitewater" men united, after superficial peculiarities wore away, in early Hoosier political alignments. "Basic issues would expose the common fundamental beliefs among these men that local conflicts had not been able to uncover."[14]

Highland County, Ohio, settlers, chiefly from Virginia and North Carolina uplands, prospered and intermarried with non-Southerners in many cases, and by 1860—in the second generation—displayed only a faint southern coloration in their politics.[15]

Politically, in Illinois, adjustment meant a gradual tempering of early southern dominance by the Yankee forces.[16] Yet this adjustment, another explains, was part of a larger design wherein "the two sections of the state, each contributing its quota to the welfare of the whole, have produced a new commonwealth which is neither Southern nor Puritan; it is Illinois, part of the great 'Middle West.' "[17]

Lesser communities such as cities and counties also have examined their cultural characteristics. The native of

Evansville, ran one such try at self-appraisal, "is not the lank, lean, sad, intense, subjective Yankee, nor the dilatory, fatty, undemonstrative, dullard of Pennsylvania, nor yet the haughty, erect and quick-tempered gentleman from the Southern States . . . but he is always florid, plethoric, laborious, wellfed, jolly and complacent."[18]

Delaware County, Indiana, had, according to a spokesman, received settlers from the principal eastern sections and had developed by the twentieth century "a thoroughly American civilization, equally removed from the dominating characteristics of the north or the south, and from the peculiarities popularly ascribed to eastern and to the western people."[19]

It may be significant that these two analyses are expressed negatively in the main. To declare what is not may be both easier and safer than to declare what is. Anyway the neutral cast of the latter statement carries a special interest: Muncie, the seat of Delaware County, is the "Middletown" of Robert and Helen Lynd.[20]

As to blending through marriage, one encounters little reluctance of either Yankee or Southerner to intermarry. This is in spite of exceptions like Yankee Samuel Whedon who preferred wife hunting in Connecticut—"such an One" as he wanted was hardly obtainable in southern Indiana.[21] A young Yankee in Illinois informed his sister in Vermont that "a cargo of Yankee girls would sell well" in that market: "We have to go to Kentucky for wives, but the Kentucky gentlemen which are here prefer Yankees."[22]

Yankees freely married the Dutch in New York. An adage ran: "A Dutch damsel can't, for her heart, resist a Connecticut schoolmaster." A historian remarks much intermarriage of Yankees with other stocks in New York City during the early nineteenth century. The Lowell *Journal* once declared that while southern gentlemen "strenuously oppose the Union of the States, [they] evince no repugnance to an Union with the rosy cheeked lasses of the North." Dr. Drake emphasized the prevalence in the Interior Valley as well as in the Deep South of unions between Yankees and Southerners unrestrained by any kind of prejudice.[23]

Among Yankees who wed Southerners in the early Northwest was David B. Sears (who developed water-power sites at Moline, St. Anthony's Falls, and on Rock River) whose wife was Kentucky-born. Cyrus H. McCormick, outstandingly loyal to Virginia, espoused a woman from the North Country of York State. Calvin Fletcher of Vermont, founder of a prominent Indianapolis family, married a Kentucky girl. The wife of "Uncle Joe" Cannon, congressman-speaker, North Carolina-bred, was a Methodist Yankee from Connecticut. Stephen A. Douglas, a Vermont native, married a North Carolinian. The father of George W. Cable was a Virginian slaveholder who in 1834 married a strict Puritan woman in Indiana. John S. Wright, Yankee editor of the *Prairie Farmer,* published at Chicago, married a belle of the Old Dominion. Potter Palmer, York State-born Chicago real estate operator and builder of the Palmer House, married a Kentuckian. These instances, encountered casually, indicate that intersectional marriages were not novel.[24]

2. "But in the Prairie, We Are All New Men"

"I can not take time to tell you the difrens between hear and thar"

As if to forecast greater changes farther West a historian remarks "something 'western' in the tradition of nineteenth-century New York, something scarcely known among the Yankees who stayed in New England."[25] Thus a westbound Vermonter found in central New York much that was unfamiliar: absence of newspapers and magazines in taverns (which latter were more numerous than in Vermont), few highway guideposts, enormous piles of hay, straw, and corn, inferior oxen and other cattle. Also buckwheat cakes (at first for breakfast, later at every meal) and people rather dull—what Vermonters called pewter- or leatherheads.[26]

Beyond the Adirondacks northward, a railway construction man found neither the land nor the people—who were "a queer mixture of all Countries"—of the pleasantest. It was not uncommon to hear French or something like it, he added.[27]

Southerners in transit to the Northwest were also struck by variance. At Wheeling, John Cocke, Jr., a proper Virginian, found the women attending market, "trafficking like true yankee dames, to make the best bargains." ". . . this is in Virginia," Cocke reflected, "but it is but a far off corner and matters here are more like New-England than the Old Dominion."[28]

But whatever the differences en route it is certain that by the time they became acclimatized to the Northwest both Yankees and Southerners were changed men, as when Ralph Waldo Emerson pronounced the people of Michigan "rough grisly Esaus, full of dirty strength," although "every forcible man among them came from New York or New England."[29]

A Virginian slave mistress found the people of southern Indiana–Illinois along the Vincennes Trace "abject and degraded," "too lazy to inhale the air which nourished their existence." Because the manners and customs were so different a teacher from Virginia concluded Indiana was a "hard place." Another advised that his sister Ann Eliza might do well teaching at New Albany, Indiana, "if she could only adapt herself to a new situation, new society, manners &c." Ill at Richmond, Indiana, in 1844, William Hurt railed, "I am amongst a set of hoosiers that will not give a rip to relieve my distress. . . ." Another Virginian was "dissatisfied with the Hoosiers and everything belonging to them."[30]

What caused change in the sentiments and ways of those who removed to the Northwest?

Objects, conditions, and ways of doing demanded at every turn a revised sense of practice or proportion.

The fishes, fruits, and vegetables of the Midwest presented strange appearance to Theodore Parker, Boston minister and scholar, even on this third visit to that region:

. . . there is a certain largeness to everything—streams, plains, trees, pumpkins, apples, swine . . . and men. . . . a certain coarseness of fibre . . . in all things; the wood is coarse-grained, the nuts are big and fat, not nice and sweet, the apples have a coarse texture—all the vegetables and all the fruit.

Did you ever see the fishes of the Ohio, They are the most uncouth-looking monsters I ever saw . . . save in the market at Rome. The cat-fish, an ugly-looking devil, with a face like an owl; the spoon-billed cat-fish, looking yet worse; the buffalo, an overgrown sculpin; the reed-horse, and the sucker. One must be hard-pushed to eat one of these wretches. The men are sickly, yellow, and flabby. In Indiana I saw but one rosy-cheeked girl, about eighteen or nineteen, "Were you born here?" "No, sir; in New Hampshire." "I thought so!" I saw 300 or 400 children in the schools at Indianapolis—not a rosy cheek. The women are tall and bony, their hair lank, their faces thin and flabby-cheeked.[31]

Since the much-traveled Parker recoiled from these details, it is a wonder that those of less experience accepted the West as calmly as they did.

No one could escape the weather. Carolinians adjusting to the Indiana climate called it "miserably cold." But Indianans wore heavier clothes. Iowa was rated "cold as Lapland." An exasperated soul denounced the chilly, sloppy winter in Ohio—a winter "not of racing blood but of running noses. . . ." Someone complained that stoves heated Indiana Quaker churches too hot while the churches of Carolina were underheated. At Chicago fogs from the Lake were blamed for the uneven temperature—morning, overcoat; noon, shirtsleeves. Fogs on the Ohio River were sometimes as chilling as the ocean fogs at Portland, Maine; while the warm vapor of others made for human languor. A printer in Rockford, Illinois, records that the heavy dews of August and September rusted their sticks badly when left near the open windows.[32]

The belief was widespread that newcomers must undergo a "severe seasoning," or a "sickly season."[33] People made or failed the adjustment through ordeals of various sorts, as suggested by a letter announcing the death of a Virginian in Illinois: "Dr. A. C. Reed died last Friday was buried on

Sabbath day. he did not live long in this country. he exposed himself to much to wet and cold run after deers, and was excited all the time." Another, enduringly bilious, mentions that her physician "talks about my getting acclimated some day." She also remarks that the western complaints were "so different" from the eastern ones. The health of a Connecticut woman in southeastern Ohio had been good "ever since the soft water has scoured out the fur in my stomach it give us all a good clensing." There were also cases like that of the Yankee who before he had been many weeks in northern Indiana, was seized with an appetite almost uncontrollable. Alarmed, he spoke of it to the family he boarded with and was consoled that such hunger (which he attributed to the hard water) was universal with newcomers and that after a season it would pass away. The first year I came here, remarked another Yankee concerning abnormal appetite, "I went hungry every day—"[34]

While it was too early, thought Theodore Parker (1854), to estimate western character, he was sure that Easterners deteriorated in the West quite as much as did Europeans in America. The climate would check the intensity of the Anglo-Saxon character and the soil, air, and other influences would deteriorate the human being for a long time to come.[35]

Perhaps Parker had been led to this belief by letters such as Minor Deming and wife wrote from Cincinnati to Connecticut. From the former:

I have not yet lost any of that elasticity and sprightliness of feeling which the climate and N-E bestows, and which the western climate robs of an eastern emigrant in a few years. How long before this will desert me I shall not attempt to predict: I hope never, as I shall be cautious in diet and exercise.

Two years later the wife of Minor Deming discussed less hopefully the same subject:

The process of acclimation is not very agreeable. All who come here from the east feel greatly the heat of the climate for 2 or 3 summers. It produces debility, want of ambition, and makes

one feel but little like making any exertion, to accomplish anything. I think the air of Litchfield would make a new creature
of me *almost*.[36]

Plain homesickness must have been important with a
majority of migrants. It would take hard doubting to tarnish
the realness of Lydia Griffith's sadness:

I was here 4 or 5 weeks before I could think I must stay Oh Dear
but I was home sick not homesick neither for I had no home to go
to but to see you. * * but Oh the woods looks dark and the Country
very rough. You would think you could not live here and if I had
not seen hills I would think so to[37]

New Englanders are said so sorely to have missed the
dandelion that they brought it to Illinois from their eastern
home.[38] They wistfully told their prairie-born children of
sleighs, ice, and snow-covered hills, "of large rocks and big
mountains" at grandfathers' back in Massachusetts. Yankees
said that they would gladly trudge fifty western miles to scan
blue hills in the distance. To feed the memory of his Maine
home, Professor Larrabee of Asbury College, now De Pauw
University, obtained an assortment of evergreens to simulate
the Maine landscape.[39]

Minor poets under titles such as "New England" and "The
Emigrant's Farewell" broadened the literature of expatriation.
One by a Miss De Forest:

> Connecticut! thy rolling shore
>   Is fading fast away,
> And I shall greet thy sight no more,
>   For many a weary day.

Another verse, "by an editor," runs:

> Old Ocean, I miss thee, my friend,
>   Thy billows and foaming white crest;
> I could wish me a life without end,
>   Wouldst thou make but thy home in the west.[40]

We also recognize moments when the newcomer was
evidently undergoing a special adjustment in feeling and

temperament. A young man from Andover, Vermont, remarked that the streams and creeks of Illinois flowed slowly
and majestically "as if conscious of their superiority, & have
none of the rude, rushing appearance of those of New
England." Another saw in the trees of Ohio which, unlike
New England trees, were symmetrical, a foreign and aristocratic grace. One Yankee wished another might see Galena
by moonlight; the evenings there were charming, far more
beautiful than even in New England. A Connecticut woman
at Newcomerstown, Ohio, had never seen "such lithning or
heard such thunder as they have here." (Also the "Females"
swore worse than she ever heard a man swear in the East.)[41]

On the final stretch (on the Ohio River) of his travel from
Boston to become a colonist on the Muskingum, Col. John May
witnessed "one of the grandest nights in all my experience."
Thunder, lightning, the howling of savage beasts, the whooping
of one kind of owl and the screaming of another, made a scene
so grand and sounds and echoes so variously awesome that
he remained up five hours to enjoy it.[42]

To certain oncomers absence of slavery must have been the
most refreshing difference. John Humphries wrote forcefully
from Indiana to Virginia: "I tell you my Friends this is not
old Va.—the curse of slavery does not exist here—it is literally
true every Man sets under his own Vine and Fig Tree and
none to make them afraid People here go ahead."[43] Another
thanked God that he had escaped the presence of slavery: "Let
fools remain [in Virginia] to breed fools." To a wage earner
free soil meant "plenty of wirke" at good wages: ". . . I don't
wish myself back you may depend on it to be a slave. . . ." A
southern-bred Chicago matron found her northern white
servants did more work and better than the blacks of Virginia.
To certain juveniles free soil meant "adopting themselves to
the habit of waiting on others. . . ." Even the daughters were
obliged "to scuffle a little," to milk cows and cook for the
family because dwelling space for servants was wanting.[44]

Another special circumstance, a "down-river" influence,

played upon certain communities. Nearly a hundred boats and more than half the people (said a New Hampshire man, 1846) of Leavenworth, on the Indiana shore of the Ohio, went trading to New Orleans and talked familiarly of that distant city.[45] Such communities were linked with a sort of fluvial cosmopolitanism, acquired from New Orleans and from inter-craft visiting of the boatmen of fifty or more river valleys. Indeed boating to New Orleans (in the view of young Addison Coffin, a Carolina Quaker) had given the people of Annapolis, near the Wabash in western Indiana, a "strong local character." The Quakers there Coffin found "very different" from others in Indiana. There was a broader, higher impulse in their characters (surprisingly, it would seem, for the young man thought the term "Wild West" originated on the Wabash). The free life of the watermen had given "tone and impress" to business and business people: "a breadth of geography and business knowledge," which surprised eastern people. Included in common speech were many "boatmen words and phrases," like the sailor language of seaports, of which they were unconscious. Old neighbors who had left Carolina within his memory had taken on the same spirit "and did not seem to know they were changed. . . ." "Hoosier Carolinians," Coffin called them.[46]

Even profound change in men occurred if the following reference to Cincinnati social life be not too much exaggerated.

The social character of its citizens is most vivid, most lively, most electrical. Never have I resided among a people so universally buoyant. Each individual seems to be an extract of the condensed essence of hilarity. For myself, once arctic and icy, living here, I have become so socially electrified that, I doubt not, I could *charge* a whole community of New Englanders, and make everyone thereof a prodigy of vivacity. * * * With you, a ball-room is nothing more, at most, than a receptacle of beautifully wrought statues, gently stimulated into a very gentle motion. With us it is a scene of the most exhilarating, the most joyous life.[47]

Charles A. Dana interpreted social adjustment at Chicago as a triumph for New England: "About this great West there is a broad, vigorous, muscular, and marrowy humanity, genial, generous, radiant, warmly courteous that somehow conquers more than all ironbound puritan strictness. . . . It is a New England expanded, vivified, under a kindlier sun, and in a wider and freer sphere of activity." But Dana's sanguine view is further interesting because unconsciously he admits the *tertium quid* which was giving new character to western life.[48]

Other random experiences and remarks by settlers sometimes point up and clarify the changes:

"I have lost my age Send it in the Next Letter if you please."[49]

Special perils beset the literate. A missionary wrote from Illinois: "I have a large and pretty well selected library with me, but my interruptions are so great, that I can use it much less than I wish."[50]

"my grammer I have forgot as I have no one to talke it to as you now practice makes Perfect."[51]

A Pennsylvania-born physician who settled around 1841 in Coles County, Illinois, noted with relief the absence of old women "brouching."[52]

"By the way, this Sucker State is a great place for raising *Suckers*. They raise six or seven here in eight to ten years."[53]

Children are seldom mentioned, but someone wrote "tell Willy & E A They must learn to say Pa & Ma [pronounced paw and maw, we may be sure] as there is nothing else said in this country."[54]

Men who came to Greene County in southern Indiana did not dream that the northern soil would bring a "revolution in farm products," placing corn and wheat and hogs on the throne so long occupied by cotton and tobacco.[55]

The West changed men's religious habituations. In a postscript a young man begged his mother to borrow no trouble about him, though he had not attended a prayer meeting since he left Maine.[56]

"I do not hardly ever tend church," wrote a young Vermonter in Ohio, "for this I feel justified, as the ministers are uncouth low bread Methodist whom I despise."[57]

"King Cheese," a ruler "as absolute and exacting as ever was King Cotton," was blamed for having all but ruined the church life of Puritan-bred people of northern Ohio, where for a generation preceding the Civil War all other concerns had been "subservient to the interests of the dairy."[58]

Words by Frederick B. Tolles concerning present-day American Quakerism suggest that religious bodies have been subject to a sort of differentiative unraveling due to locality. Not what it was on the banks of the Delaware in the days of Penn and Woolman, today's Quakerism "may be emotional, revivalistic, fundamentalist Quakerism in Oregon; rationalist, humanist, 'social-gospel' Quakerism in Southern California; conservative, plain-bonnet, 'Thee and thou' Quakerism in Iowa; respectable, churchified, quasi-Methodist Quakerism in Indiana. The historians, with one or two exceptions, have served us ill in not giving us the story of this expansion and these changes,"[59] Tolles added.

After a half decade at the West a Vermont man was making written use of the southern terms *sugar tree* and *sugar water,* equivalents of Yankee *rock maple* and *sap.*[60]

A Yankee professor in a Midwest college at first saw fault in his neighbors who built houses in the center of the lot, away from the street. But he afterward petitioned the town trustees to vacate a street and two alleys to get his cottage near the center of his lot.[61]

"Talking about water, I wish I had a good drink of Va. water. This washy, sweetish stuff of here *is* bad to take."[62]

Another, though he had almost been carried off by the gallinippers at Wheeling, found Madison, Indiana, so like New England that he forgot he was not there.[63]

Unfamiliar names such as Roup, Sumption, Reddix, Wickersham added to the strangeness of one Midwest neighborhood.[64]

From Buck Horn, Illinois, a Tarheel at Cedar Bush was assured that "thar is tools hear that you could make a wagon with a heap quicker."[65]

Another was happy because "the Sun rises and Sets in the

right place to me, which makes it all the more pleasant."[66]

A Yankee woman in Illinois describes the persevering routine by which the hard water was "broke" (as the West said it) for laundering purposes.[67]

A man assured Ohio relatives that his newly acquired wife was Kentucky-born but had not lived in Indiana long enough to become "hoosherized so as to be like the natives."[68]

An eastern farmer acknowledged it "a right smart chance if a newcomer doesn't have a 'heap' of trouble the first year or two, and by that time he will be completely 'Suckerized.' "[69]

Astonishing as it might be to a blue-hills-loving Yankee, there were those who drank healths to the flat, open corn-hog counties of the Midwest: "the fairest among a thousand. No lakes, no mountains, bogs or large rivers break the surface of the country. There is no waste land, no barrens. Her sons and daughters travel to distant parts, but return to what they believe to be the garden spot on earth."[70]

A timetable of acclimatization would be difficult to devise. A Carolinian was "much discouraged" for a year or so "but got used to it." After four years away, a Vermonter, though acknowledging negligence, did not think of home once a week. A prominent guidebook said that most individuals adjusted in a half year and that nine of ten who returned home did so during the first year.[71]

The tapering off is perhaps fairly illustrated by the letters of one George Leavitt of New Hampshire who settled in the latter 1840's in an Indiana hamlet on the Ohio River. After about three years his letters, never dull, became less vivid and his depictions more general:

I have become acquainted with quite a different state of things from that which exists in N. E. Everything here is different from what it is there and I can hardly realize that I have ever lived in a place so entirely different from this. Yet I have not so far forgot my early education as to be unmindful of the many obligations which I am under to worthy parents. . . . and the excellent rules of life they taught me.[72]

Leavitt of New Hampshire was about to blend his voice with others:

> And though I remember New England,
> The land of the brave and blest,
> Not her wealth, nor her laws, nor her manners
> Can, with me, compare, with the west.[73]

3. Settlers on Corn Belt Soil

"We are dooing better. . . ."
"—they make their money off corn & Hogs—"

"Where the corn shoots twenty feet high into the sun, and every ear yields five hundredfold, the stature of the planter is dwarfed. Man is made more than a little lower than the grain he hoes." So sings a prose-poem of America's cornfields, and cornfields deserve their poets, despite anachronisms such as hoes and very tall stalks.[74]

Perhaps no other feature of mid-America has been of greater import in moulding men and life in America than its cornfields. The maize plant is "inseparably interwoven into the spirit of America."[75] Nor has any bounty of our environment been more taken for granted. Settlement within what came to be the Corn Belt, or even its less productive fringes, must have been the significant point with countless thousands.

Corn, America's most important and distinctive crop, was itself a pioneer, growing under primitive conditions before other crops could flourish, its kernels edible a bare three weeks after pollination, and yielding twice as much food per acre as any other cereal.[76] From the beginning it rated in the West as a "sure" crop. No farmer can live without it, and hundreds raise little else, affirmed a gazetteer of Illinois in 1834. Even in valueless oversupply it afforded the best-grounded hopes for the future.[77] To stress corn is not to belittle other products of western soil—wheat, oats, hay and grass, fruits and garden produce—yet corn became the pivot around which ranged lesser crops and the different phases of animal husbandry.

Men of imagination have always stirred to the abundance,

incredible in acres or bushels, of the American maize crop. Truly told or exaggerated, marvel pieces about corn are an important part of what people believed, felt, and expected of the West. One may be impressed by the Quakerly restraint of youthful Addison Coffin, fresh from North Carolina, who saw (1844) all along the banks of the Wabash in western Indiana "corn pens with an almost unlimited supply of corn for any market that opened." Or be entertained by the harmless palaver of Hezekiah Park that on certain of his farms his 1840 crop would equal the cost of the farms. Further, he could see to corn planting in Illinois in the Spring, supervise haying in Vermont in August, then be in Texas for cotton picking in the Fall, "and take comfort the whole round."[78]

Wonder stories from the valleys of the West began to trickle eastward in the latter 1700's. It is a fact, runs a letter from the Muskingum Valley of Ohio in 1788, "that they drove a stake into a cornhill and measured the corn, and that in 24 hours it grew 9 1/2 inches." Later, fields of a thousand acres were reported from Ohio, "all of corn & *very stout*," tall enough to hide a man on horseback; which jibes unevenly with a Southerner's description in 1834 of New England maize: five feet high fully grown on rich land, with small and very yellow kernels and ears. To convey the outsize proportions of western corn taxed the imagination of more than one Yankee. It grows very tall, one of them explained, "I think about as high as the top of our old shed between the Barn[s.]"[79]

A favorite metaphor called the great cornfields "seas" or "oceans": "Only conceive in your own mind a vast plain as far as the eye can reach, waiveing as the sea, groaning under from 60 to 70 bushels of corn to the acre, and you can have some idea of the corn crop of Illinois," was one word-picture posted to Virginia.[80] A down-east youth scarcely knew whether to be more excited over the surfeiting wagonloads of Illinois watermelons or Illinois corn, but his emotion upon visiting a sixty-acre maizefield in September may well have moved others to come out and see for themselves: ". . . as I strolled

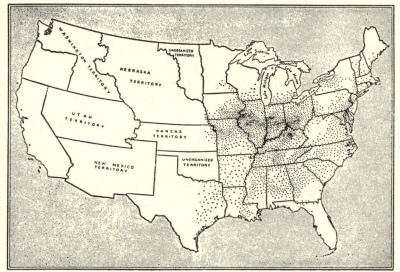

Corn Production, 1860
Each dot represents 300,000 bushels

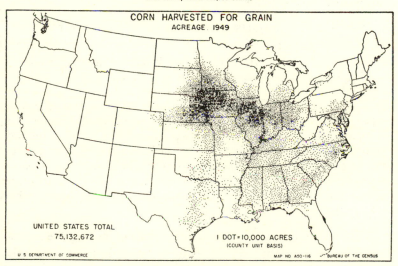

CORN HARVESTED FOR GRAIN
ACREAGE. 1949

UNITED STATES TOTAL
75,132,672

I DOT=10,000 ACRES
(COUNTY UNIT BASIS)

U S DEPARTMENT OF COMMERCE   MAP NO A50-116   BUREAU OF THE CENSUS

through it, I could but laugh heartily, for it seemed as though
I was in a world of corn. I could see nothing else except
the sun which heated the black soil so hot that I could scarcely
bear my hand on it. . . ."[81]

Wonder sometimes took the form of chronic folk query: can you hear corn grow in hot weather? An affirmative answer, nobly felt, advises you to go at night so deep into a cornfield that you are surrounded by corn higher than your head. You will have placed yourself in a special world: "But listen!" It cannot be the wind for there is no wind.

There is a whisper, a faint crackling, coming from no where and everywhere at once. It might be the ghost of a sound, imagined perhaps. But listen again!

It is the minute stretching of a billion corn leaves, stalks, husks, kernels. It is the dark chemistry of earth, working upward through roots, drawing up through the standing plants, transmitting the essences of soil into life. It is the sound of growth, a sound perhap heard by insects and other lowly creatures as a veritable roar of creation.

You are as close, here, to the inner quick of nature as ever you'll be. You are listening to the growth of corn, America's annual renewal of plant substance.[82]

In a way the proudest corn story came from a farmer near Peoria who explained for his father in Virginia how to gather one hundred bushels of corn a day, dually pleasing because it required corn *"very stout"* as well as a "good man."

It is now five O clock, Monday morning and brekfast is a bout ready will you believe that I can pick one hundred bushels in one day. well I done it one or two days. they is olly one way you can do it that is husk in lands   pick two roes by the side of the wagon   keep your left arm up your left hand pointing towards the point of the ear ketch it with your right. make but to grabs at one ear. and you can do it   make the ears pass one another if you can.[83]

But we should proceed no further without noting the second party in the corn-hog duo. It is legend that on the strong soils of the West hogs were propagated by planting pigtails bent into U-shapes as one would raise onions from sets, except that two new pigs grew from each pigtail.[84] Yet legend is scarcely less credible than the cool vital statistics of swine. A brace of writers have lately reviewed the singular efficacy of the hog as a meat animal as demonstrated in wartime when meat is wanted in a hurry.

Nature, the hog's briefholders say, takes three months, three weeks, and three days to deliver a litter of eight or more piglets. In six months more a good stockman can bring these to marketable maturity. So in ten or eleven months you can have hams on the hook or loins on the block. Moreover, the swine's reproductive cycle may be exercised twice a year, ordinarily Spring and Fall. This while the cow carries her one calf nine months, and fifteen more are required for the calf to grow into meat. Also, as a food factory the hog is the most efficient of all animals. He can store in his body up to 35 per cent of the energy contained in all he consumes. Sheep and cattle retain about a third as much.[85]

Because mountains of corn were translated into pork so were many wonder stories told in terms of swine. The crux of corn-on-the-hoof stories remained constant: "We doubt whether the annals of farming can produce many specimens of more easily grown, profitable crops," as *The Prairie Farmer* once put it.[86] Thus a Bay State friend of William Bacon, who lived near Indianapolis, thought the hundred hogs Bacon was feeding the summer of 1845 would in a single week eat all the corn in his native township of Williamstown. Bacon expected to make a thousand dollars from the venture.[87] A decade earlier an editor at Brookville, in southeastern Indiana, marvelled at the columns of hogs, totaling thirty thousand perhaps—old settlers had never seen such numbers—driven toward Cincinnati during three November weeks. Some days it seemed as if the vast arena of nature's storehouse was filled with hogs, all from one small section of the state. Wrote Calvin Fletcher from Indianapolis, "Hogs, and hens grow almost spontaneous here. . . ."[88]

It required self-restraint not to spill over in excitement at some part of the yearly pork traffic. "The ringing crack of the whip and the whoop of the driver in our streets reminds us that the Hog season is again upon us," exclaimed another editor, also at sight of swine en route to Cincinnati. For these pre-railroad times were the heyday of the drovers, said to collect a thousand hogs at once, one driver to each hundred swine. Some of these men were folk heroes of a sort, as in Rush County, Indiana, prideful of its maize and swine, where the name of "Hog" Walker is remembered.[89]

Lesser men trafficked in lesser marvels. For countless farmers from the older states the cornlands meant at first humble security for beast and man. Illinois soil reassured a Yankee who had escaped anxiety over grain rations for his livestock. Now he could work his horses every day and keep them fat and active as colts because "I have plenty of grain and *don't keep them on cob meal.*" A brother Yankee included among "good things" of that country "Plenty of Grain which makes large fat Horses and Cattle."[90]

A Virginian compared grazing in Indiana and Virginia: "Dare is Beder grass in the roads and woods here [Indiana] than eveary i had in my fields in Dare[.]" Nor did the grasslands of Illinois go unacclaimed. Acres by the million were wasting. Grass upon which cattle would become much more fat than upon the best clover pastures in Pennsylvania; on which good horses could be raised at a cost each of ten dollars a year.[91]

The gazetteer maker was doubtless on sound ground in noting (in the early 1830's) that western cows produced less milk and of lesser richness than did those of the older states.[92] But Corn Belt soil lay ready as a prime mover in making over cows everywhere.[93] Dairying with the benefit of its grass and grain was bound to bring revelations. From Quincy, Illinois, the word was: "The Prairie grass makes the Richest milk that I ever drank. It is rich with *Cream.* God willing, I hope to have a cow soon that will give butter in pound Rools—which will save the Churning." While another, buoyed by western abundance, scribed to North Carolina: "We have 2 of the best cows in Indiana one of them is worthe 3 carolina cowese."[94]

Unaccustomed ease of human subsistence went along with easy fodder. "I think as near as I can calculate I can support my

Family on less than one half the labour that I could in Maine," was a judgment reiterated before the writer had finished his sheet. Messages to Virginia were in the same tenor. "We have got more meat and bread stuf together now and got it paid for than we would have had in Virginia in a whole year," declared a couple recently settled in Indiana. Another Virginian, in Ohio, thought he was "a doing a graite Deel better then I did in thare for I have plenty of Every thing that I want."[95]

Certainly ease of subsistence varied with individual cases and from time to time and place to place. Having relatives or acquaintances in the new location was a help. But in a new country where, as a touring Englishman remarked, every ear of corn meant a meal for a hungry man, where labor could be readily bartered for provision, and in spite of indifferent care, vegetables flourished in a soil of unrivaled depth, fertility, and freshness, the specter of hunger could be only temporary. This point was not lost on a Marylander who after calling the state of Illinois by pretty names more surely based security upon the agrarian maxim "you know where the farmer can live no class need starve."[96]

All this had been anticipated by Col. John May who came out to the Yankee settlement on the Muskingum in 1788. For several days past, according to the July 24th entry in his journal, they had enjoyed plenty of vegetables. No market in the world would have a greater variety of good things than the settlement would have in the fall, the more extraordinary because six weeks before, the garden spot had borne lofty trees of the forest "from eight to ten rods long." At mid-July he had jotted: "Eat green peas today from my own garden, planted exactly five weeks ago." "Things do grow amazingly!"[97]

Tillage in the West vexed the human spirit less; though as one guidebook put it the labors of the husbandman were as arduous as in New England during the first three years; after that, much lighter. First came the hackneyed narrative—each had his own version—of a cornfield of say thirty acres, the seed covered by brushing in, never cultivated, and the ripened crop would yield twenty to thirty bushels to the acre. Back to Virginia went the assurance from a farmer who had seen how much easier cropping was in Ohio: "And I would Not [raise] Corn in thare again—Not if they would give me all the land that lyes between the Strait and the mouth of Runnions Creek." A Carolinian gave terse notice that he would rather farm in Illinois than among the rocks of his home state.[98]

Plenteous feed made horses more numerous than in the older states. Cultivation by horsepower tended to supplant the use of hoes except for chopping weeds. It is not surprising that the commerce to the East in horses increased, engaging western farmers like the one who inquired of his brother the price of horses in Massachusetts, "the most fashionable colours and all about them. it is probable I may sometime fetch you some of them if they bear a good price I can get good horses here for 50 Dolls[.]"[99]

Whatever the degree of advantage, farm making on the sodlands wrote its own chapter in ease of cultivation. Treeless prairies with names such as Two Mile, Pretty, English, Portage, Mongoquanong, Rolling, and Door were "greedily pounced upon." "I can never endure the thought since I have seen the prairies of gowing in to a timbered country to settle," wrote a Vermonter from near Chicago: "we can have our farmes as well subdued in five years here as any one can in a timbered country in twenty." To another the taming of treeless soil amounted to an "immense diminution" of labor; for Illinois, he thought, nature had done everything except fencing and breaking the sod, whereas in Ohio one had to toil and tug for years to level the forest and clear the land. Henry L. Ellsworth, one with a promoter's eye on the valley of the upper Wabash, estimated that the virgin grasslands could be brought into complete cultivation at a cost one fourth to three fourths of clearing forest.[100]

Reckonings of the comparative returns from labor probably went most directly to the heart of the matter. A young man from Maine thought that in Illinois ten bushels of corn could be produced as easily as one bushel in Maine. A Carolinian thought that farming effort in Brown County, Illinois, yielded five times its equivalent applied in the Old North State; while another Tarheel adjudged that in the same Illinois county, where eight or ten ears grew in every hill, a hand could raise 1,200 to 1,500 bushels of corn in a season. Back home the return would be around 100 bushels: "It looks like doing some good." Thus whether the gauge was bushels, acres, or effort, whether the comparison was with Maine, Carolina, York State, or Maryland, the advantage was always in favor of the West, and never much less than three to one.[101]

The cornfields made, over the decades, "corn-hog" farmers by the hundreds of thousands, who best typify the Midwest farming interest and whose sons in the twentieth century continue to hail the hog as a "mortgage lifter" and "farmer's friend when it comes to revenue for the family." They have made farmers who during a century and a quarter have been so comparatively independent with one principal source of income—the top of the cycle came at the time hogs were sold and superseded Christmas as a time for paying debts—that they have held innovation at a minimum.[102]

By the eve of the Civil War the cornlands were about to breed a host of farmers proudly rich, yet proud of their impoverished beginnings. "I have made considerable money her. and layed out considerable and I have something to show for it," remarked an Old Dominion man complacently. "Christian has got him self a home in Illinois," another Virginian wrote of his brother, "and is as saucy about it as a jay in a corn field. He has got a piece of land that can't be beat." Farmers of such prospects and feelings were on their way to financial independence. The finely engraved portraits of our ancestors, their biographical sketches and implausible lithographic farmsteads in the county histories of the 1880's witness the latter phase. Continuing satisfaction from Corn Belt realty is certain: "To have been a pioneer was an honor," wrote a county historian, "but to possess a landed estate in Warren county

in 1912 is to be happy and contented."[103] Little wonder that
on the eve of World War I these farmers felt they could feed
the world bountifully.

Men have designated the cornlands as a place of rationality,
prosperity and happiness; of intelligence, contentment, and independence; the social and economic bulwark of the nation, and
the embodiment of the best there is in the ideal Americanism.
Without attempting judgment of these qualities one may
venture that the acclimatization of men to cornland soil was
largely a matter of adapting their feelings and designs to
material abundance, of rerating their standards of effort and
personal fortune, all of which rested upon one of the best-
balanced farming economies—between men, livestock, crops,
and machines—on the planet. This means that the farmer
during three seasons has spent about half his time and that of
his motive power on his corn crop. A happy combination of
farm and factory also makes for stability. During the years
1909-1920 the Indiana corn crop fluctuated less than 10 per
cent from the average yield. In farming vernacular Corn Belt
diversity and equilibrium has meant, even in the face of a short
yield of corn, that, "If we would just have faith and trust and
work on, things will even up by the time the year will round
up."[104]

Authorities have defined the Corn Belt as that area of the
United States where corn is the major crop—the largest area
in the world with fertile soil, rainfall of 10 to 14 inches following planting, and a mean average temperature around tasseling
time of 70° to 80° Fahrenheit. Never long fixed, the bounds
of the Corn Belt proper shift with weather, the use of machinery, improved strains of seed, pests, competing crops,
prices, transport, and markets.[105]

Thus no one will suppose that the Corn Belt sprang suddenly into its twentieth-century peripheries and might. It is
interesting that no written use prior to 1882 has been reported
of the term Corn Belt.[106] As late as 1846 De Bow's *Review*
referred to North Carolina as still being a great corn-growing

state.[107]   For the year 1859, fifteen southern states claimed 52 per cent of the nation's bushels of corn.   But in this latter year Illinois took the lead, followed by Ohio and Missouri, and the corn map began to foretell its twentieth-century bounds and accents.[108]   At the turn of the new century, Professor Fred A. Shannon has pointed out, twelve North Central states (which contain almost the entire Corn Belt), with only a quarter of the nation's land and a third of its farm population, grew or had:

> 71 per cent of the nation's corn
> 64 per cent of its wheat
> 77 per cent of its oats
> 64 per cent of its hogs
> 52 per cent of its horses
> 58 per cent each of its hay, barley, and potatoes
> 44 per cent of cattle of all sorts.

With this "granary and larder," Shannon concludes, no other section could even vaguely compare.[109]

America's corn crop of 1946, for example, totaled over 3.28 billion bushels, more than three fifths of the world's crop.   It afforded 23 bushels—ten ears a day—for each American.   Yet the annual direct food-use of corn was around 65 pounds.   This means that the American people do their dining as it were in an upper chamber, on refined products such as pork, beef, dairy products, poultry, and eggs, while industry (about 12 per cent) and animal feed (about 80 per cent) account for the bulk of the crop.   Of the latter

> hogs eat 40 per cent
> cattle eat 21 per cent (dairy cows take half)
> poultry, 13 per cent
> horses and mules, 5 per cent
> sheep, $\frac{1}{2}$ per cent.[110]

Corn was more than a living.   It was for thousands a legacy.   A young Virginian, Robert Cutler, wondered who could not be "up & doing" in the midst of Indiana's rich fields and quick-moving industry; no loungers, no idlers; "grass &

corn, their principal productions & the thousand teams bearing them to the banks of the river. . . ." Cutler's stimulation may later have matched the deeds of young Enoch Honeywell, whose negotiations more than a century and a quarter ago for the growing, feeding, droving, packing, and transit of corn and swine (not to include his personal traverses between East, West, and South), were of a casualness fitting the present century.[111]

Men who had not dreamed the dream of wealth evidently did not recognize opportunity. Perhaps many of them were inveterate pone eaters (like the southern-born soldiers at Norfolk who during the second war with Britain insisted on calling wheaten bread wheat *pone*), who could substitute corn bread for poundcake at a wedding. At any rate there is a passive tone to the news from Illinois that "John Boss and Henry Boss has got more corn in their cribs than they ever had in Northcarolina."[112] Signs of collective passiveness come from southern Indiana where the farmers of Crawford County, to know whether to expect a crop of mast sufficient to fatten their shoats, would in early spring climb the beech and oak trees to observe the amount of bloom. If the bloom forecast a large crop of beechnuts and acorns, they would plant only a little corn. But in the case of a Virginian removed to central Indiana, "a plentiful country," passivity had clearly become demoralized satiety. "Father says he has Corn Enough to last him two seasons," a son remarked, "he Labours not at all."[113]

4. THE WEST DEMANDS AUTONOMY

". . . since we are not sought out, we will come out. . . ."

"The mighty West," sounded a voice at midcentury, "seems like a great cauldron, where every heterogeneous element is fermenting, foaming, and every now and then overflowing." Another contemporary was impressed by a "great unrest" during the 1850's in social, political, religious, and domestic life, due to issues such as antislavery, feminism, church polity. "Everywhere, in every channel of thought, active minds were exploring the surroundings." If the farmer now had time to think, it was largely because machinery had transformed farm and home life. Popular thrill and gratefulness reflect, in spite of spine-chilling metaphor, in verses called "Song of the Mowing Machine."

> The sinews of a dozen men
> Are in my bosom lying—
> The sinews of a dozen men,
> Ache, age and toil defying.[114]

Regional pride and desire for self-reliance were emerging. Western men chafed at importations, both material and of the mind, from the East. And it is significant that by 1850 circumstances made possible a degree of western self-dependence not previously attainable.

Complaints, protests, and demands in fact add up to a plea for western autonomy in a broad sense. If the West wanted a poem, an address, or a lecture, insisted William Turner Coggeshall, Ohio author-critic, who has been styled the most vocal of literary chauvinists, the first impulse was to telegraph for secondhand wares which some society over the mountain or over the ocean had put aside. "Why should we not send to salt water for our Governors, Senators, Representatives?" Coggeshall begged recognition *at home* for any idea, whether pertaining to the soil, the shop, the office, or the parlor, whether it should culminate in a plow, a new motor, a poem, an oration, a history, or a statue.[115]

By 1850 the grand practical results from a half century of effort were visible everywhere. The commerce of the West was touted as the controlling power of the nation, while the use of machinery was so vast and recent that only the few knew about it. The West had become "the most fruitful granary of earth. . . ." Chicago was by 1855 the world's greatest primary wheat depot (over 20 million bushels), its movement expedited by the "vast Mediterraneans of the New World" as well as by newly spiked rails. Meanwhile Cincinnati was credited with originating and perfecting "the system which packs fifteen bushels of corn into a pig, and packs that pig into a barrel, and sends him over the mountains and over the ocean to feed mankind."[116]

Coal, though traffic in it was a mere trickle, was recognized as a basic want of civilization, one of the means toward national strength. The two million bushels Cincinnati used in 1843 trebled a decade later. Looking forward, *The Western Journal* of St. Louis inventoried the "great Illinois Coal Field" as extending over forty thousand square miles, into Iowa, Indiana, and Wisconsin.[117]

Sometimes unsoberly Chicago cried its bid to become the metropolis of the Northwest. "We have the fastest horses, the fastest men, the keenest speculators, the richest merchants, the tallest stores, the most generous, hospitable, and charitable people, the smartest tradesmen, the handsomest women, and the most stunning fashions to be seen in the West. If you dont believe me, come and see."[118] In draining the level lands about the city—three successive ordinances raised the grade of the city ten feet—Chicago turned embarrassment into benefit: In one project, ran a boast, six thousand screws lifted a half block six feet to meet requirements.[119]

By the 1850's a generation born on the soil of the Northwest was feeling its weight and influence. A native of Illinois could exclaim, "I love my Prairie State! I glory in her prosperity! I rejoice in the contemplation of her free political institutions." Others explained that western birth meant western tastes, feelings, and associations: "We love its soil . . . we love the glorious, expansive, exhaustless, mighty West." Such men named "western character," straightforward and warm, as the proper representative of the general American character. They nailed the slander that the West degenerated men. They defended its climate: "not very enervating," it permitted men to work "without the hard stimulus of want to contract the mind with care of the pence, so fatal to our down-east neighbors' mental expansion."[120]

They defended the soundness, if also the novelty, of

western education. New countries, they insisted, had substitutes for colleges and academies of the old, which produced a superior quality of mind. Largeness of conception derived from the magnitude of western rivers, from long migrations, large undertakings, absence of caste and fixed institutions, wide freedom of individual choice, acceptance of new truth, and sympathy with poor young men. Also from direct presentation by leaders of public issues, the teachings of an itinerate clergy, and the opportunity of learning from migrants of many origins. Western experience remade western hearts. The farmer might therefore turn away his scythe from a clump of sweet-williams. They had greater freshness of feeling, more lively impulses, and deeper enthusiasms than those who lived in the old parts of the country.[121]

Affirmations of western strength and maturity began early and were chronic. The desire of the Northwest to produce a literature of its own intensified around mid-nineteenth century. In a letter to "Beloved Dwellers in the dear old Home-land," Mrs. H. M. Tracy plead the case. If the West kept silence, who would chronicle the history of western hearts? "We have counted the cost, and now we are ready to say, *The West must have its own Literature. . . .* She owes it to the world, to herself and to a 'higher Power,' to come out with pure and truthful thoughts. . . ." And since the West was not *sought* out it would *come* out.[122]

Native periodicals were particularly wanted. "A Magazine with the North-West in it, that is what we want . . . a distinctive, characteristic thing. . . ." Not a Blackwood, not a Harper. The agricultural press spoke its impatient piece. One half of Indiana's grain was threshed by easternmade machines declared inferior to those manufactured at Indianapolis and Richmond. Three fourths of the horsepowers in use in the state were acknowledged, protestingly, to be of New York manufacture.[123]

A correspondent from southwestern Indiana complained that not a single Indiana agricultural paper was received in his locality, yet the place was "flooded with Eastern papers."[124] We want facts, practical facts from men of Ohio and the West," insisted the *Ohio Farmer,* echoed a few years later by a neighbor : "Indianapolis—not Boston, New York or any other point a thousand miles off—is the place for the issue of such a journal. Let it grow out of the Western soil." Agents of eastern nurseries, "despite a thievish countenance," could sell a bill of fruit trees to almost every man who read an eastern journal, simply because he had seen the advertisement "in his favorite paper."[125]

Westerners resented also the monopolization of the lyceum platform by Easterners. It was "downright toadyism . . . of the same character as the millinery slavery of our females :— nothing born and bred or manufactured in Ohio is good enough." After hearing two lectures by a professor at Antioch College on the subject of war and peace, a complainant hoped that the Ohio Literary Association would soon learn that there were strong minds and eloquent tongues "nearer home than Boston and New York." A year later, another article set forth reasons for the use of western talent : "so exclusively have men from abroad monopolized the public attention, that it has almost been forgotten that the West possesses any cultivated mind."[126] That the two latter protests appeared in print at Cleveland, in a region peculiarly the child of New England, heightens the inference that the offspring was unlike the parent.

Also there was a voluble body of opinion that heaven intended for the Northwest a special destiny or mission (though Northwest was not always clearly distinguished from West, nor northwestern destiny from the national destiny). This central valley, in one view, was the heart of the Republic and might give tone to the entire system. It was attracting the attention of all the civilized world, of the more enterprising portions especially. To others the Northwest's mission was more prosaic and practical—it was the keystone in the Federal arch, in commerce, politics, and church polity.[127]

Among those who pitched the tune high was John A. Wilstach of Lafayette, Indiana, who published in 1855 an oration, *The Imperial Period of National Greatness: A Lecture on the Destiny of the West*.[128] It was the destiny of the West, he said, to furnish the fairest possible field for the development of modern ideas. Even the unsettled and the poor felt instinctively that the West was the theater of a wider, wiser, grander, purer, and loftier civilization than the world had yet witnessed. Moreover the western man saw empire opening before him, a sentiment imperfectly shared at the East.

Even livelier is the analysis of William Davis Gallagher, editor, poet, and public official, of Ohio. Of the great interior valley the most important part, according to Gallagher, was the Northwest (with which he included Kentucky, Missouri, Minnesota, Iowa). The crude components of its society were at midcentury just coming into homogeneousness and symmetry. Its latitude, with cereals, wool, flax, hemp would be sought out by men of natural sagacity. For the lower latitudes, with cotton, sugar, rice, maize, yams, oranges, and bananas, Gallagher cared not: "The men of bananas are not the men of muscle or mind. . . ." Did Gallagher forget that the papaw (the Hoosier banana) is a north-ranging tropical fruit?

In the Northwest were met all conditions for great achievement—food, clothing, commerce, manufactures, and *"we have found the men."* Here would commence a new and glorious experiment in humanity, under Christianity, the representative principle and faith that man's progress is the design of God. Here likewise would take place the experiment of Christian man.[129]

But few could have been so tipsy on the wines of destiny as Charles W. Dana when he wrote, "O, the soul kindles at the thought of what a magnificent empire the West is but the germ, which, blessed with liberty and guaranteeing equal rights to all, shall go on conquering and to conquer, until the whole earth shall resound with its fame and glory."[130]

Thoughts and feelings like these meant that the ties between western settlers and an older region were being strained or severed. The Westerner was forgetting his ancestry. What had once been "Yankee" and what had once been "Southern" had blended into something new.

5. Ending a Long Story—A Tempered Victory

"twice it sharpened into a sword"

Regardless of how they named it—Cavalier against Roundhead, Virginia against Massachusetts, Plymouth against Jamestown, North against South—more than one witness believed that Yankees and Southerners in the Northwest were playing latter scenes in a drama begun in England two hundred years before. Twice it "sharpened into a sword," in the phrase of Professor Schlesinger, once in Old England and once in America.[131]

Perhaps it was difficulty of communication during the earlier age, or slightness of attempts in collective action, that kept awareness of differences latent until about the time of the Revolution. In any case southern patriots at the Continental Congress denounced Massachusetts men as "a parcel of Canting, Hypocritical, peculating Knaves."[132]

Thomas Jefferson was enough impressed to attempt a conspectus of opposing traits. Says Jefferson in a letter to Chastellux in 1785:

I will give you my idea of the characters of the several states.

In the North they are	In the South they are
cool	fiery
sober	voluptuary
laborious	indolent
perservering	unsteady
independent	independent
jealous of their own liberties, and just to those of others	zealous for their own liberties, but trampling on those of others
interesting	generous
chicaning	candid
superstitious and hypocritical in their religion	without attachment or pretentions to any religion but that of the heart

These characteristics, continues Jefferson, who thought it well to point out vices freely, grew weaker by graduation from North to South and South to North, insomuch that any observing traveler could always know his latitude by the character of the people among whom he found himself. In Pennsylvania, Jefferson thought, the two characters seemed to meet and blend.[133]

Francis Kinloch, South Carolina aristocrat, wrote in 1786 from Newport to Thomas Boone, one-time governor of South Carolina:

I think I have heard You say, that you have been in Rhode-island, and that you were pleased with everything but the people. Your observation would be the same if you were here now. . . . they are descended, as their clothese, their wigs, & their religion prove, from those men who first raised the flame of rebellion in England in the last century, and who gloried in suffering for the good old cause—like their ancestors they are uneasy under any form of government, tyrannical to excess when possessed of power. . . .[134]

The visiting Frenchman Chevalier thought he recognized in the 1830's the same men who cut each other's throats under the names of Roundheads and Cavaliers, and who "patched up a peace" by creating a third dynasty neither Stuart nor Cromwell. In America Providence had fortunately thrown them wide apart, leaving between them the *"justes-milieux"* states of New York and Pennsylvania, with their satellites, New Jersey and Delaware. And when Lee submitted at Appomattox, Yankees with retentive memories rejoiced that the Puritan had at last "triumphed over the Cavalier."[135]

Yet compared with what took place in the Deep South when men repelled northern reformers, adjustment in the Old Northwest was a temperate affair. The doggedness of the former is displayed when a hitherto frustrated Yankee acknowledged in 1865 that it had "been easier to preach the Gospel in its fulness in Roman Catholic Italy, Mohammedan Turkey, heathen India, or barbaric Africa, than in the slave-holding States of Protestant America."[136]

In the Northwest consciousness of differences might be continuous and sometimes irritating, but no large and fundamental antipathies or interests stood in the way of eventual harmony. It is worthy of remark, wrote James Hall in his *Illinois Monthly Magazine,*

that parties, and party dissensions, do not always grow out of differences of opinion about important matters, but more frequently arise out of the veriest trifles . . . little peculiarities of belief or practice which are . . . tenaciously adhered to on one side, and contemptuously spurned on the other.[137]

While no one from this distance can tell what differences were the "important" ones, the records of everyday living are strewn with signs that Yankee and Southerner at first doubted and questioned, then accepted one another and presently came to live harmoniously together.

It has already been noted that the Yankees after about 1850 regarded themselves as victors in a "thirty years war."[138] There was much to make this view plausible. It was easy during those years to be swept into overstatement by the delirious intemperance of Manifest Destiny. But the New England triumph, however large, was never so complete as the zealots believed. One can name some of the circumstances which fed the illusion of overwhelming success.

In the first place facile transport made it easy to win general dominance in certain areas and to achieve by about 1850 commercial ties with most of the Northwest. But for the Yankees this commercial orientation of the Northwest was perhaps too easily won. Grooving of communications caused Yankee influences—votes, colleges, churches, missionaries—to become bunched and spotty on the map, which caused overoptimism from local successes. The sons of the Puritans could also place too great store by the ease of interregional visiting and letter writing which kept alive family relationships; and too readily assume that the large western circulation of eastern papers, periodicals, and books (against which western editors clamored) meant cultural identity of the two areas.[139]

Thus travelers who followed the peripheral waters of the

Northwest, for example, could easily have been misled by the number of Yankees they encountered—at Gallipolis or Galena—and failed to imagine their absence from the back country. Wrote one such circumnavigator (from Gallipolis), "We find everywhere people from New England"; from Galena: "Thus you see we meet New England people everywhere, and I have seldom felt that we were among strangers."[140]

Naturally enough the Yankees pointed gladly to local benefits from their presence. But within the larger frame their political force was uneven, though it tended to bear most firmly after the mid-1850's (each had best hazard his own summary, from the maps) upon most of Ohio, northern Illinois, southern Wisconsin, southern Michigan, extreme northern Indiana, eastern Iowa, and Southern Minnesota.[141] Claims of political success in northern Indiana and Illinois, for example, where people of enterprise and intelligence gave majorities to Frémont in 1856, discredited the southern portions of those states where "slow, lazy, thriftless, ignorant" folk gave Loco-Foco majorities.[142] And this patchy achievement lay all to the northward of the Ohio River. Of the tougher sort of political intransigeance we need only recall that somewhere to the southward of that river lies the "Solid South."

Despite a goodly number of excellent institutions, the twenty-one Congregational colleges were, like the church membership, unevenly spread throughout the Union.[143] There were in 1860 Congregational colleges in but twelve of the thirty-four states while the colleges of other principal sects were more evenly planted. Six of eleven Puritan colleges in the Old Northwest (Beloit, Knox, Milwaukee-Downer, Ripon, Rockford, Wheaton) were confined to northern Illinois and southern Wisconsin which taken along with eastern Iowa, became a special tract of Puritan influence. Also, several Congregational colleges, such as Western Reserve, Miami, Illinois, and Knox, were for several decades jointly controlled, not always in harmony, with Presbyterians under the Plan of Union of 1801. The Plan also provided that a church affiliated with either body might appoint a minister from the other and adopt the polity of either group as it saw fit. The Plan was dissolved in 1852, the same year a spokesman remarked: "They have milked our Congregational cows, but have made nothing but Presbyterian butter and cheese." And if other Puritan colleges were like Beloit, there was the further drawback of preponderant numbers of non-Yankees among the student bodies.[144]

The Yankees also undercalculated the taciturn latent strength of the upland culture which resembeled a sea which forever makes salty the fresh waters falling into it. At each new stage of western development they had to grapple with larger areas and vaster combinations. Massachusetts' veterans' land grant at Marietta was as large as Rhode Island. The Connecticut Reserve was as large as the parent state. Areas occupied by New England stock in northern Illinois were as large as Massachusetts, Connecticut, and Rhode Island.[145] Yet in 1863 Henry Ward Beecher was insisting that the Yankee diocese should be little less than the entire continent.[146]

Another error was that of expecting too much from the assimilative power of the individual Yankee, for the Yankees who went to the West were not all from the class "that conserved the type of New England civilization pure and undefiled," not on the whole the purest of New England stock. The degree to which Yankees in the West lapsed in energy and faith is a question openly debated by the Yankees themselves. The judgment that latter-day Yankees had "sold their birthright for the pottage of license and disregard of the moral law," and that the Puritan spirit was no longer in government nor in the people, supplemented the belief that, after early generations, many, perhaps a majority of Puritan–Yankees had fallen into inertia. Yet those who served the sacred calling were in turn rewarded with new energy, resourcefulness, courage, generosity.[147]

Ordinarily astute in social judgment, they undergauged the intricacies which were bringing about distinct regional cultures which were held together by common national interests. The following paragraph shows understanding that the process was enormous in scope but contains the customary and risky assumption of a "universal Yankee nation."

One of the most distinguishing characteristics of the *"universal Yankee nation,"* is the rapidity with which everything valuable is diffused throughout the length and breadth of this vast continent. Is a labor-saving implement invented—in a few weeks, by the aid of cuts, diagrams, descriptions, and the press, it is known from Maine to California. Does a new seedling prove valuable—in a few years it is in the garden or field of every intelligent horticulturist or farmer in the land. And so it is with improved stock.[148]

Meanwhile secular interest groups potentially national in scope appeared or took on new meaning. This is demonstrated in a periodical such as Porter's *Spirit of the Times,* "a chronicle of the turf, field sports, literature and the stage," whose clientele of readers extended during the 1850's well over the northern states and somewhat into the South. Volumes III and IV show reader correspondence originating in sixteen Illinois towns, eleven in Ohio, seven in Wisconsin, five in Michigan; while Kentucky and Indiana were each three times represented and Minnesota, Missouri, Arkansas, Alabama, and Louisiana appeared once each at least. The worldly linkages which united these groups—the turf, chess, cricket, billiards, footracing, fishing, the prowess of rat-killing dogs, horsebreeding, pedestrianism, rowing, hunting and marksmanship, yachting and baseball—might also have given pause to New England's children.[149]

To achieve a Yankee pattern "in the twinkling of an eye," to wield "the plastic hand of a master," would have required at any time favorable conditions, and such conditions were unlikely to obtain after midcentury. As the Yankee tone had grown shrillest, the nation stood on the threshhold of the corporate, industrial, railway, and, almost terrifying could they have foreseen, the "gilded" ages. Nor was the hope for serenity bolstered by the immigration prospect. The Civil War had cleared the air: "the reverberations of the cannon of Vicksburg were heard among the valleys of the Carpathian Mountains and along the shores of the Zuyder-Zee." Practi-

cally all of the western states were competing to attract the
thousands of Europeans eager to cross the Atlantic.[150]

Nature intervened. It forbade that the Northwest become
a replica of some other region. Its topography, the fertility of
its soil, its climate, prairies, forests, mineral resources, its in-
land waterways had no parallel elsewhere, and these alone were
sufficient to make its development follow lines of its own.[151]
The snag encountered by the Boston merchant who dreamed of
a New England village every six miles in the West is eloquently
described by a writer who must have had the same dream:

No steep and sterile mountains compel men to congregate in fertile
vallies, no common danger constrains them to unite for mutual
protection; seldom does the waterfall, or the quarry, or the mine,
attract around it a compact community. But in a country so nearly
uniform in its local advantages, with a soil so slightly varied in
surface and fertility the emigrant locates his cabin wherever his
taste, convenience or interest may dictate. Hence the peculiar
difficulty of combining and centralizing religious influence, de-
manding, as it does, the sacrifice of ease, and of local preference
and interests.[152]

Finally, the outcome of the Civil War permitted the Yankee
to feel that he had swept everything before him.[153] But it was
later than he thought. The year the "Southern Jericho" fell was
a retarded date for Beecher and others to proclaim total dominance of the South. Whatever the Yankee's impact, the Northwest became something new and different and unique in its own
right. Neither strain won out by subordination of the other,
but both were conquered as it were by the region itself, were
taken in hand by a process of blending, in which the final
outcome was neither Yankee nor Southern, but "Western."

NOTES

[1] James Hall, *Letters from the West* . . . (London, 1828), p. 245;
Chevalier, *Society, Manners and Politics in the United States*, pp. 113, 120-
21; Drake, *A Systematic Treatise* . . . *on the Principal Diseases of the
Interior Valley of North America*, pp. 644-50; headline from the *New York
Courier and Enquirer*, in *The Country Gentleman*, III (June 15, 1854), 383.

[2] Channing, *A History of the United States*, VI, 383; Turner, *The Frontier in American History*, p. 349.

[3] Wertenbaker, *The Old South*, p. 17.

[4] Henry A. Wallace and Earl N. Bressman, *Corn and Corn Growing* (5th ed. New York, 1949), pp. 6-11; William L. Brown, "The History of the Common Maize Varieties of the United States," in *Agricultural History*, XXVI (January, 1952), 2-8.

[5] Carl Drepperd, *The Primer of American Antiques* (New York, 1945), p. ix.

[6] Rexford Newcomb, "Beginnings of Architecture in Illinois," in *Journal of the Illinois State Historical Society*, XXXIX (September, 1946), 314-15.

[7] "The Illinois Farmer," in *The Chicago Magazine; The West as It Is*, I (April 15, 1857), 143.

[8] Cited by Van Bolt, "The Indiana Scene in the 1840's," in *Indiana Magazine of History*, XLVII, 345.

[9] *Recollections of the Last Ten Years*, p. 51.

[10] New York *Times*, May 11, 1947; see also Dr. James F. Bender, "Ninety Million Speak 'General American,'" in New York *Times Magazine*, August 27, 1944, p. 17.

[11] Dorson, "The Yankee on the Stage—A Folk Hero of the American Drama," in *New England Quarterly*, XII (September, 1940), 490-91.

[12] Indianapolis *Star Magazine*, February 12, 1950, pp. 8-9.

[13] George P. Schmidt, *The Old Time College President* (New York, 1930), p. 26.

[14] Van Bolt, "The Indiana Scene in the 1840's," in *Indiana Magazine of History*, XLVII, 345.

[15] Eugene H. Roseboom, "Southern Ohio and the Union in 1863," in *Mississippi Valley Historical Review*, XXXIX (June, 1952), 39.

[16] Evarts B. Greene, "Sectional Forces in the History of Illinois," in *Transactions of the Illinois State Historical Society*, 1903 (Springfield, 1904), p. 75.

[17] Mathews, *The Expansion of New England*, p. 210.

[18] Charles E. Robert, *Evansville: Her Commerce and Manufacturers . . .* (Evansville, Ind., 1874), p. 65.

[19] G. W. H. Kemper (ed.), *A Twentieth Century History of Delaware County, Indiana* (2 volumes. Chicago, 1908), I, 50.

[20] Robert S. and Helen M. Lynd, *Middletown, A Study in Contemporary American Culture* (New York, 1929).

[21] Samuel Whedon, Brownstown, Jackson County, Indiana, June 27, 1817, to his brother, Seneca Township, Ontario County, New York, IHS.

[22] Letter of one Burton, Brownsville, Illinois, to Miss Achsah Burton, Andover, Vermont, December 13, 1820, ILLSL.

[23] Fox, *Yankees and Yorkers*, p. 212; R. G. Albion, "Yankee Domination of New York Port, 1820-1865," in *New England Quarterly*, V (October, 1932), 669; Lowell *Journal*, quoted in *New England Farmer*, XI, June 12, 1833; Drake, *A Systematic Treatise . . . on the Principal Diseases of the Interior Valley of North America*, p. 646.

[24] For Sears, see *Journal of the Illinois State Historical Society,* VIII, 303; for Cannon, see an address by him, 1916, in Southern Historical Collection, University of North Carolina; for Wright, see Lloyd Lewis, *John S. Wright, Prophet of the Prairies* (Chicago, 1941), p. 100; for McCormick, Fletcher, Douglas, Cable, and Palmer see sketches of them in *Dictionary of American Biography.*

[25] Fox, *Yankees and Yorkers.* Circumstances in the Yorker's past which left their mark on the New England Yankee were, Dr. Fox believes, the Dutch tradition, contact with Iroquois, a long military experience, survival of aristocratic and feudal tradition, land speculations, the unusual prestige of the legal profession, pronounced party spirit, and absence of a tax-supported church. Introduction, pp. x, 15 ff., 21-23, 25.

The quotations in the title of this part are from Emerson (Rusk, ed., *The Letters of Ralph Waldo Emerson,* IV, 342), and from letters of Jacob Patterson, Elbridge, Illinois, to Robert Hanner, Guilford County, North Carolina, August 22, 1849, DU.

[26] Still and Herrmann (eds.), "Abner Morse's Diary of Emigrant Travel, 1855-56," in *Wisconsin Magazine of History,* XXII (December, 1938), 201-12.

[27] Jonathan Bacon, Chateaugay, New York, to Henry Bacon, North Andover, Massachusetts, September 26, 1846, Southern Historical Collection, University of North Carolina.

[28] John H. Cocke, Jr., Journal of Travels to the West, Cabell Papers (MSS 3021), UV.

[29] Rusk (ed.), *Letters of Emerson,* V, 200.

[30] Diary of Sarah Ann Quarles Chandler, 1836, pp. 10-12, ISL; William M. Keever, Poland, Clay County, Indiana, to J. D. Davidson, Lexington, Virginia, October 29, 1859, and Reverend C. B. Davidson, Evansville, Indiana, to same, Lexington, Virginia, October 14, 1854, photostats in ISL from originals in McHC; letter of William Hurt, October 8, 1844, McHC; Dr. J. A. Jordan, Indianapolis, to J. D. Davidson, Lexington, Virginia, October 25, 1837, photostat in ISL of original in McHC.

[31] John Weiss, *Life and Correspondence of Theodore Parker* (2 volumes. New York, 1864), I, 327, letter from Indianapolis, October 18, 1854, to Professor Edward Desor.

[32] Thomas, *A Tour Through the Western Country in the Summer of 1816,* p. 125; G. H. Beeler, Burlington, Iowa Territory, to Joseph Beeler, Indianapolis, November 25, 1838, ISL; *The Western Messenger; Devoted to Religion and Literature* (Louisville), IV (December, 1837), 235; Luke and Avis Woodard, Wayne County, Indiana, to Elizabeth Stanton, Beaufort, North Carolina, August, 1831, IHS; Griswold C. Morgan, Chicago, to Jasper C. Morgan, Windsor, Connecticut, September 3, 1841, CHS; Louella B. Case, Patriot, Indiana, to her brother, Levi S. Bartlett, M. D., Kingston, New Hampshire, June 2, 1847, IHS; William S. Brown, Rockford, Illinois, to friends at Dansville, New York, January 3, 1856, ILLSL.

[33] Calvin Fletcher, Indianapolis, to parents, Ludlow, Vermont, May 11, 1823, and Samuel Whedon, Brownstown, Jackson County, Indiana, to his

brother, Seneca Township, Ontario County, New York, June 27, 1817, IHS;
Oliver Soper, Wilmington, Indiana, to brother and sister Day, Phillipston,
Maine, May 31, 1851, WHS; *History of Greene and Sullivan Counties,
Indiana* (Chicago, 1884), p. 670. Down-east folk were subject to malaria.

[34] Letter, writer's name illegible, from Illinois to a friend in Ohio
County, Virginia, February 8, 1857, West Virginia University Library;
Louella B. Case, Patriot, Indiana, to her brother, Levi S. Bartlett, M. D.,
Kingston, New Hampshire, June 2, 1847, IHS; Lydia and Abel Griffith,
Winchester, Ohio, to William Town, Canandaigua, New York, September 3,
1831, OAHS; Dwinnell's Reminiscences, part 7, WHS; Calvin Fletcher,
London, Ohio, to Jesse Fletcher, Ludlow, Vermont, June 18, 1819, IHS.

[35] See *Home Missionary*, XI (March, 1839), 248; XV (May, 1842), 14.
See also Part 5, Chapter II, above.

[36] Both letters from Cincinnati, April 25, 1835, and August 7, 1837,
Illinois Historical Survey, Urbana.

[37] Lydia and Abel Griffith, Winchester, Ohio, to William Town,
Canandaigua, New York, September 3, 1831, OAHS.

[38] Willard, "Personal Reminiscences of Life in Illinois, 1830-50," in
Transactions of the Illinois State Historical Society, 1906, p. 79. A communication from G. N. Jones, associate in botany at the University of Illinois, May 16, 1943, advises that the dandelion was carried westward "in-
tentionally or otherwise (probably the latter) by the westward emigrants."

[39] Angle (ed.), "The Story of an Ordinary Man," in *Journal of the
Illinois State Historical Society*, XXXIII (June, 1940), 228; Dwinnell's
Reminiscences, part 6, WHS; *Indiana Magazine of History*, VII (Decem-
ber, 1911), 175.

[40] *The Ladies' Repository* . . . (Cincinnati), II (1842), 243; VI (1846),
283.

[41] Letter of one Burton, Brownsville, Illinois, to Miss Achsah Burton,
Andover, Vermont, December 20, 1830, ILLSL; "The Western Rivers," in
The Western Messenger; Devoted to Religion and Literature, V (July,
1838), 273; Hayes, "Letter from the West in 1845," in *Iowa Journal of
History and Politics*, XX (January, 1922), 46; Martha L. Dickinson, Newcomerstown, Ohio, to her sister, Berlin, Connecticut, July 12, 1839, Historical and Philosophical Society of Ohio. A touring Virginian was pleased
that the lightning of his home state was "far superior" to that at Albany,
New York. *Southern Literary Messenger*, I (January, 1835), 217.

[42] *Journal and Letters of Col. John May*, pp. 56-57.

[43] John Humphries, Rockville, Indiana, to Samuel Blackwood, Greenville, Virginia, January 7, 1836, ISL.

[44] "Virginians in Indiana," in *William and Mary Quarterly*, 2 series, X
(October, 1930), 312, 313; Reverend William Sickels, Indianapolis, to
Daniel Gold, Winchester, Virginia, July 15, 1828, ISL; James H. Smith,
Mt. Morris, Illinois, to David Ports, Boonesborough, Maryland, November
23, 1846, ILLSL; letter of Mrs. Leander McCormick, December 10, 1838, in
Chicago Yesterdays, garnered by Caroline Kirkland.

[45] George C. Leavitt, Leavenworth, Crawford County, Indiana, to his

parents, Chichester, New Hampshire, February 23 and May 22, 1847. From collection owned by Professor Paul W. Gates, Cornell University.

[46] *Life and Travels of Addison Coffin*, pp. 75-80.

[47] Letter written in 1835 quoted from Cincinnati *Mirror* by Virginius C. Hall, "Ohio in Knee Pants," in *Ohio State Archaeological and Historical Quarterly*, LVI (January, 1947), 12.

[48] Quoted from New York *Tribune* by *Granite Farmer*, III, September 8, 1852.

[49] Elisha Lawler, Madison County, Indiana, to Joseph Lawler, Warrenton, Virginia, August 12, 1833, DU.

[50] *Home Missionary*, III (March, 1831), 218.

[51] Lydia and Abel Griffith, Winchester, Ohio, to William Town, Canandaigua, New York, September 3, 1831, OAHS.

[52] Rutherford Collection, Illinois Historical Survey, Urbana. Charles M. Rebert, professor of psychology, St. Lawrence University, who was born in Pennsylvania, advises that "brouching" is the equivalent of "powwowing" or employing "charm" medicine.

[53] Still and Herrmann (eds.), "Abner Morse's Diary of Emigrant Travel, 1855-56," in *Wisconsin Magazine of History*, XXII (March, 1939), 338.

[54] A. C. Nevins, Cumberland, Marion County, Indiana, to Sarah Nevins, Millerstown, Perry County, Pennsylvania, May 17, 1844, WHS.

[55] *History of Greene and Sullivan Counties, Indiana* (Chicago, 1884), p. 282.

[56] Ebenezer Welch, Monmouth, Illinois, to relatives, Monmouth, Maine, September 19, 1841, CHS.

[57] Letter of Calvin Fletcher, Urbana, Ohio, November 21, 1818, IHS.

[58] *Home Missionary*, XLI (March, 1869), 267.

[59] *Mississippi Valley Historical Review*, XXXIX (March, 1953), 780-81.

[60] Journal of Calvin and Sarah Fletcher, February 9 and 10, 1833, and letter of Calvin Fletcher, Indianapolis, to his brother Michael, Staatsburg, New York, February 23, 1823, IHS.

[61] Wood, *Sketches of Things and Peoples in Indiana*, p. 38.

[62] D. L. Gold, Lawrenceville, Illinois, to William H. Gold, Winchester, Virginia, July 15, 1847, DU.

[63] M. L. Atkinson, Madison, Indiana, to Joseph Little, Newberry, Massachusetts, September 14, 1838, ISL.

[64] Dwinnell's Reminiscences, part 6, WHS.

[65] B. H. Frank, Buck Horn, Brown County, Illinois, to Alexander Frank, Cedar Bush, North Carolina, November 27, 1857, DU.

[66] Photostat of fragment of unsigned letter, in Jones family of Jonesville papers, Michigan Historical Collections, Ann Arbor.

[67] Tillson, *A Woman's Story of Pioneer Illinois*, pp. 147-48.

[68] I. N. Bereman, Madison County, Indiana, to Sally A. Bereman, New Market, Ohio, August 28, 1835, ISL.

[69] *Boston Cultivator*, XV, March 12, 1853.

[70] Mary M. Alexander and Capitola G. Dill (eds.), *Sketches of Rush County, Indiana* (Rushville, Ind., 1915), p. 68.

[71] *History of Delaware County, Indiana* (Chicago, 1881), p. 34; Calvin Fletcher, London, Ohio, to Louisa Fletcher, Ludlow, Vermont, May 1, 1819, IHS; A. D. Jones, *Illinois and the West,* pp. 149-51.

[72] George C. Leavitt, Leavenworth, Crawford County, Indiana, to his parents, Chichester, New Hampshire, December 16, 1849. From collection owned by Professor Paul W. Gates, Cornell University.

[73] *The Ladies' Repository,* V (1845), 344.

[74] Dorothy Giles, *Singing Valleys: the Story of Corn* (New York, 1940), p. 83. Of general interest is Louise O. Bercaw, *et al., Corn in the Development of the Civilization of the Americas . . . (Agricultural Economics Bibliography,* No. 87, Washington, D. C., 1940).

[75] Paul Weatherwax, *The Story of the Maize Plant* (Chicago, 1923), p. 217.

[76] Liberty H. Bailey (ed.), *Cyclopedia of American Agriculture . . .* (4 volumes. New York, 1907-9), II, 398; Edward C. Kirkland, *A History of American Economic Life . . .* (New York, 1932), p. 53; J. Howard Kempton, "Maize—Our Heritage from the Indians," in U. S. Bureau of American Ethnology, *Annual Report,* 1937 (Washington, D. C., 1938), pp. 385-408.

[77] Diary of Enoch Honeywell, p. 117, typed copy in ISL; Peck, *A Gazetteer of Illinois,* p. 29; see also John Scott, *The Indiana Gazetteer* (Centreville, Ind., 1826), p. 24; *The Plough, the Loom, and the Anvil,* VIII (August, 1855), 95; Springfield (Ill.) *Sangamo Journal,* June 25, 1846, communication signed "J.S.W."

[78] *Life and Travels of Addison Coffin,* p. 77; Hezekiah Park, Circleville, Illinois, to Thadius Bancroft, Grafton, Vermont, September 28, 1840, ILLSL.

[79] "News from the Muskingum," in *Ohio State Archaeological and Historical Quarterly,* XLVI (1936), 209, and *Journal and Letters of Col. John May,* p. 55; C. E. Eaton, Waverly, Ohio, to his brother, Candia Turnpike, New Hampshire, July 4, 1837, Eaton Letters, OAHS; *Southern Literary Messenger,* I (December, 1834), 168; Calvin Fletcher, Urbana, Ohio, to Jesse Fletcher, Ludlow, Vermont, July 25, 1818.

[80] "Emigrants to Ohio and Illinois," in *Tyler's Quarterly Historical and Genealogical Magazine,* VII (July, 1925), 92, quoting letter of James L. Welsh, Macomb, Illinois, August 31, 1860.

[81] Ebenezer Welch, Monmouth, Illinois, to his parents, Monmouth, Maine, September 19, 1841, CHS.

[82] Words of Howard T. Walden, II, cited from *Farm Journal,* by Wayne Guthrie in "Ringside in Hoosierland," in Indianapolis *News,* September 2, 1952.

[83] J. W. Davis, French Grove, Illinois, to his father, Triadelphia, Virginia, December 22, 1862, West Virginia University Library. In gathering corn, a "land" is a block of corn rows around which the wagon travels. One advantage: the wagon does not straddle and break down an unhusked row.

[84] Transcript of the memoirs of Milton Stapp, IHS. The date concerned is 1837.

⁸⁵ Charles W. Towne and Edward N. Wentworth, *Pigs: from Cave to Corn Belt* (Norman, Okla., 1950), p. 7.

⁸⁶ *The Prairie Farmer,* X (May, 1850), 140.

⁸⁷ A. W. Blair, Indianapolis, to Edwin Blair, Williamstown, Massachusetts, June 30, 1845, ISL.

⁸⁸ Quoted from Brookville (Ind.) *American,* November 29, 1834, in *Indiana Magazine of History,* XX (March, 1924), 78; Calvin Fletcher, Indianapolis, to his brother Michael, Staatsburg, New York, February 23, 1823, IHS.

⁸⁹ New Castle (Ind.) *Courier,* November 23, 1844; Alexander and Dill (eds.), *Sketches of Rush County, Indiana,* p. 49. See also various county histories.

⁹⁰ Angle (ed.), "The Story of an Ordinary Man," in *Journal of the Illinois State Historical Society,* XXXIII, 224; Buck (ed.), "Pioneer Letters of Gershom Flagg," in *Transactions of the Illinois State Historical Society,* 1910, p. 147.

⁹¹ Peck, *A Gazetteer of Illinois,* p. 41.

⁹² In 1850 the average annual yield per milch cow was 700 quarts; ninety years later it was over 2,000 quarts. See W. A. Wentworth, "Dairy Industry," in *Dictionary of American History,* II, 103.

⁹³ C. I. Swartwout, Quincy, Illinois, to Robert Swartwout, New York City, May 22, 1837, CHS; George M. Frank, Hamilton County, Indiana, to "Dear Sir" in North Carolina, April 10, 1859, DU.

⁹⁴ Matthias Bowman, Cicero, Indiana, to his brother, Rockingham County, Virginia, June 14, 1857, Wayland Papers, UV; Springfield (Ill.) *Sangamo Journal,* February 1, 1834 (quoting *Connecticut Independent Press*) and February 2, 1832; Bidwell and Falconer, *History of Agriculture in the Northern United States,* p. 497.

⁹⁵ E. E. Day, Munsontown, Illinois, to E. F. Day, Phillipston, Maine, March 13, 1846, Day collection, WHS; Anderson and Lydia Moore, Deer Creek, Henry County, Indiana, to Philip and Barbara A. Bible, Rockingham County, Virginia, January 13, 1855, and John W. Brock, Seneca County, Ohio, to Moses Bowman, Timberville, Rockingham County, Virginia, February 14, 1858, Wayland Papers, UV.

⁹⁶ Peck, *A Gazetteer of Illinois,* pp. 28, 40, 41; James H. Smith, Buffalo Grove, Illinois, to David Ports, Boonesborough, Maryland, January 28, 1840, ILLSL.

⁹⁷ *Journal and Letters of Col. John May,* pp. 83, 85, 89.

⁹⁸ A. D. Jones, *Illinois and the West,* p. 149; Ebenezer Welch, Monmouth, Illinois, to his parents, Monmouth, Maine, September 19, 1841, CHS; John W. Brock, Seneca County, Ohio, to Moses Bowman, Timberville, Rockingham County, Virginia, February 14, 1858, Wayland Papers, UV (Runyan's Creek flows through Rockingham County; Brock's reference to "the Strait" remains obscure); Jacob Patterson, Elbridge, Edgar County, Illinois, to Robert Hanner, Guilford County, North Carolina, August 22, 1849, Robert Hanner papers, DU.

⁹⁹ Peck, *A Gazetteer of Illinois,* p. 38; C. E. Eaton, Waverly, Ohio, to

Thomas Anderson, Candia Turnpike, New Hampshire, July 4, 1837, OAHS;
Asher Edgerton, Quincy, Illinois, to Elisha Edgerton, Connecticut, May 28,
1842, ILLSL; Elmore Barce, *Annals of Benton County, Indiana* (Fowler,
Ind., 1925), p. 67; Christopher R. Denny, Leicester, Massachusetts, to T. V.
Denny, Indianapolis, July 19, 1822, ISL.

[100] *History of Elkhart County, Indiana* . . . (Chicago, 1881), p. 391;
Lemuel W. Royse, *A Standard History of Kosciusko County, Indiana* . . .
(2 volumes. Chicago and New York, 1919), I, 83-84; Daniel Goodnough,
Des Plaines River, Illinois, to John M. Goodnough, Brandon, Vermont,
January 1, 1837, and James H. Smith, Elk Horn Grove, Illinois, to David
Ports, Boonesborough, Maryland, April 16, 1839, ILLSL; Springfield (Ill.)
Sangamo Journal, October 29, 1846; Barce, *Annals of Benton County,* pp.
50-51.

[101] Ebenezer Welch, Monmouth, Illinois, to his parents, Monmouth,
Maine, September 19, 1841, CHS; William and Christina Boss, Versailles,
Brown County, Illinois, to relatives in North Carolina, May 2, 1858, and
B. H. Frank, Buck Horn, Brown County, Illinois, to Alexander Frank,
Cedar Bush, North Carolina, November 27, 1857, F. L. Alexander collec-
tion, DU; Anthony M. Hoffman, Rushville, Illinois, to John Reid, Argyle,
New York, November 1, 1833, and James H. Smith, Mt. Morris, Illinois,
to David Ports, Boonesborough, Maryland, November 23, 1846, ILLSL.

[102] Whitson (ed.), *Centennial History of Grant County, Indiana,* p. 91;
Branson L. Harris, *Some Recollections of My Boyhood* (Indianapolis, c.
1906), pp. 59-60. Present dependence upon income from swine is suggested
by a report of Purdue University's farm account program: the cash income
of 587 farmers was, 1951, from hogs, 39 per cent; crops, 18 per cent; dairy
cattle and dairy products, 15 per cent; beef cattle, 14 per cent; poultry and
eggs, 7 per cent; and 7 per cent from other sources. Though the proportion
of income from swine is impressive, the 587 cases may not represent a true
cross section. See Frank Salzarulo, "The Rural Route," in Indianapolis
News, November 4, 1952.

"Of every dollar coming to the [Iowa] farm, hogs return between 40
and 45 cents." Edwin Lee Quaife and Arthur L. Anderson, "The Hog in
Iowa," in *The Palimpsest* (Iowa City), XXXIII (July, 1952), 222.

[103] J. W. Davis, French Grove, Illinois, to his father at Triadelphia,
Virginia, December 22, 1862, West Virginia University Library; James L.
Welsh, Panola, Illinois, to his mother, Rockbridge County, Virginia, August
26, 1853, in *Tyler's Quarterly Historical and Genealogical Magazine,* VII
(July, 1925), 91; Thomas A. Clifton (ed.), *Past and Present of Fountain
and Warren Counties, Indiana* (Indianapolis, 1913), p. 285.

[104] Weatherwax, *The Story of the Maize Plant,* pp. 2, 217-19; L. E.
Klimm, *et al., Introduction to Economic Geography* (New York, 1937), p.
151; Wallace and Bressman, *Corn and Corn Growing,* p. 18; Ray Allen
Billington, "Origins of Middle Western Isolationism," in *Political Science
Quarterly,* LX (March, 1945), 51; Stephen S. Visher, "The Geography of
Indiana," in *Handbook of Indiana Geology* (Indiana Department of Conser-

vation, Indianapolis, 1922), p. 25. L. M. Crist, *History of Boone County, Indiana* (Indianapolis, 1914), p. 138.

[105] Wallace and Bressman, *Corn and Corn Growing*, pp. 13-14, 15, 413.

[106] William A. Craigie and James R. Hulbert (eds.), *A Dictionary of American English on Historical Principles* (2 volumes. Chicago, 1938), I, 623.

[107] *The Commercial Review of the South and West* (New Orleans), I (June, 1846), 465.

[108] Gray, *History of Agriculture in the Southern United States to 1860*, p. 811; Bidwell and Falconer, *History of Agriculture in the Northern United States*, pp. 339-49.

[109] Fred A. Shannon, "The Status of the Midwestern Farmer in 1900," in *Mississippi Valley Historical Review*, XXXVII (December, 1950), 492-93, 495.

[110] Wallace and Bressman, *Corn and Corn Growing*, pp. 12, 16, 18, 300.

[111] Robert E. Cutler, Wilmington, Dearborn County, Indiana, to his father, Robert D. Cutler, Lovingston, Nelson County, Virginia, November 7, 1838, Tucker-Coleman papers, Colonial Williamsburg, Inc. (for a copy of this letter I am indebted to Dr. Lester J. Cappon); Diary of Enoch Honeywell, typed copy in ISL.

[112] Thomas B. Helm, *History of Allen County, Indiana* . . . (Chicago, 1880), p. 164; William and Christina Boss, Versailles, Brown County, Illinois, to relatives in North Carolina, May 2, 1858, F. L. Alexander collection, DU.

[113] H. H. Pleasant, "Crawford County," in *Indiana Magazine of History*, XVIII (September, 1922), 349; Elisha Lawler, Union Township, Madison County, Indiana, to Joseph L. Lawler, Warrenton, Virginia, March 3, 1837, DU.

[114] *Home Missionary*, XXIV (October, 1851), 132; *Life and Travels of Addison Coffin*, pp. 115-16; *Kentucky Farmer*, I (April, 1859), 145, quoting verses by J. E. Sherman in *Country Gentleman*.

[115] William T. Coggeshall, *The Protective Policy in Literature: A Discourse on the Social and Moral Advantages of the Cultivation of Local Literature* (Columbus, Ohio, 1859), pp. 15, 27. See sketch of Coggeshall in *Dictionary of American Biography*, IV, 272; also David Donald and Frederick A. Palmer, "Toward a Western Literature, 1820-1860," in *Mississippi Valley Historical Review*, XXXV (December, 1948), 418-19.

[116] The term "grand practical results" is used in *History of De Kalb County, Indiana* . . . (Chicago, 1885), p. 245; *The Chicago Magazine; The West as It Is*, I (March, 1857), 10; Cleveland *Herald*, August 20, 1844, quoted in Francis P. Weisenberger, *The Passing of the Frontier, 1825-1850* (*The History of the State of Ohio*, III, Columbus, 1941), p. 91; Cole, *The Era of the Civil War*, p. 91; James Parton, "Cincinnati," in *Atlantic Monthly*, XX (August, 1867), 232.

[117] *The Railroad Record* (Cincinnati), I (March 2, 1854), 1; *The Western Journal*, I (January, 1848), 310-12.

[118] *Spirit of the Times*, IV (April 10, 1858), 84. Article signed "Ruth Hall."

[119] *Chicago Yesterdays,* garnered by Caroline Kirkland, p. 53; *The Prairie Farmer,* XI (April, 1851), 178.

[120] *The Prairie Farmer,* XIII (December, 1853), 474; *Chicago Magazine,* I (May 15, 1857), 365 (quoting *Iroquois Republican*), and I (April 15, 1857), 141-42.

[121] Daniel Drake, *Discourse on the History, Character, and Prospects of the West . . .* (Cincinnati, 1834), pp. 6-13.

[122] Donald and Palmer, "Toward a Western Literature, 1820-1860," in *Mississippi Valley Historical Review,* XXXV, 413 ff.

[123] *Chicago Magazine,* I (April 15, 1857), 182, citing a review of one of its issues in the Chicago *Journal; Indiana Farmer,* February 18, 1860, p. 64.

[124] *Indiana Farmer,* April 14, 1860, pp. 114-15. The demand for western periodicals went largely unanswered. It was estimated in 1839, and the situation was much the same twenty years later, that the East had four quarterly reviews, twelve or fifteen monthlies, something like a score of weekly literary papers, together with fifteen or twenty large miscellaneous sheets of the family class. The western states with equal population had three of the family class, one weekly literary paper, and three monthly magazines. Coggeshall, *The Protective Policy in Literature,* p. 15.

[125] *Ohio Farmer,* January 27, 1853; *Indiana Farmer,* January 7, 1860, p. 2, and February 18, 1860, p. 64.

[126] Sandusky *Register,* cited in David Mead, *Yankee Eloquence in the Middle West; The Ohio Lyceum, 1850-1870* (East Lansing, Michigan, 1951) ; *Ohio Farmer,* III, December 9, 1854, and IV, December 1, 1855.

[127] Coggeshall, *The Protective Policy in Literature,* p. 27; *The Ladies' Repository,* IX (1849), 147; Kohlmeier, *The Old Northwest as the Keystone of the Arch of the American Federal Union;* Hutchinson, *Cyrus Hall McCormick,* II, 8, 10. McCormick believed the welfare of his country and church would be assured if the Northwest remained sanely conservative. See also Drake, *Discourse on the History, Character, and Prospects of the West,* pp. 47-53.

[128] This was published in Lafayette in 1855. See pp. 4, 9, 11, 12.

[129] Gallagher, *Facts and Conditions of Progress in the Northwest . . .* (Cincinnati, 1850), pp. 12, 19-20, 24, 26-27, 28, 38, 41, 46. See *Dictionary of American Biography,* VII, 102-3.

[130] Charles W. Dana, *The Great West, or the Garden of the World* (Boston, 1857), p. 14.

[131] Arthur M. Schlesinger, "What then is the American, this New Man?" in *American Historical Review,* XLVIII (January, 1943), 226. Also Church, *History of Rockford and Winnebago County, Illinois,* p. 161; Frazer E. Wilson, *Arthur St. Clair . . .* (Richmond, Va., 1944), p. 153; *Southern Literary Messenger,* I (April, 1835), 426.

[132] Edmund C. Burnett, *The Continental Congress* (New York, 1941), Chapter I; Miller, *Sam Adams, Pioneer in Propaganda,* pp. 315, 317.

[133] Quoted by Albert J. Beveridge, in *The Life of John Marshall* (3 volumes. Boston, 1916), I, 279.

[134] Felix Gilbert (ed.), "Letters of Francis Kinloch to Thomas Boone, 1782-1788," in *Journal of Southern History,* VII (February, 1942), 101.

[135] Chevalier, *Society, Manners, and Politics in the United States,* p. 114; *Home Missionary,* XXXVIII (March, 1866), 261; *Country Gentleman,* II (November 24, 1853), 334. See Chapter I, above, Part 5.

[136] *Franklin Farmer* (Frankfort, Ky.), II (April 27, 1839), 285; *The Cultivator,* O.S. VII (August, 1841), 135; Clement Eaton, *Freedom of Thought in the Old South* (Durham, N. C., 1940), Chapter XII; *Home Missionary,* XXXVII (April, 1865), 280, and XXI (October, 1848), 140-41.

[137] *Illinois Monthly Magazine,* I (June, 1831), 419.

[138] See Chapter I, Part 5, above.

[139] Kohlmeier, *The Old Northwest,* pp. 93-94, 112, 168-69; *New Englander,* IV (January, 1846), 36; Paullin, *Atlas of the Historical Geography of the United States,* Plates 80 B ff.; Mathews, *The Expansion of New England,* maps throughout; see also Chapter II, Parts 3 and 5, above, and Chapter V, Part 4, above.

[140] Hayes, "Letters from the West in 1845," in *Iowa Journal of History and Politics,* XX, 10, 28, 46.

[141] Paullin, *Atlas of the Historical Geography of the United States,* Plates 103 ff.

[142] Indianapolis *Indiana Daily Journal,* November 20, 1856, quoting Piqua (Ohio) *Register.* See also Madison (Ind.) *Dollar Weekly Courier,* November 26, 1856.

[143] Tewksbury, *The Founding of American Colleges and Universities before the Civil War, passim.*

[144] Schmidt, *The Old Time College President,* p. 206; Goodykoontz, *Home Missions on the American Frontier,* pp. 149-50; Charles Roy Keller, *The Second Great Awakening in Connecticut* (New Haven, 1942), p. 92; Richardson, "The Mindedness of the Early Faculty of Beloit College," in *Wisconsin Magazine of History,* XIX, 55.

[145] Bridgman, *New England in the Life of the World,* p. 356; Frederick Jackson Turner, *The Significance of Sections in American History* (New York, 1932), p. 11.

[146] *Ante,* pp. 11-12.

[147] Turner, *The Frontier in American History,* p. 215; Mathews, *The Expansion of New England,* p. 198; Church, *History of Rockford and Winnebago County, Illinois,* pp. 255-56; *History of the Formation of the Ladies' Society for Promotion of Education at the West . . . with addresses by the Reverends Edward Beecher and E. M. Kirk* (Boston, 1846), p. 15; Bridgman, *New England,* p. 7.

[148] *Moore's Rural New Yorker,* V (April 15, 1854), 117.

[149] *Spirit of the Times* (New York), III-IV (1857-58).

[150] John A. Wilstach, *A Circular for the Commissioner of Emigration . . .* (Indianapolis, 1866), p. 3.

[151] Walter Havighurst, *The Long Ship's Passing* (New York, 1941).

[152] See Chapter I, Part 2, above, and *Home Missionary,* XVI (January, 1844), 206-7.

[153] See Chapter I, Parts 4 and 5 above.

INDEX

INDEX

Abbott, Lyman, 12.

Agriculture, western, 92 ff., 137, 138, 151-62; farm land values, 27-28, 29, 30; seeds and seedlings introduced, 31; southern Indiana and Illinois, 37, 95; ease and profit in, 49, 156 ff.; farm houses and buildings, 103, 104-5; lay out of farms, 102; use of horses, 152; labor-saving machinery, 163; trade in products (c. 1855), 163-64; periodicals, 165-66. *See also* Cattle, Corn, Dairying, Hogs, Horses.

Albany (N. Y.), beginning of "water-level route," 53.

Alcott, Bronson, 93, 107.

Allen, John, 67.

American Home Missionary Society, 22-23, 117; neglect of Indiana, 70, 79-80. *See also* Missions, western.

Andover (Vt.), 146.

Ann Arbor (Mich.), 67.

Annapolis (Ind.), 147.

Antioch College, 166.

Apples, 107.

Architecture, merging of styles in West, 137.

Associate Reformed Church, 22.

Atwater, Caleb, 75, 89.

Auburn (Ill.), 92.

Auburn Seminary, colony from, in West, 13.

Bacon, William, 155.

Baldwin, Theron, 116.

Baptists, attempt to "save" the West, 7.

Barley, 161.

Barnes, Rev. Albert, 83.

Barns, 104-5.

Bartholomew County (Ind.), 81.

Beecher, Catharine, 125.

Beecher, Henry Ward, 99, 172; on benefits of Yankee control of the nation, 11-12; on Kankakee swamp, 65-66; on Indiana's backwardness, 78-79; on western farming, 138.

Beecher, Lyman, 6-7, 15.

Beloit College, 171.

Bergen (N. Y.), 13.

Berkeley, Sir William, governor of Virginia, 2, 39.

Black Swamp, in Ohio, 66-67, 75.

Boatmen, influence on Old Northwest, 147.

Bond, Shadrach, governor of Illinois, 55.

Bond County (Ill.), 85.

Boone, Daniel, 51.

Boone, Thomas, 169.

Boss, John, 162.

Boss, Harry, 162.

Boston (Mass.), 8, 10.

Bowman, Matthias, 48-49.

Bread, 111-12.

Brookville (Ind.), 155.

Brown, Dr. Ryland T., 71.

Brownsville (Ill.), 110.

Brownsville (Ind.), 117.

Buck Horn (Ill.), 149.

Buffalo (N. Y.), Yankee port of entrance into West, 28-30, 70.

Buffalo Grove (Ill.), 107.

Buffalo Trace, *see* Vincennes Trace.

Bunker Hill (Ill.), 92.

Burton, ———, 110.

(187)

Vandalia (Ill.), 138.
Vermont, 24, 98, 100.
Vermontville (Mich.), 23.
Vevay (Ind.), 26.
Vincennes (Ind.), 37.
Vincennes Trace (Buffalo Trace), 37, 38, 142.
Virginia, western population characterized, 34; love of natives for, 48; planter class, 120; reaction of natives to society and customs in Old Northwest, 142; settlers from, find easier life in West, 157.

Wabash and Erie Canal, 68.
Wabash Valley, delayed settlement of upper, 66, 70; inaccessibility, 71; impressions of, described by New England girl, 86; ease of cultivation, 158.
Walker, "Hog," 156.
"Walk-in-the-Water," Lake Erie steamboat, 30.
War of 1812, soldiers impeded by Black Swamps, 66.
"Water-level "route," 53.
Water routes, in Old Northwest, 43-44, 53, 54, 68.
Watertown (Wis.) *Chronicle,* 105.
Weather, 16, 143, 144-45.
Welland Canal, 53.
Wertenbaker, Thomas J., 136-37.
West, *see* Old Northwest.
Western Journal (St. Louis), 77, 164.
Western Methodist Episcopal Conference, 115.
Western Monthly Magazine, 48.
Western Reserve and Maumee Road, 66.
Western Reserve University, 171.
Westerner, emergence of, as type, 167-68.
Wethersfield (Ill.), Connecticut colony, 14.
Wet lands, in Old Northwest, 63-67.

Wheat, 111-12, 161.
Wheaton College, 171.
Whedon, Samuel, 110.
Wheelock, Rev. J. R., 114.
Wilder, Rev. Moses H., appeal for settlers, 17.
Wilderness Road, 38, 51.
Williamson County (Ill.), poverty of, 28.
Wilmington (N. C.), 122.
Wilstach, John A., on destiny of the West, 166.
Wisconsin, 9; financial superiority of settlers in, 33; wet lands in, 63; Yankee character of, 74; progress of religious institutions, 82; coal fields, 164; politics, 171.
Wolcott, Oliver, 10.
Wood, Aaron, on Yankee cooking and eating, 109.
Woodburn, James A., 85.
Worthington, Thomas, U. S. senator from Ohio, 31.
Wright, John S., 141.
Wright, Joseph A., governor of Indiana, 78.

Yankee, The (Portland, Me.), 125.
Yankee Notions (New York), 85-86.
Yankee, a term of derision, 126; stage character, 138-39.
Yankees, emigration to Old Northwest, 1-2, 12-17, 28-31, 32-33, 39, 63, 71-75; advice to emigrants, 94-95; western mission, 5-20, 116, 117, 118, 170 ff.; and Civil War, 7, 11-12, 14, 22, 24-25, 66, 173-74; success of mission, 11-12, 17-20, 25, 170 ff.; economic superiority, 27, 29-31, 31-32; attitude toward and relations with Southerners, 35, 36, 39, 49-50, 120 ff., 125-26, 137 ff., 142, 148-49, 169-70; literacy, 40, 42, 43; better informed on West than southern emigrant, 42-43; nationalism and attachment to